THE RISE OF CHINA AND THE CHINESE OVERSEAS

ISEAS – Yusof Ishak Institute (formerly the Institute of Southeast Asian Studies) was established as an autonomous organization in 1968. It is a regional centre dedicated to the study of socio-political, security and economic trends and developments in Southeast Asia and its wider geostrategic and economic environment.

The Institute's research programmes are the Regional Economic Studies (RES, including ASEAN and APEC), Regional Strategic and Political Studies (RSPS), and Regional Social and Cultural Studies (RSCS).

ISEAS Publishing, an established academic press, has issued more than 2,000 books and journals. It is the largest scholarly publisher of research about Southeast Asia from within the region. ISEAS Publications works with many other academic and trade publishers and distributors to disseminate important research and analyses from and about Southeast Asia to the rest of the world.

THE RISE OF CHINA AND THE CHINESE OVERSEAS

A Study of Beijing's Changing Policy in Southeast Asia and Beyond

Leo Suryadinata

ISEAS YUSOF ISHAK INSTITUTE

First published in Singapore in 2017 by
ISEAS Publishing
30 Heng Mui Keng Terrace, Pasir Panjang
Singapore 119614

E-mail: publish@iseas.edu.sg
Website: bookshop.iseas.edu.sg>

ISEAS Library Cataloguing-in-Publication Data

Suryadinata, Leo.
The Rise of China and the Chinese Overseas : A Study of Beijing's Changing Policy in Southeast Asia and Beyond.
1. Chinese—Foreign countries.
2. Chinese—Southeast Asia.
3. China—Foreign relations.
D740.4 S96 2017

ISBN 978-981-47-6264-9 (soft cover)
ISBN 978-981-47-6265-6 (E-book PDF)

Typeset by International Typesetters Pte Ltd
Printed in Singapore by Markono Print Media Pte Ltd

CONTENTS

PREFACE

I have been studying Beijing's policy towards the Chinese overseas in Southeast Asia for many years. In 1978 I published an occasional paper on the topic, which was subsequently expanded into a book entitled *China and the ASEAN States: The Ethnic Chinese Dimension* (1985). In the past thirty years since that study, many new developments have taken place. When I first conducted my study, China was still weak. But, since the end of the twentieth and the beginning of the twenty-first centuries we have witnessed a rising China, the growing overseas presence of China's state-owned enterprises (SOEs), and a new wave of Chinese migration. China has also fine-tuned its foreign policy. Within this changed context, it would be interesting to re-examine Beijing's policy towards the Chinese overseas.

Beijing's policy today shows elements of both continuity and change. But, is change more significant than continuity? Is the new policy a form of Chinese transnationalism used by Beijing to serve its own core national interest? Is the policy more effective than before as a rising China is more appealing to the

Chinese overseas? What will be the likely impact on Southeast Asia and beyond?

When I was director of the Chinese Heritage Centre at Singapore's Nanyang Technological University (CHC-NTU) from January 2006 to October 2013, I wrote a few brief articles commenting on Beijing's policy towards the Chinese overseas. However, there were then few examples to support a discussion of continuity and change. I was also busy with other responsibilities and could not do a more detailed study of Beijing's policy.

I am glad that ISEAS – Yusof Ishak Institute has given me the opportunity finally to embark on this long intended study. Nevertheless, this is a brief study, limited to Southeast Asia, the Pacific Islands, Africa, and the Middle East. The emphasis is still on the Southeast Asian region, which is my major area of interest. A comprehensive study that covers other regions should be conducted to obtain a more thorough understanding of Beijing's relationship with the Chinese overseas.

I would like to thank Mr Tan Chin Tiong, director of ISEAS – Yusof Ishak Institute, for giving me the opportunity to conduct this study. I have benefitted from the comments of some of my colleagues at the Institute as well as those of three anonymous reviewers. Nevertheless, the views expressed in this study are my own.

Leo Suryadinata
10 June 2016

GLOSSARY

ACFROCA	All-China Federation of Returned Overseas Chinese Association
CPC (not CCP)	Communist Party of China
Da Qiaowu Zhengce 大侨务政策	The Great Overseas Chinese Affairs Policy
Daguo waijiao 大国外交	Diplomacy of a Big Country
Haiwai huaren 海外华人	Chinese overseas (i.e., regardless of nationality)
Han Ban 汉办	Executive Body of the Chinese Language Council International
Huagong 华工	Chinese coolie
Huaqiao 华侨	Overseas Chinese (i.e., Chinese nationals overseas)
Huaqiao shangren 华侨商人	Chinese businessmen overseas who are citizens of China

Huaren 华人	Ethnic Chinese (Chinese overseas, mainly foreign nationals); in PRC, it refers to only those Chinese who have become citizens of foreign countries, even though in Southeast Asia it includes some *huaqiao* who have been in the region for a long time.
Huashang 华商	Ethnic Chinese businessmen
Huayi 华裔	Descendants of Chinese, referring to foreign citizens of Chinese origin, but in China, it often refers to those Chinese who have lost their Chinese culture.
Huayi Ka 华裔卡	Green Card for those of Chinese origin
Laogong Yimin 劳工移民	Labour migration
Nay Pyi Taw (Naypyitaw)	New capital city of Myanmar
OCAO	Overseas Chinese Affairs Office (see *Qiaoban* 侨办)
"One Belt One Road" (OBOR) 一带一路 Strategy/Initiative	The economic belt of overland silk road and the twenty-first century maritime silk road, proposed by President Xi Jinping in 2013.
Qiao Ai 侨爱	Love of Chinese compatriots overseas
Qiaoban 侨办	Shortened form of *Qiaowu bangongshi* 侨务办公室 (OCAO)
Qiaobao 侨胞	Chinese compatriots overseas
Qiaolian 侨联; see ACFROCA	Abbreviated form of *Zhonghua quan guo guiguo huaqiao lianhehui* 中华全国归国华侨联合会

Qiaoshang 侨商	Chinese businessmen overseas who are citizens of China
Qiaowu gonggong waijiao 侨务公共外交	Diaspora Affairs Public Diplomacy
Shijie Huaqiao Huaren Gongshang Dahui 世界华侨华人工商大会	World Overseas Chinese Entrepreneurs Conference, established in 2015 by Beijing.
Shijie Huashang Dahui 世界华商大会	World Chinese Entrepreneurs Convention (WCEC), established in 1991 by Chinese overseas.
Xin Yimin 新移民	New migrants
Yidai Yilu 一带一路	See "One Belt One Road"
Zhong Guan Cun 中关村	An area known as Chinese Silicon Valley, located in Beijing
Zhongguo Qiaoshang Touzi Qiye Xiehui 中国侨商投资企业协会	China's Overseas Chinese Entrepreneurs/Investors Association
Zhonghua Minzu 中华民族	Chinese nation

PART 1

Understanding Beijing's Policy

Chapter 1

THE RISE OF CHINA AND THE CHINESE OVERSEAS[1]

China and India, the world's most populous countries, have huge overseas populations. Nevertheless, it is the Chinese overseas who have long been a focus of attention owing to the important role they have played, their links to China, and China's policies towards them. And, that focus has become sharper since China's rise and its efforts to use the Chinese overseas as social, political, and economic capital. Moreover, Beijing's leaders perceive that the Chinese overseas are crucial for the realization of the "China Dream". This chapter will deal briefly with two important developments linked to China's changing policy towards the Chinese overseas: the rise of China and the recent massive waves of Chinese migration to both the developed and developing countries.

This study attempts to address the following questions: Why and when did Beijing's policy towards the Chinese overseas change? What are the factors that contributed to this change? Which are the countries in Southeast Asia that still have strong anti-Chinese feelings and where major anti-Chinese violence has continued to occur? What are the factors that contribute to anti-Chinese feelings and violence? Did Beijing go out of its way to protect the Chinese overseas who were affected by past outbreaks of violence? Why has Beijing adopted a differentiated approach in dealing with the Chinese domiciled in different countries? Does Beijing still differentiate between Chinese nationals and foreign citizens of Chinese descent? How have the Chinese overseas reacted to China's new policy? What have been the responses of the countries that host these Chinese?

Beijing's responses to anti-Chinese violence and anti-Chinese sentiments in selected countries in Southeast Asia and beyond since the end of the twentieth century would give us a clear understanding of Beijing's policy towards the countries in question. This study presents examples from four Southeast Asian countries (Indonesia, Vietnam, Malaysia, and Myanmar), two Pacific Island countries (Solomon Islands and Tonga) and three countries in Africa and the Middle East (Egypt, Libya, and Yemen).

As Beijing's policy towards the Chinese overseas has also been the product of its responses to internal events and needs, six internal developments have been selected for this study: the Sichuan earthquake, the Beijing Olympics, the Beijing-initiated World Overseas Chinese Entrepreneurs Conference, Beijing's so-called *Huayi* Card, its "One Belt One Road" Strategy, and the development of Chinese soft power.

From these presentations, one would be able to appreciate some changes in Beijing's policy towards the Chinese overseas. These changes have occurred amidst China's rise as an economic heavyweight, which has made Beijing more confident than in the past and allowed its state-owned enterprises (SOEs) to spread their wings across the world.

TERMINOLOGY

Several terms have been used in this study to refer to the Chinese overseas. These terms need to be explained to avoid confusion. The term "overseas Chinese" is used to refer to *huaqiao* (华侨), or Chinese nationals overseas, while the term "Chinese overseas", coined by Professor Wang Gungwu, refers to the Chinese outside China regardless of nationality, comparable to the Chinese term *haiwai huaren* (海外华人).[2] The term "ethnic Chinese" refers to the Chinese overseas, mainly foreign nationals, more or less comparable to *huaren* (华人) in Chinese. But *huaren* in the PRC refers only to those Chinese who have become citizens of foreign countries, even though in Southeast Asian usage its flexible use often allows for the inclusion of some *huaqiao* who have been in Southeast Asia for a long period of time. The term *huayi* (华裔) literarily means the descendants of Chinese, referring to foreign citizens of Chinese origin, but, in China, it often refers to those Chinese who have lost their Chinese culture.

For the purposes of this study, the term "Chinese overseas" will be used to mean the Chinese outside China.[3] This is used as a general and inclusive term to include Chinese nationals overseas and foreign citizens of Chinese descent. Chinese terms such as *huaqiao, huaren* and *huayi* can be placed under the category of the Chinese overseas. In short, all Chinese outside China regardless of their citizenship and culture are termed "Chinese overseas". Nevertheless, occasionally the term "overseas Chinese" is still used to mean *huaqiao* in a specific context.

It should be noted that after the rise of China, the term *huaqiao* or overseas Chinese is often used by China to include Chinese workers who work either for China's SOEs or for non-Chinese companies. These workers are particularly large in number in Africa and the Middle East. In fact, they are transient and different from the traditional concept of *huaqiao* as they would return to China after finishing their contracts. Nevertheless, they are considered migrant workers and are often classified by China as part of the "overseas Chinese".

As explained at the beginning, the PRC has attached particular meanings to each of the Chinese terms mentioned above. *Huaqiao* and *huaren* have legal connotations while *huayi* has both legal and cultural connotations. Nevertheless, the leadership of the PRC in the twenty-first century has a tendency to put *huaqiao huaren* together, blurring their nationality distinction and referring to them as *qiaobao* (侨胞, Chinese compatriots overseas). *Huayi* is occasionally included in this group. This blurring of citizenship is done when the leadership feels that it is in the interest of China. It is hoped that the reader will appreciate the nuances that the various terms reflect.

It should be noted that the terms "Chinese overseas" and "overseas Chinese" exclude the Chinese in Taiwan, Hong Kong, and Macao.

The number of Chinese overseas, although sizeable, has been difficult to determine with certainty. This difficulty is due to a number of factors. First, it is difficult to define a Chinese in the Southeast Asian context. Many Chinese have been indigenized, as reflected in their names. Second, many governments, such as that of pre-Suharto Indonesia, Thailand, and the Philippines, do not have "ethnic Chinese" as a category in their censuses. Even if they do, those of Chinese descent may not identify themselves as "Chinese". Third, it is difficult to know the precise number of new Chinese migrants as many governments do not provide such information. Therefore, with the possible exception of some Western countries, the numbers of Chinese overseas that are available are merely estimates or educated guesses; there are no authoritative counts.

THE RISE OF CHINA AND THE CHINESE OVERSEAS

The world witnessed the rise of China towards the end of the last century. Prior to that, China was a weak country, ideologically strong but lacking in real state power. Apart from exporting its revolutionary ideology to small movements overseas, China's ability to exert meaningful influence was limited to its immediate borders. Even the three wars in which Beijing was involved — the Korean War in 1950–53, the Sino–Indian War in 1962, and the Sino–Vietnamese War in 1979 — were all waged in its immediate neighbourhood; the Chinese military had never been sent to fight beyond its immediate borders. It is true that China provided some third world countries with economic aid but the amounts involved were small and not comparable to the aid dispensed by the developed countries. The only exception was China's aid to North Korea and North Vietnam during their wars against Western powers. But, again, these are neighbouring states.

However, China has undergone massive transformation since the late 1970s, when Deng Xiaoping launched his open door policy. He introduced market reforms, industrialization and export-oriented manufacturing. Domestically, China's rapid economic growth translated to significant poverty alleviation and improvements in living standards. Today, China has become a major economic, political, and military power. The rise of China, or more correctly, the resurgence of China became perceptible by the beginning of the twenty-first century. By the year 2000 China felt strong economically as it joined the World Trade Organization (WTO) and proposed a Free Trade Zone with ASEAN. China also played a responsible role as a major power in the international economic regime by not devaluing the Renminbi in the wake of the Asian financial crisis of 1997–98.

China has today become not only the "world's factory", manufacturing goods for export worldwide, but also an aspiring banker seeking to provide funds for infrastructural investment in Asia and beyond. In 2014, China established the Asian Infrastructure Investment Bank (AIIB) to rival, if not the World Bank, at least the Asian Development Bank.[4] China's foreign reserves have increased tremendously, enabling it to purchase vast quantities of American bonds, indirectly sustaining the American economy. Moreover, the presence of China's SOEs has become palpable in many regions, especially Africa and the Middle East as China seeks to exploit natural resources abroad.

In other signs of its growing strength and confidence, China organized the prestigious 2008 Olympic Games and successfully held major international conferences. Moreover, it has started to develop soft power by, among other things, promoting the learning of the Chinese language through the establishment of Confucius Institutes around the world.

Observers have argued that China perceives itself as a new major power, and would like to be recognized by the world, including the United States, as such; it would like to play a role in the international arena as a major power, if not a great power.

As China grows in political and economic power, its policy towards the Chinese overseas has also changed. It has gradually abandoned its earlier practice of differentiating between *huaqiao* (Chinese nationals overseas) and *huaren* (foreign citizens of Chinese descent). In fact, as late as 1998, when Indonesia was in the throes of anti-Chinese riots, Beijing was still restrained in protecting Chinese Indonesians as they were citizens of Indonesia and hence no more within China's jurisdiction. The abandonment of this "hands off" policy subsequently was probably due to several factors: the rapid rise of China and the surge in the number of Chinese migrating since the end of the last century might have caused the leadership in Beijing to reconsider its position towards the Chinese overseas.

NEW WAVES OF CHINESE MIGRATION

After the re-emergence of Deng Xiaoping in 1977, a new wave of Chinese migration from the mainland took place. The new migrants or *xin yimin* (新移民) are different from the earlier Chinese migrants in at least four aspects: their destinations, quality, geographic origins, and the nature of their migration. In terms of destination, in the past, Chinese migrants usually headed for the developing countries, especially Southeast Asia. However, about 80 per cent of new migrants have migrated to the developed countries, including the United States, Canada, United Kingdom, Australia, New Zealand, Japan, and Singapore. Only about 20 per cent migrated to the developing countries (especially Southeast Asia).[5]

The quality of the new migrants differs from that of the old ones. The new migrants are usually better educated than the earlier migrants. Many not only possess skills but also capital. In contrast, the earlier migrants were mainly poor and uneducated.

In terms of geographic origins, unlike in the past, when Chinese migrants came largely from the southern provinces, the new migrants hail from a wider cross-section of the country. One can therefore argue that the recent wave of migration is a nation-wide phenomenon. In addition, some Southeast Asian Chinese have migrated to other developed countries, but their number appears to be much smaller than that of mainland *xin yimin*.

According to Zhuang Guotu, at the end of the 1990s there were about 6 million of *xin yimin*, mainly in the West rather than Southeast Asia (see Tables 1.1 and 1.2), but by 2007–8 the number of *xin yimin* had risen to 7–8 million.[6]

The nature of the new migrants is less "permanent" than previous waves of migrants. Owing to poor education and low social mobility, coupled with China's poverty then, the earlier migrants were more likely to remain in their adopted countries and eventually integrate into local society. In contrast, some among the new migrants who are less successful in their adopted lands have chosen either to return to China, now that the country is richer and offers greater opportunities, or seek their fortunes in third countries. Some new Chinese migrants in the West are keen to reap the benefits of the two worlds and have urged China to revive its dual nationality law for the Chinese overseas.

TABLE 1.1
Number of Chinese New Migrants in Developed Countries

(unit: in thousands)

Country	1981	1992	1999	1999 (unofficial estimate)
USA	806	1,800	2,830	Over 3,000
Canada	292	750	960	1,000
Australia	123	250	380	400
UK	91	250	250	270
France	150	N.A.	200	250
Netherlands	40	60	130	150
Germany	20	70	110	130
Italy	3.5	50	70	170
Japan	60	180	250	260
Total	1,585.5	3,410	5,180	5,630+

Source: Zhuang Guotu 庄国土, *Huaqiao huaren yu Zhongguo de Guanxi*《华侨华人与中国的关系》(Guangzhou 广州: Guangdong gaodeng jiaoyu chubanshe 广东高等教育出版社, 2001), pp. 353–54.

TABLE 1.2
Number of Chinese New Migrants in Southeast Asia

(unit: in thousands)

Country	As of 2007
Brunei	Not available
Cambodia	10
Indonesia	100–120
Malaysia	100–150
Myanmar	200–300?
Laos	10?
Philippines	150–200
Singapore	200–250
Thailand	200–300
Vietnam	50–100

Source: Zhuang Guotu 庄国土, "Zhongguo xin yimin yu Dongnanya huaren wenhua" 中国新移民与东南亚华人文化, *CHC Bulletin*, no. 9 (May 2007): 9.

Many new migrants are less well integrated into their adopted countries as the ease of communication and transportation in today's globalized world allows them to maintain their links with their country of birth and retain a migrant mentality. At the same time, some host societies are not too receptive of new migrants, causing the latter to feel unwelcome. This failure or inability to integrate into their host societies serves to perpetuate the old stereotype of "once a Chinese, always a Chinese".

There are various reasons why new migrants find it difficult to integrate into local society but China's policy towards the Chinese overseas is a crucial factor in their indigenization or otherwise. If China encourages full integration for the new migrants, it is more likely that new migrants would feel obliged to do so; otherwise, they may retain their migrant mentalities.

When speaking of Chinese new migrants, the focus is usually on those who have migrated to Europe, North America, Japan, Australia, and Southeast Asia; not much attention has been given to those who have moved to the Middle East and Africa. Also, labour migrants have often been ignored. According to one estimate, there were about 4 million Chinese labourers across the world.[7] This figure has not been verified and may be inflated. However, with a labour surplus in China, it is logical to assume that many Chinese have gone overseas to work as labourers.

Labour migration was one of the major characteristics of Chinese migration in the nineteenth century. It was known as the "*huagong* (华工) pattern" or "coolie pattern" of migration. Wang Gungwu argues that this pattern "derived from the migration of large numbers of coolie labour, normally men of peasant origin, landless labourers and the urban poor."[8]

Labour migration has recurred in the twenty-first century and is known as *laogong yimin* (劳工移民). But this recent wave of labour migration differs from the historical pattern of labour migration in several aspects. One difference is that the new labour migrants are hired by China's SOEs. These SOEs operate in many resource-rich but politically unstable countries, for instance, those in the Middle East and Africa. When there was turbulence in some of these countries, the SOEs were usually affected and their Chinese labourers had to be evacuated.

Chinese labourers often work in Chinese companies involved in the building of railroads, real estate development, factories, as well as in mining and oil exploration. Strictly speaking, they are not migrants but "guest workers". They are often isolated from the local society. Usually they are obliged to leave when their projects are completed. These "overseas Chinese" are Chinese nationals and should not be counted alongside actual migrants who intend to stay and make a living in their newly-adopted lands. A mainland China scholar has argued that these labour migrants do not belong to the category of "permanent migrants" although some of them remain in the country in question indefinitely.[9] Nevertheless, the "guest workers" or "contract workers" are different from regular migrants. However, Beijing often classifies them as part of the "overseas Chinese", as seen in the case of Libya.

THE CHANGING CHINESE OVERSEAS SOCIETY

New Chinese migrants have had a major impact on the nature of the "overseas Chinese" society, especially in the developed countries of North America and Europe, and in Australia, New Zealand, and Japan (see Table 1.1). Whereas the ethnic

Chinese communities in these countries used to be small and fairly well integrated into their host societies, in a short period of time, these communities have been transformed into immigrant communities again owing to the influx of new migrants. The increase in the number of new migrants in these countries ranges from 3 times to 22 times. For instance, in the United States, there were only 806,000 Chinese migrants in 1981, but by 1999 the number had risen to over 2,830,000; in the United Kingdom, the numbers were 91,000 in 1981 and more than 250,000 in 1999; in Italy, 3,500 in 1981 and 70,000 in 1999; and, in Japan, 60,000 in 1981 and 250,000 in 1999.

The number of new migrants in Southeast Asia is not known. From Table 1.2, which is based on estimates, the number would seem to be quite significant. Nevertheless, as the Chinese communities in Southeast Asia, with the possible exception of Laos, Cambodia, and Myanmar, are long established and better integrated into their host societies, it seems that the arrival of new Chinese migrants has not had the effect of transforming these communities into the migrant communities they once were.

Many of the new Chinese migrants are better educated than previous waves of migrants and some are wealthy and have been active in the local socio-political scene. This is especially obvious in the West, where the prevailing liberal political systems are conducive to their political participation. In contrast, new Chinese migrants in Southeast Asia are generally less politically active as the political systems tend to be less liberal and where ethnic-tension between Chinese and non-Chinese remains.

Many new migrants still have connections with China and maintain contact with the Chinese embassies where they reside. This means the Chinese government could influence their behaviours, which could adversely affect the relationship between China and their host countries.

NEW CHINESE MIGRANTS AND BUSINESS

There are quite a few studies on how new Chinese migrants in the West, such as Canada and the United States, have adapted to their new lands, and the results show that the process has not been smooth.[10] However, there are few studies on the new migrants' venture into business in their newly-adopted lands to determine how successful they have been. From the sketchy information available, it appears that few new Chinese migrants have become major business figures in their new countries.

In the past few years China has encouraged and invited Chinese overseas entrepreneurs to visit and help in China's economic transformation and development, including the establishment of economic relations with other countries. For instance, at the second session of China's 12th People's Political Consultative Conference in 2014, some new migrants were invited as observers. Later, interviews with three of the successful "overseas Chinese" entrepreneurs who attended the meeting were carried in Chinese online media. These three were: Xie Chongtong of Thailand, Yi Rubo of California, USA, and Li Wenzhong of Argentina.[11] Below are their brief biographies.

Xie Chongtong (谢崇通) was born in China and received a university education there. In 1991 he went to Thailand to start his information technology business as there was not much competition in this industry from among the Chinese migrants in the country then. He gradually emerged as a giant in the industry and established the Thai Star Chinese Computer Group (泰国星华电脑集团公司) and served as its chairman. He was also the deputy chairman of Thailand's "Committee for Fostering the Unification of China" (泰国中国统一促进会). It seems that he established a family in Thailand, and his son later went to the United States to study. Xie may have become a Thai citizen. He maintains closed links with China and was instrumental in helping a Chinese company win a contract to build Thailand's high speed train.[12]

Yi Rubo (易如波) was born in China. He began to harbour the idea of going overseas in 1992 when he was still at university. After graduation, he moved to California, where he chose to invest in the property industry in Los Angeles. Initially, his business was small, but gradually he was able to establish a large company. It is not disclosed how he got rich and who his clients are. It is possible that he serves mainland Chinese who seek property in California. Yi Rubo is now chairman of the board of Zhong Ang Real Estate Group (中昂地产集团董事长) and deputy chairman of the US-Chinese Real Estate Businessmen's Association (美国华商会常务副主席). It is not known whether he is still holding a Chinese passport.[13]

Li Wenzhong (李文忠) was born in China and educated as a Traditional Chinese Medicine (TCM) doctor. In 1988 he established a private TCM hospital in Beijing. He wanted to go overseas to invest and eventually selected Argentina. There, he initially established a TCM clinic. As TCM was not popular in Argentina, he had difficulties getting accepted. However, after making countless efforts, he eventually received recognition by the local Chinese community. Li is now an adviser to the Federation of Ethnic Chinese Enterprises in Argentina (阿根廷华人企业联合会) and chairman of the board of the Li Feng Medical Group (阿根廷李丰药业集团董事长). He has been a frequent visitor to China. It is possible that he has become a citizen of Argentina, having resided there for twenty years.[14]

A highly successful *xin yimin* businessman who was not included in the interviews is Zhong Shengjian (钟声坚) of Singapore.[15] He was born in Guangdong in 1958. Not much is known about his education and life in China. He moved to Singapore in 1988 at the age of 30 and established Yanlord Land Holdings (仁恒置地), specializing in real estate. In 1993 he started building luxury apartments in Shanghai and Nanjing and became a successful businessman. He later also worked with other companies in China to invest in the paper manufacturing business and in household equipment manufacturing business. But his main business remains in property. In 2006, Yanlord Land Holdings was listed on the Singapore stock market. Zhong was identified as the seventh richest man in Singapore in 2010, with a total wealth of US$1.6 billion.[16] He was formerly deputy president of the Singapore Chinese Chamber of Commerce and Industry and was in charge of raising funds for the Singapore Chinese Cultural Centre.

The above four new migrants were all adults when they left China. At least three of them also received university education in China and one of them was already an established TCM doctor before migrating. Initially, three of them had some difficulties integrating into their host societies but they managed to stay on. Yet, their relationship with China was strong and their businesses still have close links with the country. In the interviews, the three interviewees enthusiastically expressed their desire to work for the economic interest of China.

The earlier migrants and their descendants appear to have been more successful in business in their adopted lands as they have been there longer than the new migrants and are hence better established. This is particularly the case among Chinese migrants in Southeast Asia. In contrast, the new Chinese migrants are more successful in doing business in China as they are more familiar with the situation in their native land.

The ethnic Chinese have played an important role in Southeast Asia. They dominate commerce and the business sector and form the economic elite in all of the Southeast Asian countries. Some observers exaggerate the position of the Southeast Asian Chinese, arguing that they dominate the Southeast Asian economies. But no one can deny that ethnic Chinese, or Southeast Asians of Chinese descent, do indeed play crucial roles in the Southeast Asian economies. From Beijing's perspective, the wealth of the ethnic Chinese (or what it considers the Chinese overseas) and their crucial roles in the local economies would be valuable for China as it becomes a global economic and political heavyweight. Thus the Chinese in Southeast Asia have become targets of Beijing's changing policy on the Chinese overseas, introduced after China's phenomenal economic success.

XI JINPING'S "CHINA DREAM" AND THE CHINESE OVERSEAS

Xi Jinping replaced Hu Jintao as the general secretary of the Communist Party of China (CPC) in November 2012 and president of the People's Republic of China (PRC) since March 2013. It appears that President Xi is more dynamic than previous presidents of the PRC. Once he came to power, he proposed the so-called "China Dream" (中国梦), that is, "the great rejuvenation of the Chinese nation (*Zhonghua minzu de weida fuxing* 中华民族的伟大复兴)". He first mentioned his "China Dream" in November 2012 during a "Rejuvenation

Exhibition"[17] and later officially proposed it at the 12th National People's Congress (17 March 2013):

> To realize a moderately prosperous society, to build a strong, democratic, civilized, harmonious and modern socialist state, to realize the great rejuvenation of the Chinese nation, these are the China Dream...that is the glorious tradition tirelessly pursued by our forefathers.... To realize the China Dream, we must coalesce for China's strength; that is, the strength of the great unity among the people of all ethnic groups (各族人民). The China Dream is the dream of our nation and of every Chinese national (每个中国人)......[18]

Initially, Xi included only "various ethnic groups" in China and "every Chinese national" in this "China Dream". However, in 2014, after he proposed his "One Belt One Road" Strategy (later, "Strategy" was changed to "Initiative" in the official English translation) to connect China and the world, he defined the sons and daughters of China (*Zhonghua Ernü* 中华儿女) to mean both Chinese in mainland China and the Chinese overseas. In the speech that he made at the 7th Conference of the World Federation of *Huaqiao Huaren* Associations on 7 June 2014, he said:

> A united Chinese nation is the common root of the sons and daughters of China within and outside China; the rich Chinese culture is the common soul of the sons and daughters of China; to realize the rejuvenation of the Chinese nation is the common dream of the sons and daughters of China. Common roots make us deeply rooted, a common soul makes us remember each other, a common dream makes us have one heart; we will be able to jointly write a new chapter in the development of the Chinese nation.[19]

He further noted:

> There are tens of millions of Chinese overseas compatriots (*haiwai qiaobao* 海外侨胞), all of whom are members of one big Chinese family (*Zhonghua da jiating* 中华大家庭). For a long time, overseas Chinese, generation after generation, inherited the excellent tradition of the Chinese nation: they did not forget their fatherland, they did not forget their ancestral province, they did not forget that in their body there is Chinese blood, [therefore] they have enthusiastically supported the Chinese revolution, China's construction, and the reform of China. They are making important contributions to the development of the Chinese nation and fostering the peaceful unification between mainland China and Taiwan and fostering close and friendly cooperation between the Chinese people and the people of other countries. The people of China will always remember the contribution of our Chinese compatriots overseas.[20]

Against this background, it is easy to understand why there has been an attempt on the part of Beijing to woo the Chinese overseas to work for the national interest of China.

Notes

1. The term "Chinese overseas" is used to mean ethnic Chinese outside China regardless of nationality. It is different from "overseas Chinese", which refers to China's nationals overseas. For a detailed explanation, see "Terminology" in this chapter.
2. See for instance, Wang Gungwu's book entitled *China and the Chinese Overseas* (Singapore: Times Academic Press, 1991).
3. For a detailed discussion of these terms and their usage, see Leo Suryadinata, ed., *Ethnic Chinese as Southeast Asians* (Singapore: Institute of Southeast Asian Studies, 1997), pp. 2–4.

4. For a brief study of the AIIB, see Stuart Larkin, "China's 'Great Leap Outward': The AIIB in context", *ISEAS Perspective*, no. 27 (9 June 2015); and his "Multiple Challenges for the AIIB", *ISEAS Perspective*, no. 33 (2 July 2015).
5. Zhuang Guotu 庄国土, "Zhongguo xin yimin yu Dongnanya huaren wenhua" 中国新移民与东南亚华人文化, *CHC Bulletin*, no. 9 (May 2007), p. 9.
6. Zhuang Guotu 庄国土, "Huaqiao huaren fenbu zhuangkuang he fazhan qushi" 华侨华人分布状况和发展趋势, *Yanjiu yu Tantao*《研究与探讨》, Zhonghua qiaowu diyi kan 中华侨务第一刊, 2010年 No. 4 <http://qwgzyj.gqb.gov.cn/yjytt/155/1830.shtml> (accessed 4 January 2016).
7. <News.21cn.com/zhuanti/domestic/hwlg/> (accessed 5 June 2016).
8. Wang Gungwu, "Patterns of Chinese Migration in Historical Perspective", in *China and the Chinese Overseas* (Singapore: Times Academic Press, 1991), p. 8.
9. Zhang Xiuming 张秀明, "Guoji yimin tixizhong de zhongguo dalu yimin—Ye tan xin yimin wenti" 国际移民体系中的中国大陆移民—也谈新移民问题, in *Shijie Shiye: Zouchu guomen de zhongguo xin yimin*《世界视野：走出国门的中国新移民》, edited by Zhao Hongying 赵红英 and Zhang Chunwang 张春旺 (Beijing 北京: Zhongguo hua qiao chubanshe 中国华侨出版社, 2013), p. 77.
10. See various studies in Leo Suryadinata, ed., *Migration, Indigenization and Interaction: Chinese Overseas and Globalization* (Singapore: World Scientific, 2011).
11. I have tried to look for information on the other new migrant attendees but to no avail.
12. Zhongguo Zhengxie Wang 中国政协网, "Haiwai liexi zhe: haiwai chuangyezhe de qiusuo zhilu" 海外列席者：海外创业者的求索之路，12 March 2014, <http://www.zgzx.com.cn/2014-03/12/content_8619104.htm> (accessed 10 April 2016).
13. Ibid.
14. Ibid.

15. The information on Zhong is taken from the following sources: Zhong Shengjian 钟声坚, Hudong baike 互动百科 <baike.com>; Shanwei Shimin Wang 汕尾市民网 <http://www.swsm.net/thread-313328-1-1.html>; Forbes, "Singapore's 50th Richest: #20 Zhong Sheng Jian", <http://www.forbes.com/profile/zhong-sheng-jian>; Yanlord Land Holdings website, <www.yanlordland.com/en/Corporate_Governance2.asp?>.
16. Forbes, "Singapore's 40 Richest: #7 Zhong Sheng Jian", 28 July 2010, <www.forbes.com/lists/2010/79/singapore-10_Zhong-Sheng-Jian_ZUOE.html> (accessed 12 April 2016).
17. Xi Jinping, "Shixian Zhonghua minzu weida fuxing shi zhonghua minzu jindai yilai zui weida de mengxiang" 实现中华民族伟大复兴是中华民族近代以来最伟大的梦想, in *Xi Jinping tan zhiguo lizheng* 《习近平谈治国理政》 (Beijing 北京: Foreign Languages Publishing 外文出版社，2014), pp. 35–36.
18. The English translation is by the author. For the original text see, "Zai di shier jie quan'guo renmin daibiao dahui di yici huiyi shang de tanhua" 在第十二届全国人民代表大会第一次会议上的谈话, in *Xi Jinping tan zhiguo lizheng* 《习近平谈治国理政》 (Beijing 北京: Foreign Languages Publishing 外文出版社，2014), pp. 38–43. Also in "2013 quanguo lianghui, xinhuawang" 2013 全国两会， 新华网, <http://www.news.cn/2013lh/> (accessed 31 May 2016).
19. The English translation is by the author. For the original text, see *Renmin Wang-Renmin Ribao* 《人民网-人民日报》, "Xi Jinping huijian di qijie shijie huaqiao huaren shetuan lianyi dahui daibiao" 习近平会见第七届世界华侨华人社团联谊大会代表, 7 June 2014, <http://pic.people.com.cn/n/2014/0607/c1016-25116878.html> (accessed 18 March 2016). See also Xi Jinping, "Shixian Zhonghua minzu weida fuxing shi haineiwai Zhonghua ernü de gongtong mengxiang" 实现中华民族伟大复兴是海内外中华儿女的共同的梦, in *Xi jinping tan zhiguo lizheng* 《习近平谈治国理政》 (Beijing 北京: Foreign Languages Publishing 外文出版社，2014), pp. 63–64.
20. Ibid.

Chapter 2

THE CHINESE OVERSEAS AND THE "OVERSEAS CHINESE AFFAIRS OFFICE"

Beijing's policy towards the Chinese overseas began to change at the end of the twentieth century, when there was a sudden surge in Chinese migration to the West, mainly Canada and the United States. It was reported that some of these new migrants who hold foreign citizenship started urging China to amend its 1980 single citizenship law so that they could have dual citizenship status. The Overseas Chinese Affairs Office (OCAO), also known as *Qiaowu bangongshi* or *Qiaoban* in Mandarin, which had been inactive for some years, started to strive for their cause then. OCAO officials began exercising their influence on Chinese overseas affairs and having some bearing on China's foreign policy. This chapter deals briefly with the organization of OCAO, its increasingly important role in Chinese overseas affairs, its initiative in blurring the distinction between Chinese nationals and foreign Chinese, its attempts at reviving a dual nationality law, and its links to the "One Belt One Road" Strategy.

THE CHINESE OVERSEAS

In 2015, China's OCAO estimated that there were 60 million Chinese overseas.[1] This is also the figure that Beijing's top leaders, including Premier Li Keqiang, cite. In contrast, the Taiwan Overseas Chinese Affairs Commission (侨务委员会) estimated the number to be 42 million as at end 2014.[2] This is a conservative estimate, lower even than the estimate the Chinese OCAO used in 2010, i.e., 45.4 million.[3] Scholars Dudley L. Poston, Jr., and Mei-Yu Yu assess the Taiwan Overseas Chinese Affairs Commission's statistics to be more valuable because they are "systematic and comparable overtime".[4]

If we use the Taiwanese estimates,[5] there were 39,568,000 Chinese overseas in 2010 (see Table 2.1), of which the largest concentration was in Asia, constituting about 76 per cent.[6] Of the Chinese overseas in Asia, the largest numbers were in Southeast Asia, accounting for about 91 per cent in 2010 (see Table 2.2).

TABLE 2.1
Chinese Overseas Population by Region, 2010–14

(unit: in thousands)

Year	Asia	America	Europe	Oceania	Africa	Total
2010	29,815	7,255	1,317	945	236	39,568
2011	30,041	7,498	1,565	955	249	40,307
2012	30,723	7,690	1,608	1,066	270	41,357
2013	30,656	7,903	1,696	1,129	401	41,784
2014	31,008	8,105	1,756	1,169	466	42,504

Source: Qiaowu Weiyuanhui (Taiwan) 侨务委员会 (台湾), "Haiwai huaren ji Taiqiao renshu" 海外华人及台侨人数, 29 July 2016, <www.ocac.gov.tw/OCAC/Pages/List.aspx?nodeid=33> (accessed 4 January 2016).

TABLE 2.2
Number of Chinese Overseas in Southeast Asia, 2010

(unit: in thousands)

Country	Chinese Overseas
Indonesia	8,011*
Thailand	7,513
Malaysia	6,541
Singapore	2,808
Philippines	1,243
Myanmar	1,054
Vietnam	990
Laos	176
Cambodia	147
Brunei Darussalam	50
Total	28,536

Note: *Zhuang Guotu, writing in the OCAO publication, gave an even higher figure of over 10 million.[8] In fact, the Indonesian Census of 2010 reported that the Chinese constitute about 1.2 per cent of the total Indonesian population, which is less than 300 million. The most likely figure is around 2 per cent of the population, i.e. 5 million.

Source: Qiaowu Weiyuanhui (Taiwan) 侨务委员会 (台湾), 2011 年侨务统计年报 *2011 Statistical Yearbook of the Overseas Chinese Affairs Council*, p. 11, <www.ocac.gov.tw/OCAC/File/Attach/313/File_2430.pdf> (accessed 4 January 2016).

It should be noted that the percentage of the Chinese overseas in Southeast Asia has significantly declined in the past fifty years owing to the new wave of Chinese migration to the developed countries. In the mid-1950s, for instance, 96.7 per cent of the Chinese overseas were found in Asia, compared to 2.4 per cent in America.[7] But, by 2010, the Chinese in America had increased to 18.6 per cent (7,255,000) of the population.

The migration of the Chinese began more than 1,000 years ago. For the purposes of this discussion, the modern period is more relevant. During the Qing dynasty (1644–1911), the Chinese overseas were initially ignored. Only later did the Qing dynasty realize the importance of the Chinese overseas and begin to amend the policy of abandonment to that of protection. Nevertheless, this was a bit too late as the revolutionaries had already been able to garner the support of the Chinese overseas. The Chinese overseas became the funding source, if not the political force, behind the 1911 Xinhai Revolution in China.

The Xinhai Revolution has widely been interpreted as a revolution based overseas as Dr Sun Yat Sen, being an overseas Chinese himself, received support from his overseas counterparts. Not surprisingly, after its establishment, the Republic of China (ROC) introduced a policy to include the Chinese overseas as part of the new Chinese nation. Once someone was born a Chinese, he or she was considered a Chinese, i.e., a national of China, regardless of birthplace.

Hence, many Chinese overseas possessed dual nationality. Nevertheless, China was weak and it did not have the power to "protect" the Chinese overseas. Numerous anti-Chinese movements or riots took place in several countries but China, led by the Chinese Nationalist Party — Kuomintang (Guomindang or KMT, for short) — was unable to do much.

After the Communist Party of China (CPC) established the People's Republic of China (PRC) in 1949, it inherited the KMT's policy towards the Chinese overseas and held to it initially. But this policy began to change when PRC Prime Minister Zhou Enlai attended the Afro-Asian Conference in Bandung in 1955. Beijing then encouraged the Chinese overseas to integrate themselves into their respective societies. This change of policy was aimed at gaining the support of the Southeast Asian states by resolving their historical dual nationality problem.[9] China was willing to sign a treaty with countries that had sizeable numbers of Chinese. Nonetheless, no PRC nationality law as such was promulgated. A law came into being only in 1980 after Deng Xiaoping's visit to Southeast Asia at the end of 1978, when he discovered that the problem of Chinese loyalty was still an issue for the governments of some of the countries. Deng heard firsthand from some Southeast Asian leaders, especially Singapore's Lee Kuan Yew, who expressed the idea that while China should not expect the Southeast Asian Chinese to make sacrifices for China, the latter should not expect China to make sacrifices on their behalf either.[10] This view may have led Deng eventually to formulate the 1980 nationality law.

After the promulgation of the law, China disclaimed the Chinese overseas who had obtained foreign citizenship on their own free will. Once a Chinese overseas obtained foreign citizenship, he or she ceased to be a Chinese national and hence was outside China's jurisdiction. Legally, the nationality problem of the Chinese overseas was resolved, and China was reluctant to get involved in the affairs of non-Chinese citizens.

However, this situation changed after the rise of China and the recent influx of Chinese migrants to the developed and developing countries. China has started to show interest not only in the *huaqiao* but also in the *huaren*. The organization that has been eager to push the new policy towards the Chinese overseas is OCAO.

OVERSEAS CHINESE AFFAIRS OFFICE (OCAO)

When the PRC was established in 1949, OCAO was known as the Chinese Central Government Overseas Chinese Affairs Committee (中央人民政府华侨事务委员会), abbreviated as Zhong Qiao Wei (中侨委). It was part of the Chinese Central Government

Administration Council (中央人民政府政务院). In 1954 the Administration Council was replaced by the State Council (国务院), Zhong QiaoWei was then renamed Overseas Chinese Affairs Committee of the PRC (中华人民共和国华侨事务委员会) and placed under the newly-formed State Council. The institution became inactive during the Cultural Revolution (1966–76). However, after Deng Xiaoping re-emerged, the Overseas Chinese Affairs Committee was renamed Overseas Chinese Affairs Office (国务院华侨事务委员会办公室), abbreviated as Qiaoban (侨办), although remaining under the State Council.

The main tasks of OCAO are to draft laws and regulations regarding the Chinese overseas and recommend policy on the Chinese overseas for the State Council to consider. It undertakes research and investigation on the Chinese overseas, mobilizes them to be patriotic and to invest in China with a view to helping realize the "socialist construction of the PRC". Furthermore, OCAO advises the State Council on matters regarding the protection of the legitimate interests of the Chinese overseas.[11]

OCAO directly manages two overseas Chinese-linked universities, i.e., Jinan University (located in Guangzhou, Guangdong) and Huaqiao University (located in Quanzhou, Fujian). It is also in charge of the Chinese News Agency Overseas and China Travel. In 1993, it was reported that OCAO was established in almost every province and prefecture. There were 30 provincial OCAOs and 1,400 prefecture level OCAOs.[12]

The OCAO became influential after a rising China began to see the expanding number of Chinese new migrants as a potential resource to tap. Initially it focused on returned overseas Chinese but gradually it has begun to also deal with the

Chinese still residing overseas. One of the functions of OCAO is to promote Chinese education outside China and encourage economic and scientific interactions between the Chinese overseas and the Chinese in the mainland.[13]

As OCAO also deals with many Chinese who are foreign nationals, it has established a separate entity known as China's Overseas Exchange Association (中国海外交流协会) to alleviate sensitivities over its intentions.[14] In fact, this entity is the OCAO in disguise because its personnel overlap with that of OCAO. For instance, Qiu Yuanping, who is the director of OCAO, is also the chairperson of China's Overseas Exchange Association. According to Professor Zhou Nanjing, a leading scholar on the Chinese overseas at Peking University, OCAO officials have been overly eager to promote the dual citizenship law (dual nationality law) for the Chinese overseas.[15]

Apart from the OCAO, another organization dedicated to Chinese overseas affairs is the nominally non-governmental organization known as the All-China Federation of Returned Overseas Chinese Association (ACFROCA, *Zhonghua quanguo guiguo huaqiao lianhehui* 中华全国归国华侨联合会), abbreviated as Qiaolian (侨联), which is present throughout China. Established in 1956, the organization became inactive during the Cultural Revolution (1966–76) but was revitalized after Deng Xiaoping assumed power. As of 1993, there were about 2,700 Qiaolians at the prefecture level.[16] The ACFROCA is based in Beijing. Its main task is to help resettle returned overseas Chinese, assist the Chinese government to convince other Chinese overseas to invest their capital in China, encourage the professionals among the latter to work for China and to establish their own overseas Chinese enterprises.

DEBATE ON DUAL CITIZENSHIP STATUS

In November 1999, a Chinese leader from OCAO stated during the National Overseas Chinese Affairs Working Committee Meeting held in Qingdao, Shandong province, that there were plans to promulgate a dual citizenship law for the Chinese overseas.[17] In the same year, during the second session of the Ninth People's Political Consultative Conference (PPCC), Chen Duo, Ye Peiying and ten other committee members proposed that the dual status of Chinese citizens should not be abrogated (Proposal No. 2171). In 2004, during the second session of the Tenth PPCC, another proposal (No. 0222) was made to the effect that the part of the PRC Constitution relating to the citizenship law be amended so that Beijing can selectively recognize dual citizenship. At the end of 2004, Hong Kong's Fenghuang Weishi TV organized a debate on the dual nationality issue, which sparked exchanges on social media.

Professor Zhou Nanjing took the opportunity to organize a *bitan hui* (written debate) on this important issue and subsequently compiled the arguments into an informative book.[18] Those who supported dual nationality status (dual citizenship status) based their arguments on the following grounds:

1. The majority of the countries across the world allow dual citizenship and China should follow suit.
2. The single citizenship policy was made when China was weak.
3. Reintroducing dual citizenship status would allow the Chinese overseas to enter and leave China freely and make major contributions that would be in China's national interest.

4. The Chinese overseas would also be able to participate in the politics of China and foster the unification of China.
5. When these Chinese overseas commit crimes while on Chinese soil, they can be tried in accordance with PRC law.

Those who opposed the abrogation of the single citizenship policy based their arguments on the following grounds:

1. The majority of the Chinese overseas are in Southeast Asia. Owing to historical and political legacy, the local people of the region continue to be suspicious of the loyalties of the Chinese overseas and are resentful of their superior economic positions.
2. The indigenous governments would like the ethnic Chinese to integrate themselves into their respective societies and be loyal to their adopted lands.
3. The reintroduction of the dual citizenship law would only reinforce the stereotypes of the ethnic Chinese among the local populations of Southeast Asia, namely, that the ethnic Chinese constitute a "yellow peril", a "fifth column" waiting to penetrate their countries. These rekindled suspicions could affect China's relations with many of the countries that host ethnic Chinese.
4. If China wanted to attract the ethnic Chinese in the West to return to China to work, it could give them "green cards" so that they could have long term residency and work rights in China.[19] There is no need for a re-introduction of the dual citizenship law.

Support for a dual citizenship law is strongest among OCAO officials, who are China-centred, scholars who do not have much experience with Chinese overseas issues, and new Chinese migrants in north America, especially in Canada, who feel that they can get away with the dual citizenship law. However, ethnic Chinese leaders in or scholars on Southeast Asia and ethnic Chinese who have been relatively well integrated into their respective societies (including those in the United States) oppose dual citizenship status for ethnic Chinese. They feel that the time is not ripe for a dual citizenship law and that the loyalties of the ethnic Chinese would always be suspected if a dual citizenship law were to be re-introduced. Life would become more difficult for them and ethnic tensions in their host countries would be higher.

The debate on the citizenship issue seems to have made Beijing realize that the single citizenship law was still relevant and served the national interest of China. Consequently, no amendment was made to the 1980 Citizenship Law.

The OCAO realized that it was difficult to push the dual citizenship law. In June 2005, Chen Yujie, OCAO director, remarked that "not recognizing dual nationality was for the sake of protecting Overseas Chinese interest."[20]

Nevertheless, behind the scenes, OCAO officials continued to blur the distinction between Chinese citizens and ethnic Chinese who are not citizens. Professor Zhou Nanjing mentions OCAO's establishment on 16 January 2008 of an association known as Zhongguo Qiaoshang Touzi Qiye Xiehui (China's Overseas Chinese Entrepreneurs/investors Association) as an example of this practice. The word *qiaoshang* (or *huaqiao shangren*) in the association's title means "Chinese businessmen overseas who are citizens of China", but the association's members "include ethnic Chinese businessmen (*huashang*), foreign citizens of Chinese descent (*waiji huaren*), and Hong Kong and Macao compatriots who have invested in mainland China".[21] The honorary chairman of the association at the time of its founding was Guo Dongpo (then the director of OCAO), its president was Xie Guomin (Thai name: Dhanin Chearavanont), and its executive members included Lin Wenjing (Indonesian name: Sutanto Djuhar), Chen Jianghe (Indonesian name: Sukanto Tanoto), and Li Wenzheng (Indonesian name: Mochtar Riady).[22] These businessmen are clearly not *qiaoshang* but foreign citizens of Chinese descent.

Zhou Nanjing maintained that the OCAO should not target Chinese who were foreign citizens as the object of its policy as this constituted intervention in the affairs of foreign countries. He further noted that "we do not want other countries to intervene in our Taiwan and Tibetan affairs. As the ethnic Chinese have become foreign citizens, why should [OCAO] consider them as our own citizens, what was the intention of such a move?"[23] He quoted the Confucius saying, "What you do not want done to you, do not do to others."

Nevertheless, OCAO has not heeded Zhou Nanjing's advice. It continues its practice of blurring the distinction between Chinese citizens and foreign citizens of Chinese descent.

DUAL CITIZENSHIP FOR HONG KONG CHINESE?

At this juncture, it is important to discuss the 1980 Nationality Law with regard to Hong Kong. On 15 May 1996, prior to the return of Hong Kong to the PRC, the Standing Committee of the National People's Congress passed a law which clearly stated that all Hong Kong residents of Chinese descent were Chinese nationals and that those who were also British Nationals (Overseas) were allowed to use their foreign documents to travel overseas but could not expect the British Consulate to protect them while they were in Hong Kong.[24]

In short, Beijing would not recognize the British nationality of Hong Kong residents. Not surprisingly, when then British Foreign Secretary Philip Hammond asked Beijing for information on the disappearance in December 2015 of Hong Kong bookseller Lee Bo, who was considered a British national, China's foreign minister, Wang Yi, responded that Mr Lee was "first and foremost a Chinese."[25]

Hong Kong Chinese are considered special and the 1980 Chinese Nationality Law does not apply to them. The 1996 "amendment" to the law was confined to Hong Kong residents of Chinese descent, and it has not been applied to the Chinese in foreign countries. It is, therefore, safe to assume that the 1980 Chinese Nationality Law still holds. (For the text of the 1980 Chinese Nationality Law, see appendix.)

CHINESE OVERSEAS AS SOCIAL CAPITAL

The Beijing leadership seems to assess that the Chinese overseas are no longer a liability but an asset for China. Beijing considers the Chinese in Southeast Asia and beyond as members of the "Chinese nation" that could support China both economically and politically, especially in China's quest to become a major power. When China was weak and underdeveloped, its attraction was minimal for the Chinese overseas. Furthermore, China was not strong enough to exercise a more assertive policy with regard to the Chinese overseas. However, China's economic strength today has enhanced Beijing's capability in the foreign policy arena and it wants to show its influence to Asians, if not to the rest of the world. China's new foreign policy stance has been reflected in various events in recent years.

First of all, Beijing began to relax the distinction between *huaqiao* and *huaren* from 2001,[26] when it revived the semi-official organization Zhongguo guiqiao lianhehui (中国归侨联合会) or Federation of Returned Overseas Chinese Associations (Qiaolian (侨联) for short) and invited *huaren* (foreign citizens of Chinese descent) throughout the world to be its "advisers" and "overseas committee members". In the same year OCAO organized a meeting of the World Federation of *Huaqiao Huaren* Associations (世界华侨华人社团联谊会), inviting both Chinese citizens overseas and foreign citizens of Chinese descent to participate.

In 2006 during an outbreak of anti-Chinese violence in the Solomon Islands, China began to repatriate all affected Chinese, regardless of their nationality, to Guangdong and Hong Kong.[27] In May 2008, when a massive earthquake occurred in Wenchuan county in Sichuan, Beijing appealed to the *huaqiao* and *huaren* to show their solidarity with China by making contributions.[28] In the same year, Beijing again appealed to all Chinese overseas, regardless of their citizenship, to help China ensure the success of the Beijing Olympic Games and to participate as volunteers during the occasion.[29] Beijing emphasized that the Chinese overseas were still members of the Chinese nation (*Zhonghua Minzu* 中华民族), thus promoting Chinese transnationalism.

In 2004, China established Han Ban (汉办) or the Executive Body of the Chinese Language Council International to promote the teaching of the Chinese language (or the Han language, as it is known in mainland China) and culture. This is being done by establishing schools known as Confucius Institutes in Southeast Asia and beyond.

In 2011, China introduced a Great Overseas Chinese Affairs Policy (大侨务政策), emphasizing the inclusion of *huaren* within its "Overseas Chinese Affairs" programme. This policy became clearer when Xi Jinping assumed the presidency in 2013. It began to be implemented in 2014 when President Xi proposed the "One Belt One Road" Strategy in which the Chinese overseas were envisaged to play a part. The first World Overseas Chinese Entrepreneurs Conference (世界华侨华人工商大会) was held in Beijing in early July 2015, competing with the ethnic Chinese-initiated "World Chinese Entrepreneurs Convention" (世界华商大会), which has been held periodically since its launch in Singapore in 1991. Towards the end of 2015, the pilot project of the *Huayi Ka* (华裔卡, Card for those of Chinese origin) was proposed by the Beijing authorities, aimed at attracting professionals from among the Chinese overseas to work in Zhong Guan Cun, China's Silicon Valley.

The above are the domestic drivers of Beijing's changing policy towards the Chinese overseas. But, the policy must also be seen against the backdrop of China's foreign policy and how it has responded to external events. This will be the subject of discussion in the next chapter.

Notes

1. The Chinese American Professors and Professionals Network 美国华裔教授专家网, "Guowuyuan qiaoban: haiwai huaqiao huaren da 6000 wan Zhongguo jiang zhubu jiangdi 'luka' menkan-qianzheng" 国务院侨办: 海外华侨华人达 6000 万中国将逐步降低"绿卡"门槛-签证, 3 May 2014, <scholarsupdate.hi2net.com/news.asp?NewsID=14335> (accessed 4 January 2016).
2. Qiaowu Weiyuanhui (Taiwan) 侨务委员会 (台湾), "Haiwai huaren ji Taiqiao renshu" 海外华人及台侨人数, 29 July 2016, <www.ocac.gov.tw/OCAC/Pages/List.aspx?nodeid=33> (accessed 4 January 2016).
3. Zhuang Guotu 庄国土 in OCAO's publication ["Huaqiao huaren fenbu zhuangkuang he fazhan qushi" 华侨华人分布状况和发展趋势, *Yanjiu yu Tantao*《研究与探讨》, Zhonghua qiaowu diyi kan 中华侨务第一刊, 2010 年 No. 4, <http://qwgzyj.gqb.gov.cn/yjytt/155/1830.shtml>

(accessed 4 January 2016)] noted this figure. In fact the figures were for 2007–8.

4. Dudley L. Poston, Jr. and Mei-Yu Yu, "The Distribution of the Overseas Chinese in the Contemporary World", *International Migration Review* 24, no. 3 (1990), cited in Peter S. Li and Eva Xiaoling Li, "The Chinese Overseas Population", in *Routledge Handbook of the Chinese Diaspora*, edited by Tan Chee Beng (London and New York: Routledge, 2013), p. 19.
5. The Taiwanese estimates of the number of Chinese in Southeast Asia are still high, compared to my own estimate.
6. See Table 2.1. More than 94 per cent of the Chinese population in Asia was in Southeast Asia.
7. Taiwanese figures, cited in Li and Li (2013), p. 21.
8. Zhuang Guotu 庄国土, "Huaqiao huaren fenbu zhuangkuang he fazhan qushi" 华侨华人分布状况和发展趋势, *Yanjiu yu Tantao* 《研究与探讨》, Zhonghua qiaowu diyi kan 中华侨务第一刊, 2010 年 No. 4, <http://qwgzyj.gqb.gov.cn/yjytt/155/1830.shtml> (accessed 4 January 2016).
9. For an analysis on the changing policy of China towards the Chinese overseas, see Stephen Fitzgerald, *China and the Overseas Chinese: A Study of Peking's Changing Policy 1949–1970* (Cambridge: Cambridge University Press, 1972), pp. 102–15; 149–55.
10. "Our Future in S-E Asia–Lee", *Straits Times*, 13 November 1978.
11. Fang Xiongpu 方雄普, Xie Chengjia 谢成佳, eds. 主编, *Huaqiao huaren gaikuang* 《华侨华人概况》 (Beijing 北京: Zhongguo huaqiao chubanshe 中国华侨出版社, 1993), pp. 337–38.
12. Ibid., p. 338.
13. The State Council the People's Republic of China, "Overseas Chinese Affairs Office of the State Council", 12 September 2014, <http://english.gov.cn/state_council/2014/10/01/content_281474991090995.htm> (accessed 19 February 2016).
14. Zhou Nanjing, "Guanyu Yindunixiya huaren rongru zhuliu shehui de ruogan wenti" 关于印度尼西亚华人融入主流社会的若干问题, first published in *Qiandao Ribao* (Surabaya), 13 November 2007,

republished in *Nushantala huayi zongheng*《努山塔拉华裔纵横》, by Zhou Nanjing 周南京 (Hong Kong 香港: Hong Kong Press for Social Science Ltd. 香港社会科学出版社, January 2011). For information on China's Overseas Exchange Association, see pp. 46–47.

15. Zhou Nanjing, ibid., p. 46.
16. Ibid., p. 341.
17. Zhou Naning 周南京, ed., *Jingwai huaren guoji wenti taolun j*《境外华人国籍问题讨论辑》[The Citizenship Problems of the Chinese Overseas: A Collection of Documents and Articles] (Hong Kong 香港: Hong Kong Press for Social Science Ltd. 香港社会科学出版社, 2005), p. 1. The following information on the OCAO's attempts to amend the 1980 citizenship law is also taken from the same page.
18. Ibid. For a review of the book, see Leo Suryadinata's book review published in *Journal of Chinese Overseas* 1, no. 2 (November 2005): 286–88.
19. The Green Card system was introduced in China in 2004.
20. James Jiann Hua To, *Qiaowu: Extra Territorial Policies of the Overseas Chinese* (Leiden: Brill, 2014), p. 122.
21. Zhongguo qiaoshang touzi qiye xiehui chengli dahui 中国侨商投资企业协会成立大会, <www.chinaqw.com/zt/zgqsxh> (accessed 19 February 2016).
22. Ibid. See also Zhou Nanjing, "Guanyu Yindunixiya huaren rongru zhuliu shehui de ruogan wenti", op. cit., p. 46.
23. Zhou Nanjing, "Guanyu Yindunixiya huaren rongru zhuliu shehui de ruogan wenti", op. cit., p. 48.
24. See GovHK 香港政府一站通, "Explanations of Some Questions by the Standing Committee of the National People's Congress Concerning the Implementation of the Nationality Law of the People's Republic of China in the Hong Kong Special Administrative Region (Adopted at the 19th Session of the Standing Committee of the 8th National People's Congress on 15 May 1996)", <http://www.gov.hk/en/residents/immigration/chinese/law.htm> (accessed 15 May 2016).

25. Cited in Frank Ching, "Beijing Seeks Loyalty from Ethnic Chinese Settle Abroad", *Business Times*, 4 May 2016.
26. James Jiann Hua To, citing an article published in China's *People Daily* on 8 January 2001, stated that "...when referring to qiaowu [overseas Chinese affairs], the terms 'foreign nationals of Chinese descent', 'foreigners of Chinese origin', and 'people of Chinese origin residing abroad' are often used interchangeably with 'Chinese nationals overseas'". See To, *Qiaowu: Extra-Territorial Policies of the Overseas Chinese*, op. cit., p. 112.
27. For a short discussion of the Solomon Islands affair, see Grace Chew Chye Lay, "The April 2006 Riots in the Solomon Islands", *CHC Bulletin*, nos. 7 and 8 (May and November 2006): 11–21.
28. Yang Bao'an 杨保安, "Zhongguo younan, huaren zhiyuan" 中国有难，华人支援, *Zaobao Xingqitian* 《早报星期天》, 8 June 2008.
29. For a brief discussion of this topic, see Leo Suryadinata, "A New Orientation in China's Policy towards Chinese Overseas? Beijing Olympic Games Fervour as a Case Study", *CHC Bulletin*, no. 12 (November 2008): 1–6.

Chapter 3

CHINA'S FOREIGN POLICY VIS-À-VIS THE CHINESE OVERSEAS

The importance of the Chinese overseas for China has been rather controversial. In the past, some Western scholars argued that the Chinese overseas were crucial to Beijing and that China's relations with each country hosting the Chinese depended on the latter's treatment of its Chinese minority. Other Western as well as non-Western scholars maintained that the Chinese overseas were not high in China's foreign policy agenda and hence would not be the major determinants of its foreign policy.[1] With the rise of China since the end of the twentieth century, the position of the Chinese overseas has become more important. But does this mean that the first view prevails over the second view now? Would China protect the interests of the Chinese overseas at all costs?

CHINA'S NATIONAL INTEREST AND THE CHINESE OVERSEAS

Foreign policy tends to serve the national interest of a country, and the national interest is defined by its leaders. This also applies to the PRC.[2] It is not easy to define the national interest of China as it may change from period to period. Nevertheless, the PRC, like other countries in the contemporary period, has been concerned with its national security, territorial integrity, political ideology represented by the Communist Party of China (CPC), and social and economic development. In addition, China, as a major power, would like to be the leader of the third world and eventually a world leader. It should be noted that China is an emigrant state that has a large number of Chinese overseas. Therefore, in the earliest PRC Constitution of 1954 and the latest one of 2004, despite several amendments, there has always been a clause to the effect that China would "protect the legitimate interests of *huaqiao*". From this, one can categorically maintain that the protection of the "overseas Chinese" is part of the national interest of China.

The national interest of China has many components. Among these , national security is paramount. National security for China refers to the security of the Chinese nation-state, which involves the survival of China as an entity, domestic political stability, and the survival of the CPC and the ruling elite. National security may also refer to security from external military invasion and from the containment of China by hostile powers, especially the major powers, as well as the security of the sea lanes through which China's raw materials and trade flow. National security has the added dimension of territorial integrity. Since the establishment of the PRC, minority groups have posed a threat to China's territorial integrity. China still faces separatist movements in Xinjiang and Tibet.

Beijing also considers Taiwan to be an integral part of China and would like to eventually unite it with the mainland. In 2009, China circulated a so-called "nine-dash line" map claiming 90 per cent of the South China Sea as its territorial waters, which effectively extends its national interest beyond East Asia to include Southeast Asia.[3]

China has territorial disputes with several Southeast Asian countries that also claim the South China Sea as part of their territorial waters and Exclusive Economic Zones (EEZ).[4] There is no sign that China is prepared to abandon its claims. On the contrary, under Xi Jinping's presidency, China's activities in the South China Sea have become more assertive, with construction activity on several rock-islands intensifying. As a result, tensions in the area have heightened. The South China Sea has now become a major issue in China's relations with the Southeast Asian countries in general and the claimant states in the region in particular.

Prior to attaining global power status, China would like to be perceived at least as a regional power, recognized in Asia and slowly building its sphere of influence in the Southeast Asian region. Now, the rise of China in Asia poses a challenge to the United States, which has long been present in the region. Both China and the United States are learning to accommodate each other in order to prevent major conflict between them. As with any regional power, China does not want an external power to intervene in regional matters, especially on the issue of the South China Sea.[5] Where possible, China would like to exclude the United States from Southeast Asia, which appears to be difficult, if not impossible, at least at the present time.

Communist ideology was once important for China but its importance has been declining. During the Mao era, China exported revolution and expected "national liberation movements" to succeed in Asia and Africa, if not in the whole world. It supported Communist movements, advocating armed struggle rather than the peaceful transfer of power in developing countries. Although many argued that Chinese Communism has blended with Chinese nationalism, the fact remains that during the Mao period, class was important. This was especially the case during the Cultural Revolution (1966–76), when class became the standard to judge the worthiness of an individual.

However, after the re-emergence of Deng Xiaoping in 1977 and the relative success of economic reform, China adopted the so-called "Socialism with Chinese characteristics" and began to de-emphasize class struggle in favour of "harmonious society". This "Socialism with Chinese characteristics" is a form of state capitalism that is market-driven. With market liberalization and rapid industrialization, China emerged a major manufacturer and looked for overseas markets for Chinese goods. At the same time, it had to import raw materials and resources to fuel industrialization. Today with surplus capital, China has also emerged as a major capital exporter. Thus, with the growing primacy of the market mechanism, Communism as an ideology no longer appeals to the Chinese people at large.

However, for Beijing's leadership, maintaining the CPC in power is considered to be the highest priority in China's national interest. To maintain itself in power, the CPC has to ensure that there is sustainable economic growth. In other words, economic performance is a means of legitimizing the CPC's rule. But, for economic growth to be sustainable today, annual growth rates cannot fall below 6.5 per cent.

The importance of socio-economic development has increased tremendously as economic openness has led to enhanced expectations among the Chinese population. China needs rapid economic growth as it wants to enhance the living standards of its people and become a developed country. To this end, China is now competing overseas with other powers in a scramble for resources to fuel production.

As China becomes rich and strong, its desire to become a world leader has intensified. Although the PRC continues to claim that it is still a developing country, China has now become the second largest economy in the world, surpassing Germany and Japan, and only next to the United States. Nevertheless, economic development in the country is uneven, with stark contrasts between highly developed sectors and areas, on the one hand, and those that are still underdeveloped and backward.

As the expansion of China's economy overseas continues, the post-Deng Xiaoping leadership considers the Chinese overseas as an important asset for realizing China's economic transformation. The Chinese overseas are also considered an important element in China's "One Belt One Road" Strategy. Thus, gradually China's interest in the Chinese overseas has moved up the ladder of China's national interests and has begun to coincide with its higher priorities.

THE CHINESE OVERSEAS IN CHINA'S FOREIGN POLICY

While the Chinese overseas are seen as part of China's national interests, China's national interests have different levels of priority. Concerns over national security (including the survival of the CPC) and territorial integrity are the highest priority. Concerns over social and economic development and political ideology also rank quite high, although the nature of political ideology has changed since 1978, with Chinese nationalism having become China's new political ideology. The protection of the legitimate interests of the *huaqiao*, is subservient to these higher priorities.

From past studies, it appears that the *huaqiao* would only be protected if doing so did not come into conflict with, or tended to coincide with, the higher elements in China's national interest. When the *huaqiao's* interests came into conflict with China's higher national priorities, they were ignored. This author has put forward this argument elsewhere and given detailed examples to illustrate that the PRC would not protect the interests of the Chinese overseas and go to war with third countries if doing so clashed with China's higher order national interests.[6]

The PRC's foreign policy serves China's national interests. To protect its national interests, the PRC has used diplomacy, foreign aid, party-to-party relations, and economic tools; the most extreme means, war, has only been employed as a last resort. Looking at the history of the PRC, Beijing was involved only in three wars, namely, the Korean War (1950), the Sino–Indian border war (1962), and the Sino–Vietnamese War (1979). If we examine the reasons for Beijing's involvement in these wars, it appears that they had links with the two highest priorities in Beijing's national interests: national security and the territorial integrity of China, and implicitly, also the survival of the CPC. All of these wars took place with countries along China's borders; no war has been waged by China in the interest of the Chinese overseas.

In fact, the history of the PRC's foreign relations is replete with examples where China ignored the interests of the *huaqiao* when they came into conflict with the higher priorities in China's foreign policy objectives. The most well-known examples are the anti-Chinese riots in Indonesia in 1959–60, the anti-Chinese violence in Cambodia in 1975, and the anti-Chinese campaign in Vietnam (beginning in 1976 and culminating in 1978).

THREE EXAMPLES OF ANTI-CHINESE VIOLENCE IN THE TWENTIETH CENTURY

In 1959 Indonesia introduced a regulation (known as Peraturan Presiden No. 10 or PP 10) prohibiting *warga negara asing* or foreign citizens (read: foreign Chinese) from engaging in retail trade in the rural areas. This resulted in the forced departure of the Chinese from Indonesia. Initially, Beijing sent ships to repatriate the affected Chinese but it stopped immediately when it realized that this policy had weakened the anti-colonial regime of Sukarno and given rise to the pro-West Indonesian military.

In 1975 the Pol Pot regime in Cambodia (then known as Kampuchea) introduced a policy of genocide not only towards the Khmer people but also towards the ethnic Chinese in the country. Many Chinese then rushed to the Chinese embassy for help but they were turned away as Beijing then considered Cambodia a political ally against the Soviet–Vietnamese camp. Beijing refused to protect the ethnic Chinese as it feared it might lose an ally to defeat the Vietnamese and strengthen the Soviets.

In 1976 Vietnam began to introduce a socialist transformation programme after unification, and many Chinese were forced into new economic zones. As the economic situation gradually became intolerable, many Chinese left the country as "boat people". However, China "taught Vietnam a lesson" by launching an attack against it only in February 1979, after the Vietnamese had signed a "Friendship Treaty" with the Soviet Union, occupied Cambodia, and installed a puppet regime there in December 1978. China's invasion was not prompted by the sufferings of the ethnic Chinese but by larger strategic considerations. Beijing saw the signing of the "Friendship Treaty" and the occupation of Cambodia as part of a Soviet–Vietnamese encirclement of the PRC, jeopardizing its national security. Therefore, it decided to resort to a "border war". Beijing did not send ships to repatriate the Chinese from Vietnam. One can, therefore, argue that the war was not caused by Hanoi's anti-ethnic Chinese policy. It is worth noting that the exodus of the ethnic Chinese from Vietnam did not stop even after the Sino–Vietnamese war had ended.

In 1998, Beijing's attitude towards the Chinese overseas changed somewhat. It no longer wanted to intervene in anti-Chinese violence where most of the Chinese involved were foreign citizens. This was in the early period of China's rise. Notably, Beijing adopted a "hands off" policy towards the ethnic Chinese in Indonesia during the May 1998 anti-Chinese riots. This non-interference, too, can be explained by Beijing's reluctance to compromise China's higher order national interests. This incident is analysed in Chapter 4.

CONCLUSION

By the end of the twentieth century, with significant socio-economic change in China, the expansion of China's economic interests overseas, and the wave of new Chinese migration, China's policy on the Chinese overseas had changed. The rapid surge in the number of overseas Chinese around this time prompted a re-thinking of Beijing's stance. It would appear that the interests of the overseas Chinese have suddenly become higher in the PRC's national priorities, as shown in the speeches of its national leaders and its foreign policy behaviour. This has been especially the case since Xi Jinping's presidency.

This study will examine China's position closely to determine whether the interests of the Chinese overseas have indeed become a higher order priority for Beijing. Have the interests of the Chinese overseas become the highest priority in China's national interests? Or have their interests simply coincided with the highest priority in China's national interests? Or does the situation depend on the issue, the country concerned, and circumstances? The following chapters will address these questions by examining a few specific examples. First, this study will look at China's responses to external events involving anti-Chinese violence or anti-Chinese tension. This will be followed by an examination of China's responses to internal needs that caused an adjustment in its policy towards the Chinese overseas.

Notes

1. For the first view, see Harold Hinton, *Communist China in World Politics* (Boston: Houghton Mifflin, 1966). For the second view, see David Mozingo, *China's Policy toward Indonesia 1949–1967* (Ithaca: Cornell University Press, 1976); Leo Suryadinata, *"Overseas Chinese" in Southeast Asia and China's Foreign Policy: An Interpretative Essay*, Research Notes and Discussion Paper (Singapore: Institute of Southeast Asian Studies, 1978).
2. For a discussion of China's foreign policy and "Overseas Chinese", see Leo Suryadinata, *China and the ASEAN States: The Ethnic Chinese Dimension* (Singapore: Singapore University Press, 1985).
3. For an official Chinese view on the South China Sea, see *Jiefang Ribao* 《解放日报》, "Deng Xiaoping ruhe jiejue zhongguo yu zhoubian geguojian de zhengduan?" 邓小平如何解决中国与周边各国间的争端?, 15 September 2010. For a Singapore reporter's view, see Yang Bao'an 杨保安, "350 wan pingfang gongli haiyu de geda" 350万平方公里海域的疙瘩, *Lianhe Zaobao* 《联合早报》, 8 December 2011. For a Western scholar's view, see David Arase, "Strategic Rivalry in the South China Sea: How can Southeast Asian Claimant

States Shape a Beneficial Outcome?", *ISEAS Perspective*, no. 57 (13 October 2015).

4. Four Southeast Asian states have overlapping claims with China in the South China Sea: Vietnam, the Philippines, Malaysia, and Brunei Darussalam. Two of them, Vietnam and the Philippines, have come to conflict with China over these conflicting claims. In the case of Indonesia, there is no territorial dispute over the Natuna Islands between Beijing and Jakarta but Indonesia's EEZ may overlap with the "nine dash-lines", which Jakarta does not recognize. For a discussion on the Natuna Islands and Sino–Indonesian relations, see Leo Suryadinata, "Did the Natuna Incident Shake Indonesia–China Relations?" *ISEAS Perspective*, no. 19 (26 April 2016).
5. On 12 July 2016, the Permanent Court of Arbitration at The Hague announced its verdict on the Sino–Philippine territorial dispute, rejecting China's claim that its "nine-dash line" has legal basis. The tribunal also ruled that the Spratly islands were legally rocks that are not entitled to EEZs on behalf of any country. The ruling benefited the Philippines, and China strongly rejected the verdict, called it "illegal, false and null". China insisted that the South China Sea was its territory and conducted a military exercise in the disputed areas, preventing other vessels from entering them. This behaviour is clear indication that China wanted to be regarded as the dominant power in the South China Sea, excluding the United States and Japan. See for instance, "Zhongguo jinqi zai nan Zhongguo haijunyan, jinzhi chuanzhi feiji shiru" 中国今起在南中国海军演，禁止船只飞机驶入, *Lianhe Zaobao*《联合早报》, 19 July 2016, for a report on China's military exercises in the disputed areas.
6. See Leo Suryadinata, *China and the ASEAN States: The Ethnic Chinese Dimension* (Singapore: Singapore University Press, 1985).

PART II

Responses to External Events

Chapter 4

NON-INTERVENTION: THE 1998 ANTI-CHINESE VIOLENCE IN INDONESIA

The first example illustrating how a rising China has conducted its foreign policy on issues involving the Chinese overseas is the May 1998 anti-Chinese violence in Indonesia, which precipitated the downfall of then President Suharto. China's response to this episode shows the level of priority accorded to the interests of the Chinese overseas in China's overall foreign policy objectives. To put the episode in wider perspective, this chapter also deals with the factors that contributed to the violence and how the events unfolded. The question that arises from this episode is whether China's "hands off" position in this instance was an exceptional case during the early period of China's rise.

BACKGROUND

Although Indonesia proclaimed independence in August 1945, it gained full independence only in December 1949, when a Roundtable Agreement was signed between Jakarta and The Hague. The PRC, founded in October 1949, established diplomatic ties with the Republic of Indonesia soon afterwards, in 1950. Sino–Indonesian relations have fluctuated since then until 2015. Various factors have determined the nature of these relations, of which the most important has been the national interest of China. Thus, in some instances of anti-Chinese riots in Indonesia, Beijing sent ships to evacuate the Chinese in the country, but it stopped doing so when such action conflicted with higher priorities in China's national interest (see chapter 3).

Anti-Chinese violence occurred more frequently during the Indonesian struggle for independence and soon after independence. What were the factors contributing to ethnic conflict, especially anti-Chinese violence? The wealth of the ethnic Chinese relative to the *pribumis* or indigenous Indonesians is often cited as a major factor. Some among the indigenous elite even argued that the Chinese Indonesians "controlled" the Indonesian economy. Many indigenous Indonesians wanted to undermine the economic position of the Chinese. Another factor behind anti-Chinese sentiments was the prejudice of the indigenous Indonesians deriving from the perception that Chinese Indonesians were not loyal towards their adopted land.

Domestic politics also played an important role in the outbreak of anti-Chinese violence. Some among the indigenous elite wanted to foment and use ethnic conflict to achieve their political objectives. There has been a recurring pattern in the occurrence of ethnic violence, with the Chinese being made scapegoats for expedient reasons. Anti-Chinese violence has been especially frequent during periods of economic difficulty or prior to general or presidential elections.[1] Ruling and opposition groups appear to be fond of using ethnic Chinese issues to gain political mileage. For the ruling elite, limited anti-Chinese conflict was a useful way of allowing the indigenous population to vent their anger or to divert their attention away from politically inconvenient developments, while the opposition often saw ethnic conflict as a means of de-stabilizing the government.

If we look at modern Indonesian history, anti-Chinese riots have occurred on and off, but only very rarely did they take place on a large scale or extend nation-wide. The exceptions include the 1940s following the Indonesian revolution, when many Chinese were branded as Dutch sympathizers; the early 1960s following the issuing of Presidential Regulation No. 10/1959 (known as PP 10/1959), which prohibited foreign citizens (read: alien Chinese) from engaging in retail trade in rural areas; in the mid-1960s, following the abortive coup, in which Beijing was blamed for alleged involvement; and, the May 1998 anti-Chinese violence prior to the fall of Suharto. The responses of the PRC towards each of these major instances of anti-Chinese violence differed.

During the 1960 anti-Chinese violence, many Indonesian Chinese lost their livelihoods as a result of PP 10/1959. They were forced to leave the rural areas for the cities. China then sent ships to repatriate the Chinese who had been affected by the regulation. More than 100,000 Chinese left Indonesia, mainly for China. The repatriation was a great financial burden for China, and, more importantly, the large departure of Chinese contributed to economic difficulties for the Sukarno government, which undermined the president's influence. This weakening benefited the Indonesian army, whose leaders had differences with Sukarno. The Soviet Union, China's communist rival, then was able to move in to try to exert its influence. Seeing this negative turn of events, Beijing immediately stopped the repatriation and accepted Indonesia's discriminatory policy towards the Chinese. Gradually, Sukarno regained power, the implementation of PP 10/1959 was suspended, and the situation returned to normal.[2]

The 1965 anti-Chinese violence differed slightly from the 1960 riots as it was more ideological in nature than ethnic. The major focus here was the PRC, which was believed to be behind the Partai Komunis Indonesia (PKI) or Indonesian Communist Party, which allegedly led to a coup.[3] After the coup was aborted, the new Indonesian military authorities, led by General Suharto, targeted the PRC embassy and those Chinese who were believed to be supporters of the PRC and the PKI. In the wake of the anti-Chinese pogrom that followed, Beijing also sent ships to repatriate some Chinese. However, as China was then in the throes of the Cultural Revolution, no more than 10,000 Indonesian Chinese left for China.[4] It is estimated that 500,000 "suspected communists" were killed then, among whom only 2,000 were Chinese since relatively few Chinese were actually members of the PKI.[5] Beijing was critical of the new military regime and urged the Indonesian people to resist the "Fascist Suharto-Nasution regime". In 1967 Jakarta under Suharto severed ties with Beijing.

1998 ANTI-CHINESE RIOTS

Sino–Indonesian relations were restored twenty-three years later, in 1990. Eight years later, between 13 and 15 May 1998, major anti-Chinese riots broke out in Indonesia, shocking the world. These riots were believed to be the most uncivilized instance of anti-Chinese violence in the history of the Republic of Indonesia. They were unique as they were aimed at ethnic Chinese in Indonesia, not at the PRC, unlike previous instances of anti-Chinese violence. The riots took place in several parts of Java but the most serious ones were those in Jakarta and Surakarta (or Solo). They not only involved burning and looting but also the systematic rape of Chinese women and killing, which were rare in Indonesian history. The riots were also unique in Sino–Indonesian relations as Beijing was restrained throughout their course and refused to intervene. As a result, Beijing came under criticism from Chinese communities worldwide.

This chapter attempts to briefly narrate the course of events and discuss the reasons for the 1998 anti-Chinese riots and the new Jakarta government's responses to the tragedy. The responses of the PRC government and the likely reasons behind this behaviour will be analyzed in the context of Beijing's foreign policy behaviour after the rise of China.

THE FACTORS BEHIND THE ANTI-CHINESE RIOTS

During the last phase of Suharto's rule, the power struggle within the ruling elite intensified while the gap between the rich and the poor widened against the background of the monetary crisis of 1997 and 1998, which resulted in widespread hardship. Students and opposition groups began to demonstrate. A massive demonstration took place after the killing of four students from Trisakti University, which some elements seemed to have used to foment widespread violence. According to a *Jakarta Post* report:

> The May riots inflicted losses of at least Rp.2.5 trillion (US$268 million). Thirteen markets, 2,479 shop-houses, 40 malls, 1,604 shops, 45 garages, 383 private offices, nine fuel stations, eight public buses and minivans, 1,119 cars, 821 motorcycles, and 1,026 houses were destroyed during the riots. The violence claimed 2,244 lives, according to the latest data from the

> Volunteers' Team for Humanity. The largest number of dead came from the area of Yogya Plaza department store and supermarket with 288 killed.[6] Anti-Chinese sentiment was sparked in the anarchy which was followed by looting, burning, and the rape of Chinese-Indonesians.[7]

It was also reported that about 150,000 people left Indonesia during the May riots, 70,000 of whom were believed to be ethnic Chinese.[8] Between 13 and 15 May there was virtual anarchy in Jakarta. The police and the military police were nowhere to be seen. There were no attempts by the authorities to calm down the situation.[9] This created the impression that the non-action was a deliberate attempt to let the mobs ransack Chinese property and harm the Chinese.[10] Some argued that the riots were engineered by the state or, at least, elements in the ruling elite, both civilian and military; there were claims that many of the perpetrators who instigated the crowds looked like military personnel.

Many indigenous Indonesians condemned the barbaric acts. There was also an international outcry, pressurizing the Indonesian government to investigate the riots and punish the perpetrators. Under both international and domestic pressure, B.J. Habibie, the new president succeeding Suharto, eventually announced on 22 July 1998 that a Joint Fact-Finding Team (TGPF) would be formed to investigate the violation of human rights, not only the Chinese but all communities.[11]

Since the composition of the fact-finding team was mixed — including officials from the government and military and non-officials — there were differences in opinion, understandably. The team report, which was scheduled for release after three months, was delayed by a week — it was only released on 3 November 1998. It stated that 52 Chinese women had been raped although other sources believe the number was far higher.[12] It found no proof that the riots and rapes had been planned or that the ethnic Chinese, who formed the majority of the victims, were especially targeted. The government firmly denied that there was any organized terrorism against the Chinese, although independent reports concluded otherwise.[13]

The May riots resulted in the resignation of President Suharto. But the tension between ethnic Chinese and indigenous Indonesians continued to simmer. In several small towns in Java, the two ethnic groups often clashed as a result of minor incidents but these clashes never developed into major riots as the state was no longer involved.

Many theories have been advanced to explain the anti-Chinese violence. Jemma Purdey, who conducted research in Indonesia during that period, argued that "the impetus for the violence was an elite power struggle between factions vying to be Suharto's successor".[14] She notes that "Suharto's highly ambitious son-in-law, Lt. Gen. Prabowo Subianto, then Commander of Kostrad (Army Strategic Reserve), was widely considered to be responsible for the violence."[15] He or the other faction of the Suharto group tried to divert the people's attention away from the government's role in the country's economic crisis and other failures. This was done by pinning the blame on the Chinese community. Not surprisingly, discontent against the Chinese community surfaced as various anti-Chinese activities were engineered, creating fertile grounds for the May 1998 violence.[16]

It is difficult to pinpoint with certainty the masterminds behind the anti-Chinese violence. Many observers identified Prabowo and General Sjafrie Sjamsoeddin, the commander of the Jakarta Military Zone, as the major suspects. But both men denied any involvement in the violence.[17] As of the time of writing, the masterminds have yet to be arrested, and two major suspects, especially Prabowo, have continued to play crucial roles in post-Suharto Indonesian politics.

One theory argues that the intention of the perpetrators of the violence was to terrorize Chinese Indonesians so that they would leave the country. The economic role of Chinese businessmen could then be taken over by indigenous Indonesians. If this was indeed the intention behind the fomenting of anti-Chinese violence, it was probably a flawed venture as it is not clear that indigenous Indonesians could have easily filled the role of Chinese businessmen soon enough. Nevertheless, the violence did indeed frighten Chinese Indonesians, and many fled the country, taking their family and capital with them. Many migrated to neighbouring countries. Singapore, Australia, and the United States were their favorite destinations, followed by Malaysia, where the cost of living was lower. Some even sent their children to Hong Kong, Taiwan, and China, just to escape the turmoil.

Nevertheless, the majority of the Chinese Indonesians — more than 98 per cent — had nowhere to go. They had to stay and fight for their rights. During the riots, some Chinese moved to other areas in Indonesia where there was less anti-Chinese sentiment, such as Bali and North Sulawesi. However, it should be pointed out that the majority of those Chinese who fled the riots eventually returned to Indonesia as they were unable to lead comfortable lives overseas.

THE ATTITUDE OF THE PRC REGARDING THE RIOTS

Beijing's response to the 1998 anti-Chinese violence was noticeably restrained. It was reported that Beijing was monitoring the situation in Indonesia and also the first major anti-Chinese violence in Jakarta on 13 May 1998.[18] but it did not do anything. This restraint can be understood in the context of Beijing's broader foreign policy.

As noted earlier, Jakarta had severed diplomatic ties with Beijing in 1967 and restored them only in 1990, one year after the Tiananmen affair in China, when Beijing quashed a massive student demonstration. In fact, China was diplomatically isolated after the Tiananmen incident as the West was highly critical of Beijing's high-handed policy towards the demonstrating Chinese students. Nevertheless, the ASEAN states appeared to be more understanding of Beijing's attitude and remained friendly, helping to break China's international isolation.

The emergence of Deng Xiaoping earlier, in 1977, had led to an adjustment in Beijing's policy towards the Chinese overseas. Following Deng's visit to several Southeast Asian countries in 1978, a Nationality Law was promulgated in 1980, with Beijing declaring that it recognized only single citizenship. This meant a Chinese with foreign citizenship was no longer considered a Chinese national. In the interim, many Chinese in Indonesia had adopted Indonesian citizenship voluntarily, identifying with Jakarta rather than Beijing.

After more than two decades of peace in Indonesia and amidst a growing economy, the Chinese in Indonesia had once again come under attack beginning 1996. Rivalry between members of the indigenous elite and the economic disparity between the Chinese and the indigenous Indonesians fanned the flames of this tension. Later, many politicians tolerated, if not encouraged, the anti-Chinese riots of 1998 to achieve their political objectives of putting the blame for the economic crisis of 1997–98 on the Chinese.

Even before the May 1998 violence, many Chinese outside Indonesia criticized the PRC government, some even suggesting that Beijing should protect the Chinese there. However, Beijing had refused to intervene. Beijing–Jakarta ties had been quite cordial before the May riots and Beijing had no desire to jeopardize the relationship. Thus, when ethnic tensions began to surface in February 1998 in Jakarta and many critics wanted Beijing to intervene, Zhu Bangzao, a spokesman for the Chinese Ministry of Foreign Affairs, said on 19 February 1998: "We believe that the Indonesian government can control the situation, maintain social stability and racial harmony."[19] This was a tacit acceptance that Beijing considered the incipient conflict an Indonesian domestic problem.

Privately, a Chinese diplomat in the United States noted that Beijing would not be able to protest or send ships to Indonesia because "there is no good reason to do so as the majority of the Chinese in Indonesia are Indonesian citizens."[20] To do anything otherwise would mean intervention in Jakarta's domestic affairs, which would also generate a negative reaction in other parts of Southeast Asia. Beijing may have also calculated that intervention might impose greater difficulties on those Chinese Indonesians who wanted to continue living in Indonesia.

Reports indicate that the Chinese embassy in Jakarta would help, on a case-by-case basis, individual Chinese (presumably those who did not hold Indonesian citizenship) who encountered difficulties.[21] Understandably, the embassy was cautious in doing so as this too might affect Sino–Indonesian relations.

When serious anti-Chinese riots took place in Jakarta, Surakarta, and other areas between 13 May and 15 May 1998, Beijing's attitude remained unchanged. One begins to wonder whether the above reasons were still valid for Beijing not taking any action. In fact, one writer, Shee Poon Kim, argued that the approaching anniversary of the Tiananmen may have been a factor in Beijing's restraint:

> The timing of the anti-Chinese riots came at a sensitive period for the Chinese leadership, who feared that nationalistic feelings among the Chinese students in Beijing would be stirred up, putting pressure on the Jiang Zemin leadership, particularly since the state of the May anti-Chinese riots could rekindle the memory of the 4 June 1989 Tiananmen massacre. The Beijing authorities were worried that any playing up of the anti-Chinese riots in Indonesia by the Chinese press might rekindle Chinese students' nationalistic sentiments and cause[d] them to orchestrate another anti-establishment student demonstration in Beijing on 4 June in the same year.[22]

Many of Shee's points are important for an understanding of Beijing's attitude towards the May 1998 riots.

It should be noted that the 1998 riots were different from the 1965 anti-Chinese violence in Indonesia. The 1998 violence was directed at the ethnic Chinese in Indonesia, not Beijing, while the 1965 riots were mainly directed at the PRC and the Chinese in Indonesia who were affiliated with/sympathetic to Beijing. Given this difference in nature, Beijing initially wanted to remain neutral in the May 1998 riots.

The first official reaction of Beijing to the 1998 violence occurred two months later, in late July 1998. But on 6 July Chen Shiqiu, the new Chinese ambassador to Indonesia, visited East Kalimantan to assess the possibility of investing in the area, especially in the palm oil business. During his visit, Indonesian reporters sought his views on the May riots. He was quoted as saying that China was "concerned with the incident" and wanted the Indonesian government "to investigate the matter thoroughly."[23] He told the reporters that he had met B.J. Habibie twice — first when the latter was still vice-president and later when he had become president — and on both occasions he had discussed the riot and "hoped that the riot will not recur."[24] Chen clearly stated that, "according to international law as well as the laws of the two countries, it was the responsibility of the Indonesian government to protect its own citizens, including the citizens of Chinese descent."[25] There was no official protest on the part of Beijing.

On 27 July, a Chinese Ministry of Foreign Affairs spokesman noted that China had used diplomatic channels to express its concerns for the victims of the riots. A day later, Tang Jiaxuan, then minister for foreign affairs, met with his Indonesian counterpart, Ali Alatas, in Manila and registered China's "deep concern" over the anti-ethnic Chinese riots.[26]

On 3 August, China's *People's Daily* published a critical commentary demanding that the Indonesian authorities punish the culprits for the mayhem.[27] Later, on 4 September, the paper criticized an earlier comment by President Habibie that the extent of the rapes was exaggerated. The paper was sceptical about Habibie's promise to punish the culprits.[28]

After six months of silence, President Jiang Zemin finally expressed his concern to President Habibie when they met on 17 November 1998. Jiang noted that "we hold that a proper solution of the issue of Chinese Indonesians will not only serve the long-term stability of Indonesia, but also contribute to the smooth development of the relationship of friendly cooperation between neighbouring countries."[29] Jiang also reminded Habibie that "Chinese Indonesians should enjoy the same treatment and be given the same rights as other Indonesians."[30]

CONCLUSION

Beijing was cautious in responding to the May 1998 anti-Chinese riots in Indonesia, wanting to behave like a responsible major power. It was concerned with the faith of the Chinese Indonesians but there was no concrete action taken by Beijing to pressurize Jakarta. On the contrary, it was reported that China had pledged a US$5 billion loan to help Indonesia overcome its serious financial crisis[31] and that President Habibie was grateful for China's help. In addition, Beijing provided Jakarta with US$40 million in aid for flood victims and a loan of US$500 million.[32]

It would appear that the major consideration behind the PRC's restraint was its core national interest, i.e., to gain acceptance in ASEAN in general, and in Indonesia in particular, as it still faced diplomatic isolation after the Tiananmen. This "hands off" policy was for the short-term strategic and national interest of China.

However, according to rumours, there was a split within China's Foreign Ministry on the course of action that should be taken. Recently this author asked some foreign policy scholars in mainland China about the 1998 May riots and Beijing's responses. They commented that China would not take the same attitude if such violence recurs. In other words, China would intervene if large scale anti-Chinese violence breaks out again in Indonesia.

Notes

1. Leo Suryadinata, "Anti-Chinese Riots in Indonesia: Perennial Problem but Major Disaster Unlikely", *Straits Times*, 25 February 1998.
2. Leo Suryadinata, *Pribumi Indonesian the Chinese Minority and China: A Study of Perceptions and Policies* (Kuala Lumpur: Heinamann Asia, 1978), pp. 135–37.

3. For a discussion on the victims of the coup, see Charles Coppel, *Indonesian Chinese in Crisis* (Kuala Lumpur: Oxford University Press, 1983), pp. 58–59. Also Robert Cribb, "The 1965 Killings Constituted Genocide", in *Indonesia, Genocide and Persecution Series*, edited by Noah Berlatsky (Farmington Hills, MI: Greenhaven Press, 2014), pp. 91–102. A recent study by a Chinese scholar reveals that the Aidit faction of the PKI led the "coup" while China had some advance knowledge but without the details of the PKI's planned action. Mao, however, appeared to endorse the Aidit action. See Taomo Zhou, "30 September 1965 Movement", *Indonesia* (October 2014), pp. 1–34.
4. See David Mozingo, *Chinese Policy toward Indonesia, 1949–1967* (Ithaca: Cornell University Press, 1976), p. 250.
5. Robert Cribb and Charles Coppel, "A Genocide that Never Was: Explaining the Myth of Anti-Chinese Massacre in Indonesia 1965–1966", *Journal of Genocide Research* 11, no. 4 (2009): 447–65.
6. It was argued that some elements instigated bystanders to go to Yogya Plaza and loot the stores there and that when the looting was in progress the gates were locked and the stores were burned down.
7. Damar Harsanto, "May Riots Still Burned into Victim's Minds", *Jakarta Post*, 14 May 2002.
8. Leo Suryadinata, *Elections and Politics in Indonesia* (Singapore: Institute of Southeast Asian Studies, 2002), pp. 72–73.
9. An army intelligence officer, Brigadier-General Slamet Singgih, stated in his memoirs that he was surprised that the authorities in Jakarta did not do anything between 13 and 14 May 1998. In his view, had the authorities done something on 13 May, the situation could have been easily controlled. He noted that the reason why the authorities had not done anything has yet to be addressed. See Slamet Singgih, *Intelijen: Catatan Harian Seorang Serdadu* (Jakarta: Penerbit Kata, 2015), pp. 1–16.
10. An interesting book in Bahasa Indonesian which describes anti-Chinese violence against Chinese women is Dewi Anggraeni, *Tragedi*

Mei 1998 dan Lahirnya Komnas Perempuan (Jakarta: Kompas Pustaka Buku, 2014).

11. See Suryadinata, *Elections and Politics in Indonesia*, op. cit., p. 64.
12. Ibid.
13. "Pola kerusuhan di Jakarta dan sekitarnya" (Dokumentasi Awal no. 1), in *Sujud di Hadapan Korban Tragedi Jakarta Mei 1998* (Laporan Investigasi dan Analisa Data Tim Relawan untuk Kemanusiaan) (Jakarta: Divisi Data Tim Relawan, 1998).
14. Jemma Purdey, *Anti-Chinese Violence in Indonesia, 1966–1999* (Singapore: NUS Press, 2006), p. 106.
15. Ibid., p. 105.
16. Ibid., pp. 106–7, 140–41.
17. Ibid., pp. 153–61.
18. According to an article published in a Hong Kong magazine which specially reports inside activities of the Chinese leadership, "Qian Qichen who was then prime minister, was personally in charge of charting an appropriate policy on how to deal with the new situation." See Lee Zejing, "Beijing kan yinni bianju" [Beijing Watching Changing Situation in Indonesia], *Zheng Ming* (Hong Kong, June 1998), p. 25, cited in Shee Poon Kim, "China's Responses to the May 1998 Anti-Chinese Riots in Indonesia", EAI Working Paper No. 37 (East Asian Institute, 24 March 2000), pp. 18–19.
19. Leo Suryadinata, "China's Hands-off on Indonesia", *Far Eastern Economic Review*, 16 April 1998, p. 31.
20. Ibid.
21. Ibid.
22. Shee Poon Kim, "China's Responses to the May 1998 Anti-Chinese Riots in Indonesia", EAI Working Paper No. 37 (East Asian Institute, 24 March 2000), p. 20.
23. "Dubes RRC Sesalkan Terjadinya Perkosaan Saat Kerusuhan" [PRC's Ambassador Deplores Raping During Riots], *Suara Pembaruan*, 7 July 1998.
24. Ibid.
25. Ibid.

26. *International Herald Tribune*, 4 August 1998.
27. *International Herald Tribune*, 20 August 1998, p. 20, cited by Shee, op. cit., p. 23.
28. *Straits Times*, 5 September 1998, cited in Shee, op. cit., p. 24.
29. *Straits Times*, 18 November 1998, cited in Shee, op. cit., p. 25.
30. Ibid.
31. Reported in *Ming Pao* (Ming Bao), Hong Kong, 24 August 1998, cited in Shee, op. cit., p. 25.
32. Ibid., p. 26.

Chapter 5

DIRECT PROTECTION: EXAMPLES FROM SOUTH PACIFIC, THE MIDDLE EAST AND AFRICA

(I) ANTI-CHINESE VIOLENCE IN THE SOLOMON ISLANDS AND TONGA

The second example of China's behaviour on Chinese overseas issue involves Beijing's direct intervention in 2006 during anti-Chinese riots in the South Pacific island states of Solomon Islands and Tonga. These incidents took place about eight years after the May 1998 anti-Chinese riots in Indonesia. In the interim period, China had developed further and become more confident in the international arena. Its policy towards the Chinese in these South Pacific countries had clearly shifted from its stance towards the Chinese in Indonesia earlier. However, was this really a major change in Beijing's wider foreign policy's objectives? Had the interests of the Chinese overseas become paramount by 2006? That is, would China protect the interests of the Chinese overseas at all cost? Or was this behaviour in the trajectory of its traditional foreign policy behaviour?

BACKGROUND

The South Pacific islands, which consist of fourteen small independent states, used to be considered an "American Lake".[1] The United States was the biggest aid donor in the region, which is strategically important as a gateway to the Pacific Ocean. However, after the end of the Cold War, the United States began to downgrade its involvement in the region and its pre-eminent role has been taken over by Australia, followed by Japan, South Korea, and Taiwan.[2] The PRC moved in late 1990s and began to compete with Taiwan for diplomatic recognition in these small islands states.

Initially, in the mid-1970s, soon after it had won a seat at the United Nations, Beijing managed to establish diplomatic ties with the larger Pacific Island states, such as Fiji, Western Samoa, and Papua New Guinea (PNG), ignoring the smaller states, which it considered insignificant. Later, however, Beijing realized the strategic importance of the smaller states and the presence of Chinese new migrants there. More attention was then paid to the South Pacific. Currently, Beijing has ties with eight Pacific Island states, including the Cook Islands, the Federated States of Micronesia, Fiji, Niue, Papua New Guinea (PNG), Samoa, Tonga, and Vanuatu, while Taiwan continues to have ties with six countries.[3] including the Solomon Islands, which will be discussed in this chapter. Tonga, which recognizes Beijing, will also be examined.

The small island states in the South Pacific are economically backward and require development assistance. Their political systems are not well developed either as they gained independence only very recently. Ethnic politics often characterizes their political processes. Moreover, money politics has become the norm rather than the exception, and both Taiwan and the

PRC have exploited the situation and themselves used money politics (some refer to this as "chequebook politics") to gain the support and influence of local politicians.[4]

There are only a few thousand Chinese residents among the 8 million people living in the South Pacific islands. But, while the numbers are small the presence of the Chinese is significant as they own grocery stores, restaurants, and other small businesses.[5] Some of the Chinese are old timers, but a larger number are new Chinese migrants from mainland China who moved to the Pacific Islands in the past twenty years or so, amidst the new wave of global Chinese migration. The new Chinese migrants are very enterprising. Within a short period of time, they have been able to own shops in central business districts and other prime areas, arousing the envy of the indigenous populations. One author pointed out that whereas there was not a single Chinese-owned grocery store about twenty years ago in Nuku'alofa, the capital of Tonga, in 2007 more than 70 per cent of the groceries were reportedly owned by Chinese new migrants.[6] A BBC reporter noted that the new migrants brought with them a lot of money and desire to do business. For instance, in Honiara, Solomon Islands, they bought up beachfront sites and transformed them into hotels, and they used prime property for restaurants and shops.[7] They have changed the landscape of the area.

ANTI-CHINESE RIOTS IN THE SOLOMON ISLANDS

In April 2006, there was a large-scale anti-Chinese riot in the Solomon Islands, unprecedented since its independence from the United Kingdom in July 1978. The event that triggered the riot was the 5 April 2006 election of the Prime Minister, Snyder Rini, who was accused of rigging his victory. On 18 April, a group of opposition supporters gathered near the assembly hall demanding the resignation of Rini. The peaceful demonstration snowballed into a riot. The mob began to attack the nearby Chinatown, which was later burned to the ground.

Earlier, in 2000, the Chinese in the country had already been victimized during another political conflict. A militant organization known as the Malaita Eagle Force had occupied the capital city and kidnapped then Prime Minister Bartholomew Ulufa'alu. As tensions rose and the situation became uncontrollable, the Chinese came under attack. It was reported that about 116 Chinese were eventually repatriated by China.[8] There was relatively little media coverage of this incident, and the scale of violence was likely much smaller than that of 2006.

A brief look at the political situation in the Solomon Islands prior to the 2006 riots will provide some context for examining the reasons behind the incidents.

After gaining independence, the Solomon Islands was racked by ethnic tension between the people of Guadalcanal, the main province, and migrants from the neighbouring province of Malaita. The people from these two regions often did not see eye to eye and failed to co-exist in harmony. The political leadership failed to resolve the country's economic problems, especially those arising from the land tenure issue.[9] Economic and ethnic issues contributed to political tensions, and the Chinese were dragged into the conflict although they numbered under 2,000.[10] The Chinese included 464 residents of Honiara, among whom 180 were Chinese nationals, including 5 Hong Kongers, and 31 were Taiwanese citizens, among whom some were from the diplomatic and technical aid staff.[11] The rest were likely to be naturalized Solomon citizens.[12]

The economic success of the Chinese, especially the new migrants, was resented by the indigenous population. The Chinese were often seen in stereotypical terms as people who got rich quickly by using devious means. Many Chinese were owners of grocery stores, restaurants, and hotels, and they were accused of paying poor wages to their workers, not obeying laws and always bribing government officers to get what they wanted.[13] Local journalists often portrayed the Chinese in negative terms relative to their depiction of other Asians in the Solomon Islands, such as the Japanese and Koreans. The Chinese bore the brunt of native resentment probably because they outnumbered other Asians in the Solomon Islands.

More significantly, unlike the other Asians, the ethnic Chinese were linked to local politics, with two naturalized Solomon Islanders among the Chinese even being elected members of parliament. One of them, Thomas Chan, a business tycoon, assumed the chairmanship of the Association of Independent Members of Parliament (AIMP).[14] Snyder Rini was a member of this association. Rini was then deputy prime minister to Allan Kemakeza, who "allegedly operated a slush fund up to AUD$10 million a year to dispense political favours."[15] This fund was provided by the Taiwanese government, which spent AUD$100–150 million on aid to the Solomons each year.[16]

In 2006 Rini was nominated as prime minister by AIMP and the People's Alliance Party and he was eventually elected, inheriting the old regime. The opposition members resented his ascension and accused him of buying parliamentary votes, using local Chinese and Taiwanese money. Rini's vehement denials of any wrongdoing did not stop the opposition from demanding his immediate resignation.

About 300 voters gathered outside the Parliament building and refused to disperse until the Participating Police Force (PPF) was called in and tear gas and flash grenades were deployed. This precipitated a riot, with a mob of about 1,500 people moving into the nearby Chinatown and going on a rampage of torching and looting.[17] "Chinese families living above their shops jumped down from burning buildings and swam across a nearby river to escape rioters.... Minor injuries were reported among residents."[18] More than twenty stores owned by the Chinese were burned down, and the victims sought shelter at hospitals, churches and police stations.[19] Big hotels and restaurants owned by local Chinese were also burned down. The situation went out of control, prompting Australia and New Zealand to send extra troops, thus strengthening the Australian-led Regional Assistance Mission to the Solomon Islands (RAMSI). A curfew was imposed and violaters were arrested and prosecuted. The situation only returned to normal on 20 April.[20] According to a Hong Kong newspaper close to mainland China, "Honiara was turned into a waste land. Large-scale looting caused direct economic losses of US$10 million to the local Chinese."[21]

FACTORS CONTRIBUTING TO THE SOLOMON RIOTS

At least two major factors contributed to the riots: (i) the poor state of the Solomon economy and the economic strength of the Chinese vis-à-vis the indigenous population; and (ii) political rivalry and money politics.

Three candidates had contested the prime ministership in the 2006 election. Snyder Rini, who won, was supported by Taiwan and local tycoons. It was reported that members of parliaments were bribed to support Rini. One of the defeated candidates told Australian radio that "the election was neither fair nor free as it was corrupted by Taiwanese and business houses owned by Solomon Islanders of Chinese descent."[22] It seems that this allegation was widely accepted by opposition leaders and their followers. Nevertheless, Taiwan (then under the rule of the Democratic Progressive Party) denied its involvement in the election.

Despite Taiwan's denial, the Australian government seemed unconvinced. Australia's then foreign minister, Alexandra Downer, was quoted as saying that some of the rioting was sparked by allegations made by Snyder Rini's political opponents that Rini had received Taiwanese money.[23] Australian government agencies reportedly "raised grave concerns that some politicians involved in last week's Solomon Islands uprising were on Taiwan's payroll." The agencies were also said to be "alarmed" about China's growing influence across the Pacific.[24] Unnamed senior government sources were noted to have observed that Taiwan "has adopted the direct approach by allegedly paying off individual politicians while China has given funds to community projects."[25] An Australian Senate report expressed concern that the diplomatic competition between the PRC and Taiwan and their "chequebook diplomacy" to gain influence in the South Pacific could hurt the region's political stability and economic development.[26]

RESPONSES FROM TAIWAN AND THE PRC

While Taiwan denied its involvement in local politics, it admitted that those who were affected by the riots in Chinatown were mainland Chinese migrants, not Taiwanese businessmen.[27] It also stated that there were only two Taiwanese shops in the Solomon Islands, one a restaurant and the other a vehicle repair shop. "Neither shop was located in Chinatown or affected by the wave of riots that targeted the local Chinese."[28] There were only thirty-one Taiwanese citizens (including diplomatic staff) in Honiara, and none was affected by the riots. Nevertheless, the Taiwanese embassy assisted one family of six to take refuge in Australia. The embassy had expressed willingness to evacuate another family of ten if they, too, wanted to leave.[29] In other words, the Taiwan embassy was not concerned about Chinese victims who were not Taiwanese.

While the Taiwan embassy did not do anything to help victims who were not from Taiwan, Beijing which does not have diplomatic relations with the Solomon Islands, came forward to help the Chinese victims. On the evening of April 22, Beijing began a large-scale evacuation of Chinese refugees.[30] The Chinese government chartered four flights over three days and evacuated almost 400 people, including twenty persons from Hong Kong.[31]

As there were about 1,000 Chinese in the Solomon Islands, what happened to the rest who were neither evacuated by Taiwan (to Australia) nor by the PRC? As stated earlier, these remaining Chinese were likely to be naturalized Solomon Islanders. No information is available on their whereabouts. Some may have made their way to Australia as refugees but the majority were more likely to have remained in the country, waiting for another chance to make a livelihood.

It is worth noting that there were indeed many new migrants from mainland China who had come to the Solomon Islands in the 1990s. The majority were from Jiangmen prefecture, with Kaiping county accounting for 80 per cent. The migrants still had close connections with the Overseas

Chinese Affairs Office (OCAO) in Jiangmen. When the riots took place, Mainland China OCAO was contacted and, therefore, arrangements for evacuation could be made rapidly.[32]

Wen Wei Po (Wenhui Bao 文汇报), a Hong Kong newspaper which is close to Beijing, reported that then President Hu Jintao

> has asked the Foreign Ministry [of China] to concretely ensure the safety of all Chinese people in the Solomon Islands. The Chinese government has made the resolute decision to evacuate the Chinese, including compatriots from Taiwan as well as those Chinese persons who hold Solomon Islands passports. This type of evacuation is not usually seen internationally. This shows that China is a responsible major country with a philosophy of focusing on people, extending to the entire Chinese Diaspora whenever lives and properties are threatened.[33]

This process of evacuating Chinese from the Solomon Islands was later styled the "Solomon Model".[34] The model is important for students of Chinese foreign policy as it is based on ethnicity rather than nationality, that is, China would protect and save the Chinese overseas, regardless of their nationality, when they were caught in anti-Chinese riots. If the "Solomon Model" is indeed practised, China may come into conflict with countries where the Chinese reside, and the loyalties of those Chinese who have assumed local citizenship would be suspected by their governments and fellow citizens. In the case of the Solomon Islands evacuees, it is not known how many of them were Solomon citizens of Chinese descent. But it is clear that they were new migrants who still had strong links with China.

It is also possible that the "Solomon Model" is a special case as China does not have diplomatic ties with the Solomon

Islands, which recognizes Taiwan. Beijing's aim in this instance was to show the Chinese overseas and the world at large that China was strong while Taiwan was weak and that only Beijing could help the Chinese overseas.

China is concerned with its influence in the South Pacific islands, especially the Solomon Islands, which is the third largest country in the area in terms of population. It was reported that soon after the riots Beijing had set up a secret $1.2 million fund to support politicians in the Solomon Islands who promised to sever the country's diplomatic ties with Taiwan and switch to recognizing the PRC.[35] However, it appears that the Taiwanese may have spent much more than Beijing has on the Solomon Islands and, as a result, has been able to still maintain diplomatic ties.

"ANTI-CHINESE RIOTS" IN TONGA

Seven months later, on 16 November 2006, major "anti-Chinese violence" erupted in another South Pacific country, Tonga. Similar to the Solomon Islands riots, the riots in Tonga's capital Nuku'alofa had a political dimension. It was domestic politics that culminated in the riots. However, unlike the Solomon Islands case, Tonga has had diplomatic ties with Beijing since 1998. Therefore, there was no issue of competition between Beijing and Taipei for recognition and influence. Nevertheless, Beijing's response to the plight of the Chinese victims in Tonga was quite similar to its response during the Solomon Islands incident, that is, to send an airplane to repatriate the victims to mainland China, but the number involved appears to be fewer.

Tonga, a monarchy, was a British protectorate between 1900 and 1970, when it gained independence. Its economy is agriculture based. At the time of the riots, the majority of the population lived in poverty and the gap between the rich and the poor was wide. Against this background, a pro-democracy movement emerged. It was reported that 75 per cent of the land in the country was still in the hands of the royal family and nobility while the remaining 25 per cent was owned by the government. Unemployment rates were high and strikes occurred frequently in factories. A major strike by public servants lasting six weeks took place in 2005. King Taufa Ahau Tupou IV eventually promised to introduce reforms but he died in September 2006 and was succeeded by his son, George Tupou V, who was reluctant to introduce any significant reforms.[36]

On 16 November 2006, several thousand pro-democracy demonstrators were reported to have staged a rally during the only sitting of Parliament for that year. They demanded a vote on major democratic reform but their demands were ignored and Parliament was adjourned.[37]

Enraged by this disregard for their demands, more than 2,000 people took to the street and some started attacking and burning government buildings, a luxury hotel, restaurants and shops in Nuku'alofa. Many of the restaurants and shops were owned by new Chinese migrants. Some 80 per cent of the business district was reported to have been burnt down.[38]

There are two interpretations of the riots. One labels it an anti-Chinese riot, similar to that on Solomon Islands, while the other considers it a class conflict in which the Chinese were not the rioters' main target. Holding the latter view, Beijing's ambassador to Tonga was reported to have told China's *People Daily* that "only 25 per cent of Chinese stores [about 30] were looted or burned"[39] and the six persons who died during the riots were non-Chinese.[40]

Nevertheless, new Chinese migrants dominated retail establishments in Tongatopu, the main island in Tonga. They came to Tonga under the so-called "cash-for-passports scheme" introduced by the king that ended in 1998.[41] According to one academic, 72 per cent of businesses in Tonga are owned by the Chinese.[42] As such, any disruption to business will certainly have affected the Chinese. The total number of Chinese in Tonga then is not known with certainty although it was estimated to be between a few hundreds and a few thousands. An Australian newspaper reported that there were about 500 Chinese in Nuku'alofa before the riots.[43]

Unlike the Solomon Islands case, where the Chinese used their connections to OCAO to obtain speedy evacuation assistance, the Chinese victims in Tonga had to wait for Beijing's ambassador to the country, who was concurrently ambassador to Papua New Guinea, to make evacuation arrangements. The ambassador was able to collaborate with Tongan police to escort 150 Chinese into the embassy for refuge.[44] Those who did not go to the embassy were also given protection. It was reported that China's Foreign Ministry arranged for an airplane with a capacity of more than 250 passengers to evacuate the Chinese from Tonga. However, because Tonga did not have a large airport, the airplane could only land in Fiji. As a result, the Chinese refugees had to go to Fiji in order to fly to China. The number of Chinese affected by the riots and evacuated to China is not clear although one source claims it was about 300.[45] Like the Solomon Islands authorities, the Tongan authorities, too, urged Australia and New Zealand to send troops to help control the situation. Within days of the arrival of forces from these countries, the riots were quelled and the situation came under control.

It should be noted that many Chinese migrants chose to remain in Tonga or migrate to other South Pacific countries. Chinese migration to Tonga has continued following the return to normalcy. These new Chinese migrants play economic roles similar to those played by the Chinese prior to the 2006 riots.

CONCLUSION

The Solomon Chinese could be said to have been partially the victims of competition between Taipei and Beijing for recognition and influence. The presence of new Chinese migrants in the Solomon Islands and the wider South Pacific region is the result of globalization. In fact, many new Chinese migrants had intended to migrate to Australia and New Zealand but for various reasons had to settle in the South Pacific islands instead. Many of these migrants would have liked to make their fortunes in these islands and then move on to Australia when possible, but few were able to realize their dreams.

Defending the interests of the Solomon Chinese coincided with the higher order priorities in China's national interests. First, China wanted to project itself as a rising great power. The Solomon Islands is a gateway for China to the Pacific, yet Beijing had no diplomatic relations with the country. Understandably, Beijing wanted to replace Taipei as the representative of China. Thus, Beijing's second national interest was to show that the PRC was the only representative of the Chinese overseas, not Taiwan. When there was anti-Chinese violence in the Solomon Islands, Beijing sent its ambassador to Papua New Guinea to the country to repatriate both Chinese nationals and non-Chinese nationals (except the Taiwanese). This was intended to show the Chinese overseas and the world at large that China was now capable of protecting the Chinese overseas regardless of their nationality. But China failed to impress the Solomon Islands to switch sides from Taipei to Beijing.

The contest between Beijing and Taipei over the Solomon Islands has not ended. Both sides continue to use chequebook politics to gain local influence. Although Beijing in the earlier years appeared to have offered less money and hence was unable to replace Taipei in representing China, its affluence today makes it better placed to succeed in this quest eventually.

The anti-Chinese riots in Tonga appear to be different from the Solomon case as they did not stem from accusations that the Chinese were involved in local politics. Nevertheless, Chinese domination of local business appeared to be resented by indigenous Tongans. Therefore, the riots, which were directed at the government, also developed into anti-Chinese riots, or at least seriously affected the Chinese population in the capital. As in the case of the Solomon Islands, Beijing was able to repatriate the new migrants because they were few in number.

(II) EVACUATION OF THE CHINESE FROM EGYPT, LIBYA AND YEMEN

The third example, which I would still classify as "Direct Protection", involves the mass evacuations of Chinese workers and Chinese nationals from Africa and the Middle East (particularly from Libya). These took place between thirteen and seventeen years after the 1998 anti-Chinese riots in Jakarta. On the surface, this set of evacuations is similar to the two instances of evacuation in the South Pacific islands discussed earlier. In reality, they are quite different, at least in Libya, as the evacuated Chinese were not "overseas Chinese" but in fact guest workers who worked for China's state-owned enterprises (SOEs) and were supposed to return to China when their projects were completed. In the case of Egypt, the Chinese evacuees included Chinese tourists and visiting students, while the evacuation in Yemen was more of an international mission rather than one involving the rescue of just the Chinese overseas.

BACKGROUND

By the end of the twentieth century, China had become a "capitalist state" (or, in Beijing's language, a "Socialist-oriented market economy") which requires resources from overseas, overseas markets, and overseas projects. Two of the major targets that it has selected in this respect are Africa and the Middle East, regions that are rich in energy reserves, minerals, and raw materials. Since the turn of the century, China's trade with Africa and the Middle East had "increased twenty-fold, reaching US$200 billion with each of these regions in 2014."[46] Oil and energy investments dominate China's commercial activities in the region. Two-thirds of China's oil imports come from Africa and the Middle East.[47]

In Africa, China has invested most in five countries, namely, Nigeria, Zambia, South Africa, Zimbabwe, and the Congo.[48] A large number of Chinese SOEs are present also in Algeria, Libya, and Sudan. In the Middle East, China has invested heavily in Egypt, Yemen, Saudi Arabia and Kuwait, and China's SOEs are also present in these countries.

China's SOEs in Africa and the Middle East are engaged in building houses, bridges, roads and railways, and in the telecommunication, oil exploration, and mining industries. Given that these are heavy industries, it is not surprising that the SOEs need a lot of manpower, especially labourers. Although labour is in plentiful supply in most countries in the region, many of the SOEs prefer Chinese labourers as they are considered more efficient than the locals and do not present communication challenges.

According to Chinese reports, there are about 3.75 to 4 million Chinese labourers working overseas.[49] This number has not been verified. These labourers tend to head mostly for the Asian countries, such as Japan, South Korea, and Singapore.[50] There are no reports indicating that sizeable numbers were or still are in Africa and the Middle East.

However, one scholar maintained that Chinese workers had flooded Africa but not the Middle East, as the former does not have restrictions on the entry of foreign workers, unlike the latter.[51] For instance, Egypt allows only one in ten workers on any single project to be a foreign national; temporary exceptions are granted only for the high-tech sector.

Nevertheless, Libya and Algeria (and, to a lesser extent, Yemen) are obvious exceptions to the rule. There were an estimated 35,000 foreign workers in each country prior to the recent social unrest.[52]

EVACUATION OF CHINESE NATIONALS FROM EGYPT, LIBYA, AND YEMEN

Libya was a monarchy before the king was overthrown by Colonel Muammar Qadhafi in 1969 and the country became a republic. It was ruled for more than forty years by Qadhafi until the so-called Arab Spring revolution in early 2011. A controversial and eccentric figure, Qadhafi ruled with an iron fist. He claimed to be a revolutionary, a nationalist, and an architect of African unity. His policies were erratic. In the 1970s he introduced his so-called Third Universal Theory, arguing that Libya was an alternative between capitalism and communism. He was against Western imperialism and financed revolutions in neighbouring countries. On the domestic front, he brutally suppressed the opposition. He had introduced a state-run economy but towards the end of the twentieth century he began to privatize the economy and welcomed foreign investment. It was during this period that the PRC began to invest heavily in Qadhafi's Libya. In 2002, President Jiang Zemin visited Libya and bolstered China's investment.

According to a report, there were about fifty big Chinese projects in Libya before the Arab Spring. Thirteen SOEs were involved in the projects, which included China Railway Building Engineering Company (中国铁道建筑工程总公司, involved in building railways along the coastal area), China Engineering Company (中国工程总公司, involved in building residential homes), and China Oil and Natural Gas Group (中国石油天然气集团, involved in exploiting oil and gas).[53] However, during the Arab Spring, when an armed opposition emerged to overthrow Qadhafi, the Chinese companies found themselves caught in between. The rebels were hostile towards Chinese companies that were working on government projects. The safety of the property of these companies and of their managements and workers could not be guaranteed.

Initially, China wanted to take a business-as-usual approach, but soon the civil war appeared to get out of control. "...thousands of Chinese nationals in the troubled North African country were robbed and dozens were wounded as they tried to flee the violence."[54] China's SOEs in Libya began to ask for help from the Chinese government. Back home in China, the relatives of Chinese workers in Libya also pressurized their government to rescue their kin. Apart from these pressures, an equally important reason for Beijing's willingness to eventually evacuate the Chinese was perhaps its confidence in playing a major role in international rescue operations as its navy, air force, and army were now ready for such a task.

To evacuate more than 35,000 Chinese nationals, mainly labourers and other employees of the SOEs, was not an easy task. It required detailed planning, and the Chinese government needed to work in close collaboration with its embassies overseas, the SOEs, and the military, in what was to be the largest evacuation mission the PRC had ever conducted by sea, air, and land. By 1 March, China had pulled out about 32,000 nationals from Libya, 9,000 of whom were back in China and roughly 21,000 already in a third country, while 2,100 were on their way to a third country.[55] By 3 March, a total of 35,860 Chinese citizens had been evacuated from Libya.

The massive evacuation proved to be a great success for China. There were countless reports in China on the gratitude of those who had been able to return home and their pride in the PRC's achievement. *Xinhua Wang* (Xinhua Net) used the opportunity to declare that "...all the overseas Chinese would keep in mind: though thousands of miles apart, China — a prosperous, stable and strong homeland — is always their safe haven linking them by heart."[56] As stated earlier, these people were mainly SOE workers, but the report continued to call them "overseas Chinese", the term that is also used for "Chinese nationals overseas" (海外中国人).

Prior to the Libya saga, the "Arab Spring" affected Egypt in January 2011. As protests became widespread, the political situation in Egypt became unstable. Many Chinese in Egypt feared for their lives and asked to be evacuated. The backgrounds of these Chinese are not clear. One source said that more than 500 Chinese people had flocked to Cairo Airport on 31 January

2011, among whom more than 300 were tourists and 41 students. They were flown back to China and arrived in Beijing on 1 February 2011.[57] Another source noted that "the Chinese government organized eight flights to Egypt and brought back a total of 1,848 Chinese, including those from Hong Kong, Macao, and Taiwan."[58] The Egypt evacuation story is quite different from that of Libya not only in terms of scale and means of evacuation but also the background of the evacuees: most of them were Chinese tourists and Chinese students visiting Egypt.

In Yemen, violence spread across the country in September 2014, when Iranian-backed Shi'ite Houthi fighters seized the capital, Sanaa. The rebels managed to unseat President Abd-Rabbu Mansour Hadi only in late January 2015. Following Hadi's ouster, a Saudi-led coalition launched a week-long air strike against the rebels.[59] In March 2015, two Chinese frigates, the Linyu and Weifang, which had been on a routine patrol mission in the region, evacuated 629 Chinese citizens and 279 other foreign nationals from war-torn Yemen.[60] It is not clear who these Chinese citizens were. It is likely they were workers employed on Chinese projects. Among the other nationals who were rescued, many were Pakistanis; the rest were nationals of fifteen different countries including Singapore, the United Kingdom, Germany, and Italy.

An unnamed diplomat was reported to have remarked that the Chinese ships had been in the right place at the right time, and that the operation was risky as fighting had come close to the Chinese warships.[61] This was a historic move for China as it was the first time that the PLA Navy had conducted an evacuation operation that included rescuing foreign nationals. The 2011 Libya evacuation involved rescuing only Chinese citizens. Xi Jinping's China, it seems, had begun to play an international disaster rescue role.

CONCLUSION

Comparing the evacuations of Chinese from the Solomon Islands and Tonga in 2006, on the one hand, and the evacuations from Libya, and Egypt, both in 2011, and from Yemen in 2015, on the other hand, one can find few similarities and several major differences. Their similarity is obvious: all the evacuees (with the exception of those in Yemen) were new "migrants" and Chinese citizens. The similarity appears to stop there.

The evacuees in Solomon and Tonga were mainly traders and numbered only a few hundreds, while those from Libya were mainly project workers and employees who were linked to China's SOEs, and they were far more numerous, numbering 35,000. This latter group is a special kind of "overseas Chinese". The evacuees from Egypt were a mix of Chinese tourists, students and workers, numbering 1,800 in total, while the evacuees from Yemen were a mix of Chinese citizens and non-Chinese foreign nationals, numbering 908 people.

The three regions involved, the Pacific Islands, the Middle East, and Africa, are of different strategic importance to China. The Pacific Islands are important for China's maritime security and one of the islands (Solomon Islands) is linked to the Taiwan issue, but Africa and the Middle East are more critical for China's supply of resources and as a destination for capital investment. It is not surprising then that China's SOEs were and still are operating in the Middle East and Africa in sizeable numbers and on large scales. The critical importance of these two regions makes it a high priority for China to protect the Chinese working for China there. Understandably, Beijing would not hesitate to send its navy and air force to evacuate

Chinese in these regions. It should also be noted that the evacuations were undertaken in 2011, during Hu Jintao's presidency, when China had just started to show its military might. Nevertheless, the large-scale evacuation undertaken in Libya was the only one of its kind, with the rest of the evacuations being relatively small. For instance, the 2015 evacuation from Yemen involved fewer than 1,000 people. The Yemen evacuation is unique as it included foreign nationals, illustrating that China has the potential to play an international humanitarian role.

It is clear that the protection of the Chinese overseas after the rise of China is still within the framework of China's foreign policy interests: the interests of the "overseas Chinese" were protected because these did not come into conflict with China's higher order national interests. In fact, the above examples show that the interests of the overseas Chinese have become merged with China's key national interests.

Notes

1. Zhu Zhiqun, *China's New Diplomacy: Rationale, Strategies and Significance*, 2nd ed. (Surrey, England: Ashgate Publishing, 2013), p. 143.
2. Ibid., p. 143. In fact, it is important to note that Australia is the largest aid donor in the Pacific Islands as the region is crucial for the security of Australia. See Lowy Institute for International Policy, "Australian Foreign Aid", <http://www.lowyinstitute.org/issues/australian-foreign-aid> (accessed 23 October 2015). But Zhu did not mention Australia at all. Instead, he noted that Japan was the largest donor.
3. Lowy Institute for International Policy, "China and the Pacific Islands", <www.lowyinstitute.org/issues/china-pacific> (accessed 23 November 2015).

4. Penny Spiller, "Riots Highlight Chinese Tension", BBC News, 21 April 2006, <http://news.bbc.co.uk/2/hi/asia-pacific/4930994.stm> (accessed 2 August 2015).
5. Zhu, op. cit., p. 143.
6. Bertil Lintner, "The Sinicizing of the South Pacific", *Asia Times Online*, 18 April 2007, cited in Zhu, op. cit., p. 143.
7. Spiller, op. cit.
8. China.org.cn. "Large-scale Evacuation of Chinese from Solomon Islands", 25 April 2006, <www.china.org.cn/english/2006/Apr/166694.htm> (accessed 23 October 2015); Lin Xixing 林锡星, "Fansi suolomen qundao paihua beiju" 反思所罗门群岛排华悲剧, Yazhou Zhoukan《亚洲周刊》, 7 May 2008, p. 18.
9. Grace Chew Chye Lay, "The April 2006 Riots in the Solomon Islands", *CHC Bulletin*, nos. 7 and 8 (May and November 2006): 12.
10. One scholar argues that there were only about 1,000 Chinese in the Solomon Islands. See Lin, op. cit., p. 18.
11. See Chew, op. cit., p. 14.
12. This is my guess as the information is unavailable.
13. Spiller, op. cit.
14. Chew, op. cit., p. 13.
15. Nick Squires, "Beijing Slush Fund to Woo Solomons", *South China Morning Post*, 30 April 2006.
16. Ibid.
17. For a description of the riots, see Chew, op. cit., p. 13.
18. Reuters, "Solomons Hell for Chinese", EastSouthWestNorth Blog, 20 April 2006, <http://www.zonaeuropa.com/20060425_1.htm> (accessed 2 August 2015).
19. Nanfang Daily (*Nanfang Ribao*, Mainland China), in English translation, "The Battle of the Solomon Islands", EastSouthWestNorth Blog, 24 April 2005, <www.zonaeuropa.com/20060425_1.htm> (accessed 2 August 2015).
20. Chew, op. cit., p. 14.
21. *Wen Wei Po* (Wen Hui Bao, Hong Kong), "The Battle of the Solomon Islands", EastSouthWestNorth Blog, 24 April 2006,

<www.zonaeuropa.com/20060425_1.htm> (accessed 2 August 2015).

22. Tony Jones, "Joses Tuhanuku on the Solomon Situation", Transcript of ABC TV programme, 19 April 2006, cited by Chew, op. cit., p. 14.
23. Joel Atkinson, "Big Trouble in Little Chinatown: Australia, Taiwan and the April 2006 Post-Election Riot in Solomon Islands", *Pacific Affairs* 82, no. 1 (Spring 2009): 57–58.
24. Ian McPhedran, "Concern Over 'Buying' Islanders", *Adelaide Advertiser*, 26 April 2006.
25. Ibid.
26. Reuters, "Solomons Hell for Chinese", op. cit.
27. ETTV (Eastern Television), "The Battle of the Solomon Islands", EastSouthWestNorth Blog, 20 April 2006, <www.zonaeuropa.com/20060425_1.htm> (accessed 2 August 2015).
28. *Taipei Times*, "The Battle of the Solomon Islands", EastSouthWestNorth Blog, 21 April 2015, <www.zonaeuropa.com/20060425_1.htm> (accessed 2 August 2015).
29. VOA (Voice of America), "The Battle of the Solomon Islands", EastSouthWestNorth Blog, 24 April 2006, <www.zonaeuropa.com/20060425_1.htm> (accessed 2 August 2015).
30. *Sing Tao* (Hong Kong), "The Battle of the Solomon Islands", EastSouthWestNorth Blog, 24 April 2006, <www.zonaeuropa.com/20060425_1.htm> (accessed 2 August 2015).
31. *Wen Wei Po*, op. cit.
32. See Lin, op. cit., p. 13.
33. Ibid.
34. The term "Solomon Model" (Suoluomen moshi 所罗门模式) was used in an article written by a PRC scholar. See Hao Mengfei 郝梦飞, "Qiaomin liyi, lingshi baohu, guojia liyi" 侨民利益, 领事保护, 国家利益, in *Zhongguo guojia liyi yu yingxiang*《中国国家利益与影响》, edited by Xu Jia 许嘉, 主编 (Beijing 北京: Shijie zhishi chubanshe 世界知识出版社, December 2006), p. 152.
35. Squires, op. cit.

36. Mike Harman, "Tongan Riots, 2006", Libcom.org, 28 June 2008, <https://libcom.org/history/tongan-riots-2006> (accessed 30 March 2016).
37. Ibid.
38. Ibid.
39. The statement of Beijing's ambassador Hu Yeshun is cited in "Tongan Riots, 2006", op. cit.
40. Zhongguo Pinglun Xinwen Wang 中国评论新闻网, "Tangjia shaoluan 8 ren siwang, huaren shangdian zao xiji" 汤加骚乱8 人死亡，华人商店遭洗劫, 18 November 2006, <http://hk.crntt.com/crnwebapp/doc/docDetailCreate.jsp?coluid=7&kindid=0&docid=100251880> (accessed 30 March 2016). In the contents of the report, it was reported that six (not eight) people were dead.
41. "Tongan Riots, 2006", op. cit.
42. Academic Phil Crocombe proposed this figure in his study. Cited in "Tongan Riots, 2006", op. cit.
43. Sydney Morning Herald, "Mobs Run Riot in Tonga", 16 November 2006. Also "Tangjia shaoluan 8 ren siwang, huaren shangdian zao xiji", op. cit.
44. "Zhongguo pai zhuanji jie tangjia huaqiao huiguo" 中国派专机接汤加华侨回国，<http://www.tuiwen.org/article/2060404638/> (accessed 30 March 2016).
45. Zhang Zhenguo 张振国, "Waimei: huaren yimin zai Tangjia weihe bushou huanying?" 外媒：华人移民在汤加为何不受欢迎？Xingdao huanqiu wang 星岛环球网, 31 December 2013, <http://edchina.stnn.cc/Chinese/2013/1231/4757.shtml> (accessed 30 March 2016).
46. Luke Patey, "China's New Crisis Diplomacy in Africa and the Middle-East", *DIIS Policy Brief*, January 2016.
47. Ibid.
48. Sina 新浪网, "CHH: Zhongguo zai feizhou de touzi yuan chao meiguo" CHH: 中国在非洲的投资远超美国, <finance.sina.com.cn/stock/usstock/c/20140806/175719932066.shtml> (accessed 1 June 2016).

49. Zhongguo Xinwen Wang 中国新闻网, "Jingwai dagong bu qingchu quanli yiwu, haiwai zhongguo laogong jiufen jizeng" 境外打工不清楚权利义务海外中国劳工纠纷骤增, 9 February 2007, <http://www.chinanews.com/hr/news/2007/02-09/871487.shtml> (accessed 1 June 2016).
50. Ibid.
51. Ben Simpfendorfer, "The Impact of the Arab Revolutions on China's Foreign Policy", in *The EU-China Relationship: European Perspectives. A Manual for Policy Makers*, edited by Kerry Brown (Singapore: World Scientific, 2015), pp. 201–13 (p. 209).
52. Ibid.
53. Len Xinyu 冷新宇, "Zhongguo guoqi zai libiya shousun 188 yi meiyuan, minqi sunshi weizhi" 中国国企在利比亚受损188 亿美元, 民企损失未知, *Zhongguo jingji zhoukan* 《中国经济周刊》, 24 May 2011, <http://news.qq.com/a/20110524/000019.htm> (accessed 5 June 2016).
54. Xinhua Wang 新华网, "China's Libya Evacuation Highlights People-First Nature of Government", 3 March 2011, <http://news.xinhuanet.com/english2010/indepth/2011-03/03/c_13759953.htm> (accessed 6 June 2016).
55. Ibid.
56. Ibid.
57. "Baoji cheqiao" 包机撤侨, <www.baike.com/wiki/包机撤侨> (accessed 10 June 2016).
58. Xinhua China Daily 中国日报网, "Backgrounder: China's Major Overseas Evacuations in Recent Years", <www.chinadaily.com.cn/china/2015-03/30/content_19954649.htm> (accessed 1 June 2016).
59. Megha Rajagopalan and Ben Blanchard, "China Evacuates Foreign Nationals from Yemen in Unprecedented Move", Reuters Television and Sabine Siebold in Berlin, 3 April 2015; Joshua Keating, "Yemen's President Just Stepped Down. Now What?", 22 January 2015, <http://www.slate.com/blogs/the_slatest/2015/01/22/yemen_s_president_just_stepped_down_now_what.html> (accessed 1 June 2016).

60. Jonas Parello-Plesner and Mathieu Duchatel, *China's Strong Arm: Protecting Citizens and Assets Abroad* (London: Internatonal Institute for Strategic Studies, May 2015); also BBC News, "Yemen's Crisis: China Evacuates Citizens and Foreigners from Aden", 3 April 2015, <www.bbc.com/news/world-middle-east-32173811> (accessed 1 June 2016).
61. Rajagopalan and Blanchard, "China Evacuates Foreign Nationals from Yemen in Unprecedented Move", op. cit.

Chapter 6

EFFECTIVE PROTECTION? THE 2014 ANTI-CHINA/CHINESE RIOTS IN VIETNAM

The fourth example involves China's response to the 2014 anti-China/Chinese riots in Vietnam. This episode took place sixteen years after the anti-Chinese riots in Jakarta. By then, Xi Jinping had assumed the presidency of the PRC and had begun to adopt a more assertive foreign policy in the region, especially in the South China Sea, where China has a territorial dispute with Vietnam. The anti-China/Chinese riots of 2014 should be seen against this backdrop. Beijing was able to offer effective protection to its nationals, who were the victims of the riots. From China's foreign policy perspective, is this another example in which the interests of the Chinese overseas are paramount? Or can China's behaviour be explained in terms of its traditional foreign policy behaviour?

BACKGROUND

Vietnam was a vassal of China in ancient times although the Vietnamese people occasionally rebelled against continued domination by China. In the nineteenth century, Vietnam was colonized by France. After World War II a communist regime established itself in Hanoi in the north and started a war of national liberation against the French and their South Vietnamese allies (the First Indochina War). The United States took over as patron of South Vietnam after Hanoi forced the French to retreat in 1954 and soon the Second Indochina War began. In both wars, Hanoi received tremendous support from the PRC as well as the Soviet Union. It eventually managed to repel US forces and achieve the reunification of North and South Vietnam in 1975.

Soon after reunification, Vietnam started a socialist transformation programme, which adversely affected the ethnic Chinese in the country, especially those in the south. The Chinese, who formed the middle class in Vietnam, began to leave the country in large numbers.

Meanwhile, despite receiving help from the PRC in their fight for independence, the Vietnamese resented being continually influenced by China. In 1976, at their fourth party congress, the Vietnamese Communist Party leadership purged the pro-Beijing group in their midst, and relations between China and Vietnam became tense.[1] More importantly, Vietnam's relationship with the Soviet Union, which had begun to intensify, culminated in a formal alliance in June 1978, which was perceived by Beijing as an act to encircle the PRC. Subsequently, on 25 December 1978, Vietnam invaded and occupied Cambodia, which was an ally of Beijing. Nearly two months later, on 17 February 1979, Beijing launched an attack on Vietnam from the north, claiming that it intended to teach Vietnam a lesson. The conflict lasted only for a month and, after capturing Long San, Chinese troops withdrew. Both sides suffered heavy casualties. The end of what became known as the Third Indochina War ushered in a period of frosty relations between Hanoi and Beijing, which improved only after the disintegration of the Soviet Union in 1991.

The reasons for the Sino–Vietnamese war are complex and not related to Vietnam's treatment of ethnic Chinese and their subsequent exodus from the country, which was only one of several contributing factors. The war took place more than two years after the flight of ethnic Chinese from Vietnam began. The factor that triggered the war was Vietnam's alliance with the Soviets and its invasion of Cambodia. Even after the war had ended, the position of the ethnic Chinese in Vietnam remained difficult and the refugee outflow continued. Thus, Vietnam's campaign against the ethnic Chinese was only one of the contributing factors behind the PRC's decision to launch a war against it.[2]

The war between the two countries, both ruled by communist parties, was a conflict of two nationalisms; there was no more international communist solidarity. However, despite major conflict, the realities of proximity forced the two neighbouring countries to improve their relationship, especially as both gradually began pursuing open door economic policies. China introduced economic reform in 1978, while Vietnam introduced its own reform programme known as *doi moi* (renovation) in 1986. Although both countries continued to adopt a single party system, they nevertheless pursued liberal economic policies.

Much the same way that China welcomed capitalists among the "overseas Chinese" to participate in China's economic development, Vietnam encouraged the Vietnamese overseas (*Viet kieu*, many of them are Chinese Vietnamese) to return to help in the economic development of Vietnam. China has also invested heavily in Vietnam in the form of joint or individual ventures. According to China's Chamber of Commerce in Vietnam, as of 2014, China had 112 large and medium enterprises in Vietnam, and its investments were focused in the north of the country rather than the south.[3]

It is worth noting that after the dissolution of the Soviet Union in 1991, there was hardly any anti-Chinese violence in Vietnam. However, this does not mean that Vietnam no longer harboured anti-China/Chinese sentiments. Instead, such sentiments were kept at bay because Moscow was no longer able to provide large amounts of economic assistance and Hanoi needed Beijing's help to develop its economy and thereby maintain political stability.

What then were the factors that contributed to the anti-China/Chinese riots of 2014? Were they similar to the factors that led to anti-Chinese/China campaigns in the past? What was Beijing's response? Does it fit into one of the models discussed earlier?

ORIGINS OF THE 2014 RIOTS

On 2 May 2014 the PRC's China National Offshore Oil Corporation moved a semi-submersible oil rig into waters within the 200 mile-Exclusive Economic Zone (EEZ) of the Paracel Islands, which are claimed by both China and Vietnam. The oil rig was guarded by the PRC's aircraft and battleships during its exploration activity. In response, Vietnam sent thirty naval vessels to the area but these were repelled by the eighty PRC ships protecting the rig.[4]

Hanoi felt that the Chinese had infringed upon its national territory. Soon, peaceful anti-China demonstrations began to take place in Vietnam. It was later revealed that the Vietnamese authorities had initially endorsed a show of Vietnamese patriotism and nationalism to register their dissatisfaction with China.[5]

However, the demonstrations soon moved away from their anti-China/Chinese focus and seemed to be directed also at the Hanoi authorities, who had become more repressive of domestic criticism as well as more corrupt.[6] Peaceful demonstrations began to turn violent.

It should be noted that violent demonstrations occurred mainly in Vietnam's south near Ho Chi Minh City, especially in Binh Duong province, Ha Htinh and Dong Nai province, not in the north. If the demonstrations were meant to punish Beijing, the north would have been the focus because the 1979 Sino–Vietnamese War, which took place along Vietnam's borders, took a greater toll on the Vietnamese people in the north while those in the south were not affected. Yet, the focus for the 2014 riots was in the south.

It is also worth noting that of the few hundred factories/companies that were affected by the riots, only fourteen were owned by the PRC; the rest were owned by Taiwanese, Hongkongers, Singaporeans, and Japanese. The Taiwanese owned most of the factories in the area that were hit by the riots and their factories were the most affected. There were two explanations for this. First, Vietnam recognizes only one China, that is, the PRC. In Vietnamese school textbooks, Taiwan is described as a province of China. Taiwanese companies in the Industrial Parks had signboards bearing names written in Chinese characters. Furthermore, their employees included mainland Chinese workers. For these reasons, the rioters may have assumed that these companies were owned by mainland Chinese.[7] Second, before the riots, there had been petitions and protests against many Taiwanese companies by Vietnamese workers who felt exploited and wanted better working conditions and pay. In 2008 and 2012, industrial conflicts in these factories had led to strikes.[8]

On the evening of 12 May, 100 Vietnamese workers in a Taiwanese-owned shoe store located in the Singapore Industrial Park in Binh Duong reportedly staged a demonstration. The following morning (13 May), these workers went on strike. This action was followed by workers in other Taiwanese-owned factories as well as some factories owned by Hongkongers. Within a short period of time, 20,000 workers surrounded the industrial park. Many managed to enter the park and started ransacking and burning the factories. Many non-Vietnamese workers were injured. It appeared that there were not enough police, and the situation was out of control.

Four other industrial parks were also affected by the riots. Factories owned by mainland Chinese and Hongkongers had also been destroyed. Even some factories in Ho Chi Minh City were affected. The deputy head of Binh Duong province, Tran Van Nam, was reported to have said that on the night of 13 May, 20,000 Vietnamese workers from several industrial parks participated in anti-China activities. The workers claimed that they had meant to attack factories owned by mainland Chinese but by mistake they attacked those owned by Taiwanese and Hongkongers. On 14 May, the police arrested about 600 people and charged them with "looting and inciting the crowd."[9] The conflict resulted in 400 policemen being injured.

On 15 May, Prime Minister Nguyen Tan Dung sent notices to the security department and other ministries, saying that "in recent days, the people throughout the country have expressed their patriotism legitimately by protesting China's illegal placement of its Haiyang Shiyou 981 oil rig in Vietnam's water"[10]. However, he further noted that "[s]ome have violated the law and spontaneously damaged production units, including those of foreign investors, and oppose the authority..." and asked these illegal actions to be stopped immediately.

CHINA'S REPATRIATION OF PRC CITIZENS

On the same day, that is, 15 May, Chinese Foreign Minister Wang Yi protested to the Vietnamese foreign minister and called for a halt to anti-China activities. On 17 May, with the help of the Chinese embassy in Hanoi, China repatriated more than 3,000 Chinese nationals from Vietnam, with sixteen victims who were seriously injured being taken to Sichuan. On the morning of 18 May, China sent five more ships to repatriate more Chinese to their homeland.[11] It also dispatched a medical team by plane to Vietnam to take seriously injured victims in Ha Htinh province. Interestingly, the Chinese media did not give much coverage to the anti-China riots in Vietnam.[12] Perhaps Beijing feared that playing up the issue might stoke an outburst of Chinese nationalism, which could be difficult to manage.

On 14 May, Reuters reported that as anti-Chinese riots spread in Vietnam, twenty-one people had died, of whom five were Vietnamese and the rest mainland Chinese. In addition, 100 people had been hospitalized.[13]

On 16 May, a spokesperson from China's Foreign Ministry stated that "according to the information that I have collected, two Chinese were dead, hundred people were injured...in this event, the greatest damage suffered by the Zhong Ye Company (中冶公司) which is located in Ha Htinh."[14]

The damage suffered by the Taiwanese was more serious: at least 224 factories were affected, of which eighteen were burnt to the ground. According to Lin Xinyi, a Taiwanese investor, the chairman of the Board of Steel Factory in Ha Htinh province, "four of his mainland Chinese employees died, of which two were burned to death, one collapsed and died due to heat and the other was beaten to death.... One Taiwanese employee was shocked...and flown back to Taiwan and died."[15]

The Vietnamese authorities managed to quickly curb the riots and the situation returned to normal by 16 May. Nonetheless, the riots caused Vietnam serious economic losses and affected the country's economic development. In order to woo back foreign investment, Vietnam announced that it would offer some form of humanitarian assistance to the Chinese victims and dispatch a delegation to China to offer condolences to the families of the victims. It also decided to offer compensation for the victims involved in the riots. Hong Lei, the spokesperson of China's foreign minister, was reported to have welcomed the Vietnamese move.[16]

CONCLUSION

There is no doubt that the anti-China riots in Vietnam originated in the protest against the establishment of the oil rig in Vietnamese-claimed waters but broader factors beyond just anti-Chinese sentiments were at work. Hanoi's intention was to stage a peaceful demonstration to protest against Beijing's actions in the South China Sea, but this went out of control as various interest groups began to vent their frustrations. Nonetheless, anti-Chinese sentiments in Vietnam are still strong and anything related to China and the Chinese can easily be used to trigger riots.

The PRC appeared to keep a low profile in its response to the anti-China/Chinese violence. There was no mobilization in mainland China nor much reporting in the Chinese press about the riots. Nevertheless, when the riots took place, China immediately sent medical teams and ships to repatriate the Chinese workers who were affected, showing that it was able to protect its overseas citizens.

The riots had affected the operation of Chinese factories in south Vietnam but China did not withdraw its investments from Vietnam. From Beijing's point of view, this was just another anti-China/Chinese riot.

However, from Hanoi's point of view, the anti-China riot, which was linked to China's deployment of an oil rig into Vietnamese waters, was an important event in contemporary Vietnam–China relations. It seems to have been the trigger for a serious reassessment of its relations with China and its attempt to establish a closer link with Washington in order to balance China.[17]

The Vietnam example shows that China places its territorial integrity above the interests of Chinese overseas. However, when its actions affected the Chinese nationals overseas, Beijing was able to protect them by sending planes and ships to repatriate them. Nonetheless, China would not be able to prevent anti-Chinese violence.

Notes

1. William S. Turley, "Vietnam since Reunification", *Problems of Communism* 26 (March–April 1977): 38; also William J. Duiker, *The Communist Road to Power in Vietnam* (Boulder: Westview Press, 1982), especially p. 340, for the names of Vietnamese leaders who were purged because of their pro-Beijing attitude, see Jaap van Genniken, *The Third Indochina War: The Conflicts between China, Vietnam and Cambodia* (Amsterdam, n.p., 1983), p. 16.
2. For a brief analysis of ethnic Chinese and the Sino–Vietnamese war, see Leo Suryadinata, *China and the ASEAN States: The Ethnic*

Chinese Dimension (Singapore: Singapore University Press, 1985), pp. 53–58.

3. "2014 nian 5 yue yuenan paihua zhenxiang, luji ganbu: yuenan baomin jiushi yao baofu taishang xuehan gongchang" 2014 年 5 月越南排华真相, 陆籍干部: 越南暴民就是要报复台商血汗工, 19 May 2014, <http://blog.udn.com/t612/13456054> (accessed 16 December 2015).
4. Paul J. Leaf, "Learning from China's Oil Rig Standoff with Vietnam", *The Diplomat*, 30 August 2014, <thediplomat.com/2014/08/learning-fromchinas-oil-rig-standoff-with-vietnam> (accessed 15 December 2015). It should be noted that China was scheduled to withdraw the platform on 15 August, but by 16 July it had already done so.
5. Zhongguo Ribao Wang 中国日报网, "Meimei: yuenan jiang wei fanhua shaoluan fuchu jingji daijia" 美媒: 越南将为反华骚乱付出经济代价, 19 May 2014, <http://world.chinadaily.com.cn/2014-05/19/content_17517952.htm> (accessed 16 December 2015).
6. Jason Morris-Jung, "Reflections on the Oil Rig Crisis: Vietnamese's Domestic Opposition Grows", *ISEAS Perspective*, no. 43 (30 July 2014); Huong Le Thu, "The Anti-Chinese Riots in Vietnam: Responses from the Ground", *ISEAS Perspective*, no. 32 (27 May 2014); also Joshua Kurlantzick, "Vietnam Protests: More Than Just Anti-China Sentiment", *Council on Foreign Relations*, 15 May 2014, <http://blogs.cfr.org/asia/2014/05/15/vietnam-protests-more-than-just-anti-china-sentiment/> (accessed 16 December 2015).
7. Apple Daily, "Paihua baodong waijiaobu yintiezhi gongtaishang quge/jishixinwen" 排华暴动外交部印贴纸供台商区隔/即时新闻, 15 May 2014, <http://www.appledaily.com.tw/realtimenews/article/new/20140515/398104> (accessed 16 December 2015).
8. China.org.cn., "Taiyang: yuenan paihua yuanqi nanhai, gen zai guonei" 太阳: 越南 "排华" 缘起南海, 根在国内, 24 May 2014, <http://www.china.org.cn/chinese/2014-05/24/content_32472465.htm> (accessed 16 December 2015). However, Huong Le Thu

argued that the instigators "allegedly hired to lead the mass protests", not the workers, and most of the victims were Taiwanese factories, not those of mainlanders, she suspected that China was perhaps behind the anti-Chinese riots as China intended to sabotage Vietnam's stability. But no strong evidence was provided. See Le Thu, "The Anti-Chinese Riots in Vietnam: Responses from the Ground", op. cit., pp. 7–8.

9. Reuters, "Up to 21 Dead, Doctor Says, as Anti-China Riots Spread in Vietnam", 15 May 2014, <http://www.reuters.com/article/us-vietnamchina-riots-casualties-idUSBREA4E03Y20140515> (accessed 16 December 2015).
10. The Socialist Republic of Vietnam, Online Newspaper of the Government, "PM Orders Urgent Measures to Maintain Security, Order", 15 May 2014, <http://news.chinhphu.vn/Home/PM-orders-urgent-measures-to-maintain-security-order/20145/21039.vgp> (accessed 16 December 2015).
11. The five ships were able to accommodate 5,000 passengers, but it is not known how many eventually board the ships. According to China Daily Net, in May 2014, China pulled back 3,500 Chinese citizens affected by the riots in Vietnam. Xinhua China Daily 中国日报网, "Backgrounder: China's Major Overseas Evacuations in Recent Years", <www.chinadaily.com.cn/china/ 2015-03/30/content_19954649.htm> (accessed 1 June 2016).
12. Zhongguang Xinwen Wang中广新闻网, "Yuenan fanzhong baodong, lu mei chao ditiao" 越南反中暴动，陆媒超低调, 17 May 2014, <https://tw.news.yahoo.com/越南反中暴動-陸媒超低調-062949679.html> (accessed 16 December 2015).
13. Reuters, "Up to 21 Dead, Doctor Says, as Anti-China Riots Spread in Vietnam", op. cit.
14. Embassy of the People's Republic of China in the Republic of Singapore, "2014 nian 5 yue 16 ri waijiaobu fayanren Hua Chunying zhuchi lixing jizhe zhaodaihui" 2014年5月16日外交部发言人华春莹主持例行记者招待会, 16 May 2014, <http://www.chinaembassy.org.sg/chn/fyrth/t1156836.htm> (accessed 16 December 2015).

15. Qiang wai lou 墙外楼, "Taisu zhaokai xinwen fabuhui: zai yue gangchang 4 ming dalu ji laogong siwang" 台塑召开新闻发布会: 在越钢厂 4 名大陆籍劳工死亡, 20 May 2014, <https://commondatastorage.googleapis.com/letscorp_archive/archives/71132> (accessed 16 December 2015).
16. *The Sun Daily*, quoting the Bernama News, "China Welcomes Vietnam's Compensation on Anti-China Riots", 26 August 2014, <www.thesundaily.my/news/1151177> (accessed 16 December 2015).
17. Nguyen Manh Hung, "The Politics of the United States–China–Vietnam Triangle in the 21st Century", *Trends in Southeast Asia*, no. 21 (Singapore: Institute of Southeast Asian Studies, 2015), p. 28.

Chapter 7

FROM NON-INTERVENTION TO INTERVENTION? THE "NUDE SQUAT" EPISODE AND CHINESE AMBASSADOR SAGA IN MALAYSIA

The fifth example revolves around China's attitude towards the Chinese in Malaysia during two different periods: (i) a low ethnic tension period in 2005 involving the so-called "Nude Squat" (also known as "the lock up girl") episode, and (ii) a high ethnic tension period in 2015 involving the Chinese ambassador's behaviour and speech. In the latter case, the Malaysian authorities considered the ambassador's actions to be an intervention in their domestic affairs but it did not develop into a diplomatic uproar. Does this case represent a shift in Beijing's policy towards the Chinese overseas and in China's foreign policy principles in general?

BACKGROUND

Malaya was a British colony that became independent only in 1957. Owing to its long struggle against a domestic communist insurgency, which was dominated by ethnic Chinese and also perceived to be supported by the PRC, the Malayan government adopted an anti-PRC attitude. The anti-communist and anti-PRC policy continued after 1963, when Malaya, together with three other British colonies, formed Malaysia.[1] It was only in 1974 that Malaysia established relations with the PRC, when the then prime minister, Tun Razak, sought to woo ethnic Chinese votes during the general election. Nevertheless, even after diplomatic ties were established, the Malaysian government imposed restrictions on interactions between Chinese Malaysians and mainland Chinese. The bilateral relationship improved only after the end of the Cold War, long after Deng Xiaoping had introduced market reforms in China.

Malaysia is a multi-ethnic country. It has a large number of ethnic Chinese, but the Malays are the dominant ethnic group. There has long been some degree of tension between the Malays and the Chinese, which erupted in 1969 in a major racial riot. This resulted in the entrenchment of Malay pre-eminence, encapsulated in the political doctrine of *Ketuanan Melayu* (Malay supremacy), to which the Malay elite, especially the Malay-based ruling party the United Malays National Organization (UMNO) is strongly committed until this day. Although no anti-Chinese riots have taken place since the events of 1969, the relationship between the two ethnic groups remains fragile.

Notwithstanding the uneasy relationship between the Malays and Chinese Malaysians, state-to-state relations between China and Malaysia improved, especially after China's phenomenal economic growth. Chinese tourists began visiting Malaysia in fairly large numbers. However, there were reports that many Chinese tourists, especially women suspected of being involved in prostitution, received harsh treatment by the Malaysian police. Chinese tourists also complained that they were forced to pay bribes. In addition, mainland Chinese women who married Chinese Malaysians have encountered unpleasant experiences.

THE "NUDE SQUAT" EPISODE

On 3 November 2015, three female Chinese citizens — Yu Xuezhen (35) and Gu Xiuhua (40), both married to Malaysians, and Wu Xiaohua (34), a secretarial student living in Malaysia — were travelling together in a car driven by a friend when police stopped them at a roadblock in Sungai Buloh.[2] They were detained by police on suspicion that their passports were fake. While under police custody, they were forced to perform squats in the nude. Yu's husband was said to have later brought down their marriage certificate to the police station but failed to secure the release of Yu. The three were eventually released four days later without any charge after the Immigration Department certified that their passports were genuine.[3]

Yu was later accompanied by Theresa Kok, an opposition parliamentarian from the Democratic Action Party (DAP), to lodge a police report.[4] At the end of the same month, the Chinese press (*Zhongguo Bao*) broke the news that a video was circulating of a "Chinese" woman who had been forced to perform a nude squat in front of a policewoman. Kok also received the video from an unknown source and she revealed this in Parliament.[5] It was reported that the video, or a clip lasting 70 seconds, had been widely circulated on social media.[6] Ministers and members of parliament had also watched the video clip.

The existence of the video reinforced the three Chinese women's accusations of police abuse. However, the identity of the woman in the tape could not be determined; the assumption was that she was ethnic Chinese, but her ethnicity or citizenship could not be determined with certainty.[7]

Malaysia's then Prime Minister Abdullah Badawi was embarrassed by the accusations and decided to set up an independent inquiry to investigate the matter, pledging that there would not be any cover-up. His then deputy, Najib Razak, supported the move.[8] However, some of the other ministers as well as the police expressed different views, undermining Abdullah's efforts to search for the truth. For instance, Noh Omar, deputy internal security minister, told the press that he saw nothing wrong with the police action and asked those foreigners (*orang asing*) who thought that "Malaysian police is cruel" to go back to their own country.[9] His statement prompted Abdullah to criticize him for his choice of words. Noh later blamed the press for misquoting him.[10]

The Chinese ambassador in Malaysia expressed his concern over the matter. A spokesman of China's Ministry of Foreign Affairs, Liu Jianchao, stated that "the Chinese government has always considered it important to protect the legitimate rights and interests of Chinese citizens from being violated."[11] Liu went on to stress that "China will continue to urge Malaysia to investigate and deal with these cases in a serious and just manner and bring trouble makers to justice, so as to really protect the dignity and safety of Chinese citizens and prevent such cases from recurring."[12]

It was also reported that China's Deputy Foreign Minister Wu Dawei summoned the Malaysian ambassador, Syed Norulzaman, to lodge a protest over the video case, stating that "[t]he Chinese government attaches great importance to safeguarding the dignity and safety of Chinese citizens and is deeply concerned with the incident."[13] Norulzaman was reported to have said that he had also been shocked to watch the video.

Syed Hamid Albar, who was then Malaysia's foreign minister, responded to the protest of China's foreign minister: "As a sovereign country responsible in protecting its citizens,... it is fair (for China) to present a protest note, and we will take action."[14]

In fact, the Malaysian Cabinet sent Azmi Khalid, minister for home affairs, to China as Malaysia was concerned that a negative image in China would affect the inflow of Chinese tourists.[15] It is also possible that Azmi wanted to explain the Malaysian government's attitude to the incident. In mid-December, Chinese Prime Minister Wen Jiabao visited Malaysia, as previously scheduled, signalling that the incident had not affected Malaysia–China relations.

In 2006 the report of the Malaysian inquiry into the incident was eventually released. The report stated that the action taken by the police was not acceptable and should be discontinued.[16] The surprise finding was that the woman in the video was an ethnic Malay arrested for a drug offence, not a Chinese.[17] The DAP member of parliament Teresa Kok and the lawyer for the four Chinese women were convinced that the woman was a Malay, but many still did not believe that the woman was a non-Chinese.[18]

BACKGROUND TO THE CHINESE AMBASSADOR SAGA

The second case took place ten years later, i.e., in 2015. The political situation then was quite different from that in 2005. In the 2008 general election, the UMNO-led coalition, known as Barisan National (National Front), lost its two-thirds majority.

The Malay elite was split, which saw a fall in UMNO's share of Malay votes at the expense of the opposition parties, i.e., Parti Keadilan Rakyat (PKR) and Parti Islam Se-Malaysia (PAS). The Malaysian Chinese Association (MCA), part of the ruling coalition, which usually garnered much of the ethnic Chinese support, lost votes to the opposition Democratic Action Party (DAP). The results of the 2013 general elections were even worse for the ruling Barisan, which gained fewer popular votes than the opposition parties in the country's first-past-the-post electoral system. The majority of the Chinese votes appeared to have gone to the DAP. Many analysts argued that to retain UMNO's dominance Prime Minister Najib Razak began to stress ethnicity, especially the *Ketuanan Melayu* concept, as if Malay supremacy was now being challenged. This is the context against which the China ambassador saga must be examined.

Just before the saga, Kuala Lumpur was gripped by ethnic tension. On 13 July 2015, a Malay man allegedly stole a smartphone from a Chinese trader at a shop in the Low Yat Plaza in the Bukit Bintang suburb of Kuala Lumpur. The man was caught and handed over to the police. Later in the day, the upset man took a group of friends to the shopping mall to take revenge on the Chinese trader. This triggered a racial riot, injuring five persons.[19] A video of the incident went viral on social media, further polarizing the Chinese and the Malays. The tension lasted several days.

In the same month, reports emerged on a major scandal involving Prime Minister Najib, who was accused of channelling to his personal bank account over RM2.67 billion (nearly US$700 million) from One Malaysia Development Company (1MDB), a government-owned strategic development company.

Najib did not respond to the charges until August, claiming that the money transferred to his account was from a Saudi Arabian donor, not 1MDB. Unconvinced, ex-Prime Minister Tun Dr Mahathir Mohammad and some opposition members called on Najib to resign. There was also criticism of Najib from within the ranks of UMNO, resulting in the embattled prime minister dismissing those who did not support him, including Deputy Prime Minister Muhyiddin Yassin.

A civil society movement, Bersih 4.0 (also known as the "Yellow Shirt" movement), organized a mass demonstration on 29 August 2015, one day before Malaysia's National Day, accusing Najib of corruption and calling on him to step down. However, Najib and UMNO purposely played up the Chinese angle, asserting that the demonstration was led by the Chinese, although many non-Chinese also participated. Jamal Yunus, a pro-Najib UMNO leader, then organized a "Red Shirt" counter-demonstration on 16 September, the day of the formation of Malaysia, demanding to safeguard the "Respect of Malays". The demonstrators demanded that Kuala Lumpur's Chinatown be opened up to Malay hawkers. To achieve the maximum impact, it was reported that the pro-Najib "Red Shirts" planned another demonstration on 26 September, this time in Chinatown.

CHINESE AMBASSADOR HUANG'S SPEECH

However, on 25 September, the PRC Ambassador, Huang Huikang, visited Chinatown to greet the residents in connection with the Moon Cake Festival. During his visit, the ambassador delivered a prepared speech, which was widely quoted in the local and foreign press. The ambassador was reported to have said:

> The government of China practises peaceful co-existence in its diplomatic policy in international relations. It has never interfered in the domestic politics of other countries; it has not involved itself in other countries' domestic affairs. However, we will not stand by idly as others violate the national interests of China, infringe upon the legal rights of Chinese citizens and companies, undertake illegal behavior that impedes the friendly relations between China and the local country in question. ... The government of China opposes any kind of terrorism, opposes any form of racism or extremism that focuses on a certain race and ethnic group, opposes violent behavior which would destroy public order and social stability.[20]

On 27 September, it was reported in local newspapers that the Chinese ambassador had interfered in the domestic affairs of Malaysia and had been summoned by Malaysia's deputy foreign minister to clarify his remarks during his visit to Chinatown. As Foreign Minister Anifah Aman was overseas then, his deputy, Reezal Merican, issued the summons. This was considered a breach of protocol as another full minister had, in fact, been nominated acting foreign minister during Anifah's absence. Acting Foreign Minister Hamzah Zainuddin, hence cancelled the summons and invited Ambassador Huang to his office for a talk. Ambassador Huang visited Hamzah the following morning, and the two men talked for more than two hours. Hamzah did not issue any statement on the contents of the talk, stating only that the Foreign Ministry would release a statement later, which it never did.

However, the Chinese held a press conference in Beijing. A spokesman of China's Foreign Ministry, Hong Lei, backed Ambassador Huang's position, stating that the ambassador's visit to Kuala Lumpur's Chinatown was "normal, friendly behavior" (正常的亲善行为) and that China had no intention to intervene in other countries' domestic affairs.[21]

On 28 September, Ambassador Huang attended a forum, on the Maritime Silk Road, during which he made another speech. In his speech, which was reported in the press, Huang said, among other things:

> We sincerely hope that the *huaqiao huaren* who live in this beautiful land of Malaysia will live happily, succeed in their careers, and live in harmony with our friendly race. I would like to stress once more, overseas *huaqiao* and *huaren*, no matter where you go, no matter how many generations you are, China is **forever** your warm "maternal home" (niang jia 娘家)![22]

MALAY RESPONSES

While the Malaysian government did not make any statement, UMNO politicians, however, reacted negatively. They were offended by the visit of Ambassador Huang to Chinatown and the speech he had made during the visit, insisting that he had interfered in the domestic affairs of Malaysia. The editorial column of the *Utusan Malaysia*, a Malay daily controlled by UMNO stated that the Chinese ambassador had interfered in the domestic affairs of Malaysia and had "touched on the sensitive nerve of the Malaysian people."[23] It demanded that Beijing apologize and promise not to interfere again. It further said that China had enough problems of its own and should not create trouble in other countries. It even stated sarcastically that "it would be better if the ambassador gives more focus to the issue of large numbers of Chinese nationals in the prostitution and massage industry (in Malaysia) as Chinese government is more stern in dealing with such matters in their own country."[24]

Rais Yatim, former foreign minister of Malaysia and now chairman of the Islamic University, made a statement that the behaviour of the Chinese ambassador was beyond the scope of his ambassadorial duties.[25] He said if the ambassador wanted to be friendly with the people, he should have not become an ambassador.[26]

UMNO Youth chief Khairy Jamaluddin noted that Ambassador Huang had no right to meddle with Malaysia's internal affairs, and that "Malaysia's pride must not be put at stake simply to take care of the feelings of China or other bigger countries."[27] Arman Azha Abu Hanifah, UMNO Youth exco member, stated that the ambassador's speech was a form of "provocation and an insult to the Malays."[28]

MALAYSIAN CHINESE REACTIONS

Malaysian Chinese reactions to the ambassador's speech fall into two categories. The Chinese-dominated political parties appeared to take a sympathetic approach, while some of the Chinese media were rather critical of the ambassador's speech.

The President of the MCA, Liow Tiong Lai, and his deputy, Wee Ka Siong, commented that Ambassador's Huang speech had been taken out of context. They maintained that he had no intention to intervene in the domestic affairs of Malaysia.[29] Liow even argued that Ambassador Huang knew his limits as an ambassador and had conveyed an appropriate message, i.e., calling on people to oppose terrorism, extremism and racism. This is the stand of China; this is also the Malaysian stand.[30] An ex-president of the MCA, Ong Tee Keat, was sarcastic in his response. He stated that Malaysia had wrongly targeted Chinese Ambassador Huang; it would have been more appropriate if the target was the Indonesian ambassador to

Malaysia. By targeting the latter, "Malaysia could have passed a message about the suffering of the Malaysian people owing to the Indonesian haze and could have asked the ambassador to explain the factors that contributed to the haze and what effective solutions Indonesia had in mind."[31]

Not many comments can be found on the Chinese ambassador's speech by DAP leaders. If the remarks of Fong Kui Lun, the DAP member of Parliament for Bukit Bintang, can be used as an indicator, the DAP's view appeared to be similar to that of the MCA. Fong noted that Ambassador Huang had not interfered in the domestic affairs of Malaysia and that Malaysia's Foreign Ministry was not familiar with diplomatic protocols.[32]

SIN CHEW JIT POH'S RESPONSE

Sin Chew Jit Poh (星洲日报), a large and influential Malaysian Chinese newspaper, appeared to be less critical in its initial reporting of the ambassador's visit and speech. It only cited Ambassador Huang's explanation that he did not have any intention of intervening in the domestic affairs of Malaysia and that he had visited Chinatown with good and friendly intentions. The newspaper also carried the Chinese embassy's statement, which noted that Ambassador Huang had visited Chinatown during the Moon Cake Festival and "had friendly chats with ethnic Chinese and Malay shop owners, asked them about their businesses and wished them a happy Moon Cake Festival."[33]

However, on 29 September, *Sin Chew Jit Poh* published an editorial by its Chief Editor Guo Qingjiang that questioned the wisdom of the Chinese ambassador's speech at a sensitive venue.[34] This strongly worded editorial was a rare criticism of

China by the newspaper, which is owned by a tycoon who has been seen to be close to Beijing.

The editorial began by explaining developments after the ambassador's Chinatown speech. It claimed that an attempt had been made subsequently to ensure that no side would lose face, but that the attempt failed as "a hawkish group" in UMNO was now in power and the prime minister was on their side. The editorial then noted:

> Petaling Street (foreigners call it Chinatown) as a symbol of the Malaysian Chinese, had just faced provocation on 16 September by the "Red Shirt Army". Ambassador Huang elected to visit Petaling Street again when the extremists warned to create problems in Petaling Street on 26 September. Both the place and the timing are considered to be sensitive; they are bound to give rise to different interpretations.[35]

The editorial went on to say:

> In Malaysia all events are politicized and this is very normal. The hawks in UMNO are now in power. From their perspective, Ambassador Huang visited Petaling Street (Chinatown) at this particular time and made a speech. It is easy for politicians to take the speech out of context for their own purposes, easy for them to hijack it and put it forward.
>
> Nevertheless, Ambassador Huang must have weighed the risk before visiting Petaling Street and evaluated the overall situation. He also knew the gains and losses of doing so.
>
> Ambassador Huang said the Chinese government was against all forms of terrorism, against all forms... of racism and ethnic extremism, against serious violence which destroys social order and social stability. This is a general statement, and also has its universal values. However, once it was said, how it was interpreted by others and played around would be beyond his control."[36]

The editorial seemed to be implicitly disapproving of the ambassador's statement. It noted that the statement would only harm the interests of the ethnic Chinese in Malaysia. The editorial also took the opportunity to comment on Beijing's attitude towards the Chinese overseas in general and Chinese Malaysians in particular. It said:

> Besides these points, China often refers to overseas Chinese as *huaqiao*. In fact this does not suit the Chinese in Malaysia (*Da Ma huaren*, 大马华人). Both within and outside Malaysia, the new generation of Malaysian Chinese regard themselves as Malaysians. They don't like to be called *huaqiao*. This is the situation that China should understand. We do not want the Malays to keep doubting our loyalty to Malaysia and suspecting that we do not identify ourselves with Malaysia.
>
> We have been independent for 58 years, but our racial relations are still very fragile. We often say and feel proud that we have "racial harmony", but "racial harmony" in fact has become a fragile leaf. If it is held in the hand it will be broken easily.[37]

OTHER COMMENTS

A month later, a veteran Singaporean diplomat, Bilahari Kausikan, published a long article on Singapore–Malaysia relations. The article touched on the Chinese ambassador's speech:

> Under other circumstances these sentiments would perhaps have passed unnoticed. But the timing and context laid the ambassador's words and actions open to disquieting interpretations.
>
> Was it just bad judgment? What was he trying to do? If the ambassador was trying to help the Malaysian Chinese, then he failed miserably. He probably made things worse for

> them by confirming the worst suspicions of the Malay right wing.
>
> But were the interests of Malaysian Chinese even a consideration? Was the intention to highlight a rising China's clout? The Chinese Foreign Ministry spokesman defended the ambassador's visit to Petaling Street as "normal" and emphasised China's adherence to the principle of non-interference. But this was of course what she would have said irrespective of China's intentions.[38]

Bilahari went further to discuss current Sino–Malaysian relations:

> More telling perhaps was the apparent confusion over whether or not the Chinese ambassador should be summoned to explain himself. This should have been obvious. A retired Malaysian diplomat who used to deal with China pointed out the dangerous precedent that would be set if no action was taken. But different Malaysian ministers contradicted each other, with a clearly frustrated Foreign Minister Anifah Aman finally telling them all to leave it to Wisma Putra.
>
> Was this the consequence of China's influence? Possibly. In the end, some sort of meeting with Wisma Putra has occurred. Deputy Prime Minister Ahmad Zahid Hamidi subsequently announced that the Malaysian Cabinet decided to "call in" the Chinese ambassador (he was careful to make clear the ambassador was not being "summoned").[39]

Bilahari's comments have clarified a number of questions regarding the event and its impact on Beijing–Kuala Lumpur relations.

CONCLUSION

The first case described above, which occurred in November 2005, involved three female Chinese citizens who were locked up by Malaysian police and forced to do squats in the nude as they were suspected to be using fake passports. The police suspicions were later proven to be untrue. Two weeks after the incident, a video of a "Chinese" woman being abused by the police was distributed, which shocked Malaysia. Assuming that the woman in the video was a Chinese citizen, Beijing's Foreign Ministry summoned the Malaysian ambassador and lodged a stern protest, urging the Malaysian government to bring justice to bear on the perpetrators of the ill-treatment. The Malaysian government accepted responsibility and launched an investigation. An official inquiry later found that the "Chinese" woman in the video was a Malay woman, not a Chinese.

The second case was different. It took place ten years later and involved the Chinese ambassador's visit to Kuala Lumpur's Chinatown and his remarks during his visit, which became a diplomatic issue between Beijing and Kuala Lumpur. However, although this issue was played up by some Malay extremists at that time, it was soon defused as both governments, especially Malaysia, did not want to make it a bigger issue.

Nevertheless, it is quite clear that Beijing's ambassador, had begun to be more active than before in building up relations with the local Chinese community. More importantly, he also made remarks that tended to include Malaysian Chinese in the category of *haiwai qiaobao* (海外侨胞) or Chinese compatriots overseas. It appears that Beijing was able to get away with the ambassador's remarks owing to Malaysia's need to retain the goodwill of a rising China to which it had become economically beholden. The Najib government had benefited much from trade with China and the inflow of Chinese investments and managed to prevent the issue from spiralling out of control. Nevertheless, if such an event were to recur, would Kuala Lumpur be restrained again? Would it affect Malaysia's cohesion as a nation? Or is it only a ripple in a teacup? These are some questions that remain unanswered.

From the foreign policy perspective, the Chinese ambassador saga indicates that Beijing wanted to show its concern for the Chinese overseas, which is tantamount to interference in the internal affairs of Malaysia, but when such an act came into conflict with its core national interests, i.e., to maintain good relations with third countries and to extract economic benefits, it did not push the issue further. The Malaysian government, for its part, also had core national interests at stake and chose not to escalate the dispute.

The response of Chinese Malaysians to Ambassador Huang's speech is worth noting. The community appeared to be divided, but both the MCA and DAP were quite happy with the ambassador's speech. They saw it not as "an intervention" but as disseminating an anti-terrorism and anti-racism message. Perhaps the Malaysian Chinese parties were in a weak position when faced with Malay extremism and intended to use an external force — i.e., the Chinese ambassador's speech — to counterbalance it without foreseeing the likely impact of doing so on the future of ethnic Chinese politics in Malaysia.

Notes

1. One of these colonies, Singapore, left Malaysia in 1965.
2. For the background information on the episode, see Nurul Nazirin, "Chinese Nationals to Sue for Cruelty, Torture", 14 November 2005, <soc.culture.malaysia.narkive.com/a0sR3EjE/chinesenationals-to-sue-for-cruelty-torture> (accessed 12 April 2016); Parveen Gill, "Police Made Me Strip, says Chinese National", *The Star*, 12 November 2005, <http://www.thestar.com.my/news/nation/2005/11/12/police-mademe-strip-says-chinese-national> (accessed 16 April 2016); and *South China Morning Post*, "Malaysia: Stripping Scandal Inquiry Widens", 1 December 2005, <web.international.ucla.edu/institute/article/34741> (accessed 16 April 2016). Gill's report only

mentioned two women being in the car. Yet, other reports noted that three of the women were arrested on 3 November.

3. Ibid.
4. Nurul Nazirin, "Chinese Nationals to Sue for Cruelty, Torture", op. cit.
5. Carolyn Hong, "Malaysia: Policewoman in Abuse Video Identified", *Sunday Times*, 27 November 2005.
6. Ibid.
7. *Kyodo News*, "Official Chided for Humiliation of Chinese Women", 2 December 2005, <http://www.chinadaily.com.cn/english/doc/2005-12/02/content_499957.htm> (accessed 12 April 2016).
8. Hong, "Malaysia: Policewoman in Abuse Video Identified", op. cit.
9. *Kyodo News*, "Official Chided for Humiliation of Chinese Women", op. cit.
10. Ibid.
11. China View, "China asks Malaysia to probe Assault Cases", 29 November 2005, <http://news.xinhuanet.com/english/2005-11/29/content_3853442.htm> (accessed 16 April 2016).
12. Ibid.
13. *South China Morning Post*, "Malaysia: Stripping Scandal Inquiry Widens", op. cit.
14. The statement was reported in the news agency *Bernama*, quoted in *South China Morning Post*, "Malaysia: Stripping Scandal Inquiry Widens", op. cit.
15. Jonathan Kent, "Video puts Malaysia Police in Dock", 25 November 2005, <http://news.bbc.co.uk/2/hi/asia-pacific/4470422.stm> (accessed 16 April 2016).
16. Malaysiakini, "Suruhanjaya: Bogel dan ketuk ketampi haram", 23 January 2006, <http://www.malaysiakini.com/news/46110> (accessed 16 April 2016).
17. The person in picture was later revealed as a Malay woman named Hemy Hamisa Abu Hasan Saari. See Hafiz Yatim, "Ketuk Ketampi bogel 2005: K'jaan bayar pampasan", 27 July 2011, <https://www.malaysiakini.com/news/171157> (accessed 16 April 2016).

18. Carolyn Hong, "Doubts Linger over Nude Video", *Straits Times*, 5 January 2006.
19. *Malay Mail Online*, "Low Yat was about Racism, deal with it", 14 July 2015, <http://www.themalaymailonline.com/opinion/boo-sulyn/article/low-yat-was-about-racism-deal-with-it> (accessed 10 February 2016).
20. Li Yanyun 李艳云, "Zhongguo dashi yanlun ganshi neizheng, damajiang chuanzhao" 中国大使言论干涉内政，大马将传召, BBC, Boxun.com, 27 September 2015, <http://www.bbc.com/zhongwen/simp/world/2015/09/150927_malaysia_china_diplomacy> (accessed 10 February 2016). This author's translation. The ambassador made his speech from a prepared text; he did not make off-the-cuff remarks. See Huang Jinfa 黄进发, "Haiwai guchu gukushen?" 海外孤雏孤苦甚?, Sui Huo Pinglun 燧火评论, 2 October 2015, <http://www.pfirereview.com/20151002> (accessed 10 February 2016).
21. Li Yanyun 李艳云, "Malaixiya dai waizhang yuejian dashi yu liangxiaoshi" 马来西亚代外长约见大使逾两小时, BBC, Boxun.com, 28 September 2015, <http://www.bbc.com/zhongwen/simp/world/2015/09/150928_china_malaysia_meeting> (accessed 10 February 2016).
22. Embassy of the People's Republic of China in Malaysia, "Huang Huikang dashi zai haishang sizhou zhilu Zhongguo-Malaixiya luntan ji Zhongguo-Dongmeng shangwu xiehui, Malaixiya chengli yishi shang de zici" 黄惠康大使在海上丝绸之路中国-马来西亚论坛暨中国-东盟商务协会（马来西亚）成立仪式上的致辞, 1 October 2015, <http://my.chinaembassy.org/chn/sgxw/t1302809.htm> (accessed 5 October 2015).
23. Li Yanyun, "Zhongguo dashi yanlun ganshi neizheng, damajiang chuanzhao", op. cit.
24. Ibid., also Malaysiakini, "Utusan to Chinese Envoy: Deal with Prostitutes, not Petaling Street", 27 September 2015, <http://www.malaysiakini.com/news/313634> (accessed 5 October 2015). The citation is from the second reference.

25. See also Timothy Achariam, "Rais Slams Ambassador Over Petaling Street Visit", 27 September 2015, <www.thesundaily.my/news1564767> (accessed 5 October 2015).
26. Li Yanyun, "Zhongguo dashi yanlun ganshi neizheng, damajiang chuanzhao", op. cit.
27. Malaysiakini, "Don't Put China's Pride Above Malaysia's, says Khairy", 28 September 2015, <www.malaysiakini.com/news/313794> (accessed 5 October 2015).
28. Li Yanyun, "Zhongguo dashi yanlun ganshi neizheng, damajiang chuanzhao", op. cit.
29. Michael Murty, "MCA Attacks DAP's 'Calculated Distortion' of China Ambassador's Speech", *Rakyat Post*, 28 September 2015, <http://www.therakyatpost.com/news/2015/09/28/mca-attacks-dapscalculated-distortion-of-china-ambassadors-speech> (accessed 26 January 2016).
30. Li Yanyun, "Zhongguo dashi yanlun ganshi neizheng, damajiang chuanzhao", op. cit.
31. Ibid.
32. *Lianhe Ribao* 《联合日报》, "Fang Guilun: Dashi wu ganzheng, waijiaobu budong lijie" 方贵伦: 大使无干政，外交部不懂礼节, 28 September 2015, <www.kwongwah.com.my/?p=21101> (accessed 8 February 2016).
33. Li Yanyun, "Zhongguo dashi yanlun ganshi neizheng, damajiang chuanzhao", op. cit.
34. Guo Qingjiang 郭清江, "Zongbianji shijian, laolian guabuzhu" 总编辑时间・老脸挂不住", *Sin Chew Jit Poh* 《星洲日报》, 29 September 2015, <http://www.sinchew.com.my/node/260087> (accessed 30 September 2015).
35. Ibid.
36. Ibid.
37. Ibid.
38. Bilahari Kausikan, "Singapore is Not an Island", *Straits Times*, 6 October 2015.
39. Ibid.

Chapter 8

TO HELP OR NOT TO HELP? THE KOKANG CHINESE PROBLEM IN MYANMAR

This chapter deals with the sixth example of China's approach to Chinese overseas issues. It involves China's response to the 2015 Kokang Chinese rebellion in Myanmar (formerly Burma), in which Beijing appeared to have adopted a pragmatic attitude.[1] It should be pointed out here that when we speak of the Chinese overseas we usually refer to "non-homeland minority groups", i.e., groups of Chinese who do not have their original "homeland" within their respective countries of residence. The only exception to this general characteristic are perhaps the Kokang Chinese in Myanmar, who are a "homeland minority group", i.e., their original homeland is within Myanmar. It should also be noted that the homeland of the Kokang Chinese is an area that borders China. Hence, there has been a lot of interaction between the Kokang Chinese and the Chinese of mainland China. Owing to these unique characteristics, the Kokang Chinese issue needs to be treated differently from other Chinese overseas issues. Although this study treats the Kokang Chinese case alongside other "overseas

Chinese" cases, China's treatment of this special category of Chinese overseas differs from its approach to other groups of Chinese overseas.

INTRODUCTION

On 9 February 2015, the Myanmar National Democratic Alliance Army (MNDAA), led by Peng Jiasheng (彭家声, also known as Phone Kyar Shin or Pheung Kya-shin), suddenly returned to Laukkai, the Kokang capital, from an unknown hideout and attacked the security forces of the Myanmar government. Serious fighting took place, which resulted in the exodus of many of the Kokang Chinese people, mainly to Chinese territory. The fighting lasted several days and there were many casualties on both sides but the MNDAA failed to capture Laukkai, fled to the border, and allegedly entered Chinese territory. The Myanmar army pursued the rebels and fired shells at areas believed to be the hiding place of the MNDAA. The Myanmar air force joined the fighting and on 13 March a Myanmar fighter plane bombed the Chinese side of the border, killing five Chinese villagers and wounding another eight.[2] Beijing protested against this incursion, and Nay Pyi Taw (Naypyitaw) apologized.[3] High-level meetings were then conducted between the two countries to look for a solution.

Nevertheless, fighting continued for more than three months. On 2 June, China conducted live firing exercises in Chinese territory along the Sino–Myanmar border.[4] Tensions immediately rose between the two countries. Nevertheless, scholars close to the People's Liberation Army (PLA) noted that the purpose of the exercise was to pacify China's domestic critics; the exercise was not aimed at the Myanmar government.[5] This was because

> Myanmar is a key exit to the sea for south-western China. It also plays a crucial role in both the safety of the Sino-Myanmar oil pipeline and the development of China's future maritime silk road. Meanwhile, the United States and Japan have eagerly drawn Myanmar to their sides to put China in a dilemma, especially on the shelling issue. On the one hand, China would like to stop the civil war in Myanmar from hurting Chinese citizens but, on the other, it would also like to prevent the Sino-Myanmar conflict from escalating. Therefore, China has to move cautiously.[6]

On 10 June, a National League for Democracy (NLD) party delegation led by Aung San Suu Kyi, who was then in opposition, arrived in Beijing following an invitation from the Communist Party of China (CPC)[7]. It appears that Beijing wanted to mend its relations with Myanmar's opposition. Many interpreted this as part of China's dual track policy towards Myanmar, meant to show its dissatisfaction towards the ruling military junta.[8] Several questions can be posed: What is China's position on the Kokang Chinese issue? How does Myanmar see the issue? Will China's position affect Sino–Myanmar relations? Will the Kokang Chinese problem be solved soon? To get some answers, it would be useful to look at the history of the Kokang Chinese in Myanmar.

HISTORICAL LEGACY

Kokang (Guo Gan 果敢 in Mandarin, meaning the Brave), a part of the Shan state of Myanmar today, was once Chinese territory under the Qing dynasty until 1897. In that year, under the Anglo-Chinese Agreement, the Qing government ceded Kokang to British India, of which Burma was then a part. Kokang was incorporated into the Shan region after 1937, when Burma became a separate British colony.[9]

During the colonial period, the British had some presence in Kokang through an appointed regent but, after Burma's independence in 1948, Kokang was left to govern itself. The Yang family, which had traditionally exercised leadership over Kokang, became *de facto* rulers of the area. Soon, the region came under the control of the Kuomintang army, and, later, the Burmese Communist Party (BCP), which received support from the CPC. It was virtually independent of Myanmar's central government. Kokang self-defence troops, which were led by a Kokang Chinese named Peng Jiasheng, joined the BCP to fight the central government. But Peng and his forces split from the BCP in 1989 to sign a ceasefire agreement with the Myanmar government. The Myanmar government then renamed Kokang the "Kokang Special Region".[10] Peng was allowed to retain his army, which was renamed the Myanmar National Democratic Alliance Army (MNDAA) and entrusted with maintaining border security. Later, a power struggle developed between Peng and a member of the Yang family, Yang Maoliang, in which Peng emerged as the winner.[11] Yang was ousted and eventually left Kokang. His family now lives in Yangon. Peng was also engaged in another power struggle. He sought to replace his deputy, Bai Suocheng, with his own son, Peng Deren. This resulted in a split between Peng and Bai.[12]

Meanwhile, the military government of Myanmar drafted a new constitution in 2008, which declared that there could only be one union army. The armed forces of the various ethnic groups were required to demobilize and form a Border Guard Force (BGF), which would have some representation from the Myanmar military and would be trained according to its guidelines.[13] Refusing to comply with the guidelines, Peng rebelled against the government on 8 August 2009 but was defeated by the Myanmar army and fled. His former deputy, Bai Suocheng, was then appointed by the government as the new leader of the Kokang region, and, under his management, Kokang appeared to be peaceful.

Earlier, when Peng and Bai were still on good terms and working together, Peng had initiated moves to eradicate opium cultivation and Bai was the chairman of the Ban Opium Committee. In 2002 they announced that the area was free of poppy cultivation, the first region in Myanmar to eradicate opium. Until then, the livelihood of the Kokang Chinese had been dependent on poppy cultivation. Poppy cultivation was replaced by the cultivation of rubber, sugar cane, tea, and corn.[14]

Peng then disappeared from the scene for about five years. Baidu Baike, China's version of the free online collaborative encyclopaedia Wikipedia, claims that he moved to Thailand, Malaysia, and Singapore, before returning to Kokang in 2014. However, his overseas movements cannot be verified as he was considered an outlaw and could not have used a Myanmar passport. Other sources note that he might have been hiding in China's Yunnan province or northern Myanmar all along as his son was married to the daughter of the leader of Mong La, which is adjacent to Kokang. Peng also had contacted the Kachin Independence Army (KIA). According to rumours, he staged some attacks in Kokang together with the KIA, but this information, too, cannot be verified. In any case, the Myanmar army was caught by surprise by Peng's sudden onslaught in February 2015. Apparently, the government intelligence agency had failed to gather information on Peng's movements from the Kokang Chinese population.

THE KOKANG CHINESE COMMUNITY

Although the Kokang Chinese community had become part of Shan State, it was never really integrated into the Burmese nation, just like many of the other ethnic minorities along the country's northern border areas. The situation of the Kokang Chinese is also unique, compared to that of the other ethnic minorities: owing to its history and proximity with Yunnan, many Kokang Chinese still retain strong Chinese characteristics.

According to Myint Myint Kyu, a Kokang Chinese scholar who conducted field work and completed her thesis in October 2011, Kokang is largely inhabited by the ethnic Chinese who call themselves Kokang Chinese. They constitute about 90 per cent of the region's population. They comprise a mix of local-born and newer migrants from China. The administrative language of Kokang is Mandarin, the currency is Renminbi (not the Myanmar Kyat), and the time used is China standard time. The Kokang are thus special compared to other Myanmar minorities. Nonetheless, the Kokang Chinese are not a homogeneous group. Some of them are quite well integrated into the local society and are able to speak local languages used in and around the Shan region, but these Kokong are a minority.

Not all Kokang Chinese reside in Kokang. In fact, quite a few live in some of the major cities of Myanmar. Some even live in Yangon and other parts of the world, assuming Myanmar's identity. For instance, the former drug lord Law Sit Han (Lo Xinghan, 1935–2013), who was a leading businessman, lived in Yangon, together with his son U Tun Myint Naing (alias Steven Law) who is a business tycoon.[15] Law Sit Han had close relations with the Myanmar government, and was credited with persuading Peng Jiasheng to leave the BCP in 1989.[16] As for Peng, he was born in Kokang and his ancestors came from China's Sichuan province.[17] Bai Suocheng, Peng's former deputy, was also born in Kokang but his ancestral origins are unknown. Peng appears to have multiple identities. Earlier he emphasized his Kokang identity. However, after the recent attacks on Myanmar security forces, when he was pushed back to the China–Myanmar border, he declared himself to be "Han Chinese" in an attempt to appeal to the Chinese of China and to recruit them as fighters. This kind of identity shift is possible as the majority of Kokang Chinese still speak Chinese and practise Chinese traditions. Not many Kokang Chinese who live within Shan province speak the Shan language, let alone Burmese.

Because of this dual ethnic identity, the military junta that preceded the current Myanmar government refused to consider the MNDAA led by Peng as representative of the Kokang minority and excluded it from the nationwide ethnic peace agreement that it signed with several minority groups in October 2015.[18] In fact, the Myanmar government is in a dilemma. On the one hand, it recognizes the Kokang Chinese as one of 135 "national ethnic races",[19] but, on the other hand, it considers Peng and his followers in MNDAA as not representative of the local population. A peace agreement without the participation of the MNDAA may be problematic.

Myanmar is still in the process of nation-building as many minority groups still have strong ethnic identities. In the past, as the military government was preoccupied with other domestic issues, including other rebellions, it was unable to integrate the Kokang Chinese into mainstream Burmese society, and hence tolerated the *de facto* autonomy of the Kokang leaders. However, with the transition to constitutional rule, the military government began to pay attention to its border areas and sought to integrate its border minorities into the Burmese nation. It began to assert its authority over the border areas and became less tolerant of the Kokang Chinese, who are culturally and traditionally Chinese. However, the Kokang Chinese, especially some of their leaders who had enjoyed virtual independence in the past, resisted the "intrusion" of the central Government. This is especially the case with Peng Jiasheng, now an eighty-one-year-old man, who perceives himself as the ruler of Kokang.

PERSPECTIVES OF MYANMAR AND CHINA

When Peng declared himself a "Han Chinese" and appealed to the Chinese in Yunnan for support, there were two conflicting reports of China's response. One said that the Yunnan Chinese supported him while the other said that the support was in fact minimal.[20] Beijing also stated that it did not and would not support Peng militarily but that the Myanmar military did not believe it.[21]

Does China consider the Kokang people as Chinese? Beijing acknowledges that many of the Kokang Chinese are of Chinese (or Han) descent, have inherited Chinese traditions, and possess other traits of the Chinese, but stresses that they are not Chinese by nationality.[22] Instead, they are Myanmar's ethnic minority ("national ethnic race", as it is known in Myanmar). Therefore, the conflict between the Kokang Chinese and the Myanmar central government is an internal affair of Myanmar and not a national problem of the PRC. With regard to the rebellion led by Peng Jiasheng, Beijing asserted that it was not supporting Peng; it wanted the Myanmar authorities to solve the problem peacefully. It seems that China has been careful in responding to the Kokang rebellion as it may have domestic implications for China. If China intervenes in Kokang Chinese matters while the world watches developments in Myanmar closely, it may create a problem for itself in dealing with its own minorities in Xinjiang and Tibet.

While China does not want to get involved in Kokang Chinese matters, fearing that it would be seen as interfering in the internal affairs of another country, China nevertheless will not help Myanmar crush the rebels either as this is not Beijing's business. Yun Sun, a scholar, argues,

> As a national policy, China does not support Peng Jiasheng. However, if Peng does successfully consolidate his control of Kokang, China will not opt to oppose him. China will accommodate such a reality, even if it indicates more uncertainties and risks.... To manage uncertainty and resolve conflict requires strengths and wisdom from the Burmese authorities. Any suspicion of China undermining the process is as equally misplaced as any hope for China to solve the problem for Burma.[23]

Yun Sun's argument is based on her observation of Chinese foreign policy behaviour in other regions. She says: "[I]n similar cases of internally divided and unstable countries, such as Pakistan and Afghanistan, China has developed a record of smoothly working with both local tribes/warlords and the central governments."[24] The analogy is inappropriate, however. The tribes in Pakistan and Afghanistan are not linked to the Han Chinese and the situation in each of these two Islamic states is beyond Beijing's control. Moreover, the two countries are strategically less important to China than Myanmar is. China could do something in Myanmar if it wanted to. However, Beijing's policy would be decided by its foreign policy objectives. If it is in the national interest of China to deepen its relations with Myanmar, Beijing would adjust its policy towards Peng Jiasheng accordingly.

Another more realistic argument regarding Beijing's foreign policy behaviour is put forward by another Chinese scholar, Xue Li. Xue argues that Myanmar is important for China's new strategies and security, and he maintains that China's current passive policy does not serve its interests. He, therefore, suggests that China needs to take the initiative to create a favourable environment for peace in Kokang by asking Peng to lay down his weapons and negotiate with the Myanmar government, which would also provide a "suitable arrangement" for Peng to solve the problem. If Peng refuses, China should cut all illegal weapons supplies to Peng. Xue goes on to say that a prosperous Kokang would serve the interests of both China and Myanmar:

> Establishing a Kokang Special Administrative Area (a step forward from the current autonomous area), where the Myanmar government is only responsible for defence and diplomacy, might be a viable solution. This will need Myanmar's government to genuinely implement the Panglong Agreement,[25] and to go beyond the 2008 constitution, which is not recognized by local ethnic minorities.[26]

Xue's view is that a prosperous Kokang and a more stable Myanmar will benefit China as well. China cannot afford to let the situation worsen as this will only benefit Beijing's rivals. His argument is proving to be correct, at least in the short term. On 11 June, one day after Aung San Suu Kyi arrived in

Beijing, the MNDAA suddenly announced that it had decided to start a unilateral ceasefire, ending four months of fierce fighting. It also noted that "the government of China has strongly urged that the peaceful situation should be restored along the Sino–Myanmar borders. This is one of the factors which contributed to the [unilateral ceasefire] decision."[27]

It is also worth noting that Aung San Suu Kyi visited Yunnan province during her China trip and a Chinese newspaper reported that she thanked the Chinese government for accepting the Kokang refugees and giving them shelter. She was also impressed by the development of Yunnan, which might be a model for Myanmar. The report noted that President Xi Jinping stressed the territorial integrity of Myanmar and expressed China's strong wish to maintain friendly relations with Myanmar.[28] The BBC Chinese network commented that this low-profile visit was not widely reported in other media and no report on what transpired during the discussion between Aung San Suu Kyi and the Chinese leaders was made available.

CONCLUSION

Myanmar has not made any official response to Peng's declaration of a unilateral ceasefire during Aung San Suu Kyi's China visit, but it does not seem to have initiated any attack on Peng's forces. Nevertheless, one Western scholar noted that "the government has still refused to reconsider its military solution so far."[29] In a separate development, on 30 June 2015, Reuters reported that the chief of the Myanmar air force, Major-General Lwin Oo, had been replaced by Brigadier-General Maung Maung Kyaw in a move that appeared to be a response to China's anger over the bomb that fell on Chinese territory three months earlier.[30]

The Kokang Chinese, with their long history of autonomy, if not independence, of the central government and their unique culture and tradition pose a far more complex problem than that posed by the country's other minority groups, who do not have and have never declared links with the Han Chinese. It seems that the Myanmar government wants to undertake state-building first rather than nation-building, i.e., it wants to control the area rather than bring about the cultural integration of the Kokang Chinese. It wants to disarm the Kokang Chinese, firmly control the area, and establish a "national administration". This may also involve some sort of nation-building in the sense of using Myanmar currency and both the Burmese language and Chinese as the administrative languages of Kokang. This would be an uphill task and the problem is not easy to resolve. Nevertheless, the Kokang Chinese problem can be contained if an understanding is reached between China and Myanmar.

Strictly speaking, the Kokang Chinese are different from other Chinese overseas as they have their own homeland, which borders China. Their close link with Chinese culture makes it difficult, if not impossible, for them to be integrated into the mainstream Myanmar society. Nonetheless, Beijing maintained restraint in its reaction to the Kokang rebellion in order to win the cooperation of Myanmar and guarantee China a southwestern passage to the sea. Myanmar is also crucial for China's economic security as well as for the realization of its Maritime Silk Road.

Notes

1. This chapter is based on my published paper, "Can the Kokang Chinese Problem in Myanmar be Resolved?" *ISEAS Perspective*, no. 37 (15 July 2015).

2. Xue Li, "Can China Untangle the Kokang Knot in Myanmar?" *The Diplomat*, 20 May 2015, <http://thediplomat.com/2015/05/can-chinauntangle-the-kokang-knot-in-myanmar> (accessed 22 May 2015).
3. Shannon Tiezzi, "Myanmar Apologizes to China for Deadly Strike", *The Diplomat*, 3 April 2015, <http://thediplomat.com/2015/04/myanmarapologizes-to-china-for-deadly-strike> (accessed 21 May 2015).
4. Peng Nian 彭念, "Wengshan Suzhi fang hua de xuanji" 翁山淑枝访华的玄机, *Lianhe Zaobao*《联合早报》, 11 June 2015.
5. Yangguang Huaxia 阳光华夏, "Zhongmian bianjing gao junyan, jiefangjun yishi liangniao" 中缅边境搞军演, 解放军一石两鸟, 2 June 2015, <http://hk.on.cc/hk/bkn/cnt/commentary/20150602/bkn-20150602012349241-0602_00832_001.html> (accessed 10 June 2015).
6. Ibid.
7. Deng Yuwen 邓聿文, "Beijing dui miandian de liangshou zhengce" 北京对缅甸的两手政策, *Lianhe Zaobao*《联合早报》, 10 June 2015.
8. Peng Nian, 彭念 "Wengshan Suzhi fang hua de xuanji", op. cit.
9. Myin Myint Kyu, "Spaces of Exceptional Shifting Strategies of the Kokang Chinese along the Myanmar/China Border", M.A. thesis, Graduate School of Chiang Mai University, October 2011, p. 202.
10. Ibid., p. 204.
11. Baidu Baike 百度百科, "Peng Jiasheng" 彭家声, <http://baike.baidu.com/view/932349.htm> (accessed 20 May 2015).
12. Baidu Baike 百度百科, "Bai Soucheng" 白所成, <http://baike.baidu.com/view/2764210.htm> (accessed 20 May 2015).
13. Myin Myint Kyu, "Spaces of Exceptional Shifting Strategies of the Kokang Chinese along the Myanmar/China Border", op. cit., p. 206.
14. Myin Myint Kyu, "Spaces of Exceptional Shifting Strategies of the Kokang Chinese along the Myanmar/China Border", op. cit., p. 5.
15. Daw Win, "Law Sit Han", in *Southeast Asian Personalities of Chinese Descent: A Biographical Dictionary*, edited by Leo Suryadinata (Singapore: Institute of Southeast Asian Studies, 2012), p. 495.

16. Ibid.
17. Huanqiu Shibao《环球时报》, "Zhefu wunian chongchu jianghu ting 84 shui 'guogan wang' jiang mianbei jushi" 蛰伏五年重出江湖听 84 岁 "果敢王" 讲缅北局势, 29 December 2014, <http://world.huanqiu.com/exclusive/2014-12/5307556.html> (accessed 20 May 2015).
18. I would like to thank Dr Tin Maung Maung Than for providing me with this information.
19. It should be noted that the Kokang Chinese are recognized by the Myanmar government as one of the country's ethnic minority groups, unlike the Rohingyas, who are not. See Embassy of the Republic of the Union of Myanmar in Belgium, "Composition of the Different Ethnic Groups under the 8 Major National Ethnic Races in Myanmar", <http://www.embassyofmyanmar.be/ABOUT/ethnicgroups.htm> (accessed 18 June 2015).
20. Radio Free Asia (RFA), "Kokang Army Recruiting Chinese Nationals as Mercenaries in Yunnan: Sources", 24 March 2015, <http://www.rfa.org/english/news/myanmar/recruit-03242015121255.html> (accessed 22 May 2015).
21. Sean Gleeson, "Chinese, Burmese Officials Meet to Defuse Kokang Tensions", *The Irrawaddy*, 9 March 2015, <http://www.irrawaddy.com/news/burma/chinese-burmese-officialsmeet-to-defuse-kokang-tensions.html> (accessed 22 May 2015).
22. Global Times Editorial, "North Myanmar Peace Imperative for China", 16 February 2015, <www.globaltimes.cn/content/907884.shtml> (accessed 15 April 2015).
23. Yun Sun, "The Kokang Conflict: How Will China Respond?" *The Irrawady*, 18 February 2015, <www.irrawaddy.com/contributor/kokang-conflict-will-china-respond.html> (accessed 21 May 2015).
24. Ibid.
25. On 12 February 1947 the Burmese government under Aung San reached an agreement at Panglong with the Shan, Kachin, and Chin people. The Panglong Agreement accepted "full autonomy in internal administration for the frontier area" in principle. See The Panglong Agreement referring to the agreement at the University of

North Carolina's Public Library and Digital Archive, "The Panglong Agreement, 1947", <http://www.ibiblio.org/obl/docs/panglong_agreement.htm> (accessed 21 May 2015).

26. Xue Li, "Can China Untangle the Kokang Knot in Myanmar?" op. cit.
27. *Lianhe Zaobao*《联合早报》, "Zai Beijing shiyaxia, Mian tongmengjun jieshu yu zhengfu jun jizhan" 在北京施压下, 缅同盟军结束与政府军激战, 12 June 2015.
28. BBC Zhongwen Wang, BBC 中文网, "Miandian fandui pai lingxiu ang shan su ji jieshu lishixing fang hua" 缅甸反对派领袖昂山素季结束历史性访华, 14 June 2015, <http://www.bbc.com/zhongwen/simp/world/2015/06/150614_burma_aungsansuukyi> (accessed 17 June 2015).
29. Jurgen Haacke, "Why Did Myanmar's Opposition Leaders Just Visit China?" *The Diplomat*, 15 June 2015, <thediplomat.com/2015/06/whydid-myanmars-opposition-leader-just-visit-china> (accessed 18 June 2015).
30. See *Straits Times*, 30 June 2015. The report said that Reuters got the information from a senior official in the Myanmar President's Office but "it is unclear when the switch happened."

PART III

Responses to Internal Needs

Chapter 9

THE USE OF CHINESE TRANSNATIONALISM, THE SICHUAN EARTHQUAKE AND THE BEIJING OLYMPIC GAMES

This chapter deals with China's response to two major domestic events in 2008, in which the Chinese overseas were mobilized, namely, the Sichuan earthquake and the Beijing Olympic Games. Both these events show Beijing's changing policy towards the Chinese overseas. In order to achieve certain objectives, Beijing has begun to treat the Chinese overseas as a single entity, regardless of their citizenship. By appealing to their primordial Chinese sentiments Beijing hopes to use the Chinese overseas as a form of social capital.

THE SICHUAN EARTHQUAKE: THE USE OF SOCIAL CAPITAL?

An earthquake struck Sichuan province on 12 May 2008, resulting in 62,000 dead, 23,000 missing, and 350,000 injured.[1] The earthquake left about 5 million homeless, although the actual number could have been as high as 11 million.[2] The disaster immediately attracted the attention of the world. Many countries expressed their sympathies and offered aid. After a two-day hesitation, Beijing abandoned its self-reliance policy and accepted the help of foreign countries, allowing their personnel to enter the disaster area.

While accepting the aid of foreign countries, China did not go out of its way to solicit their help. However, its attitude towards the Chinese overseas was vastly different. Many Chinese overseas, regardless of their citizenship, voluntarily staged campaigns to collect funds for the earthquake victims, showing their sympathy for their ethnic kin. But Beijing, for its part, had a conscious policy to get the Chinese overseas involved.

With the PRC's healthy foreign reserves position, China, in fact, did not need the financial contribution of the Chinese overseas. Nevertheless, China was not only happy that the Chinese overseas were paying attention to the earthquake victims, but also intentionally appealed to them to continue to give donations for the victims. Beijing acknowledged the role of the Chinese overseas in rebuilding the disaster area in subsequent years. The Overseas Chinese Affairs Office (OCAO) in the State Council declared in June 2008 that it would use the donations of the Chinese overseas (*huaqiao huaren*) to build 100 Qiao Ai Schools and 100 Qiao Ai health clinics in the following three to five years. The term *qiao ai* means "love of Chinese compatriots overseas".[3]

Donations by the Chinese overseas can be divided into a few categories. The top category comprised donations made by Chinese entrepreneurs. Their donations were the largest in terms of amount. These donations could have been motivated by sympathy for the victims in some cases and by business considerations in other cases. Many of these *huashang* (Chinese entrepreneurs) had by then made major investments in China.

Therefore, they needed to show some sort of corporate social responsibility by providing donations to the earthquake victims. These Chinese entrepreneurs competed among themselves to give donations; each wanted to outdo the other in terms of the amount of money donated.[4]

The second category of donors comprised those who hold Chinese passports, including Chinese nationals overseas, Chinese students overseas, and new Chinese migrants (*xin yimin*). These people do not have large resources, but their hearts are still linked to China. Some even have relatives in the disaster area. These are also the people who were mobilized a month before the earthquake to guard the Olympic torch relay when anti-Beijing elements sought to disrupt it. They waved the PRC flag and sought to ensure that the torch relay progressed safely. This point will be discussed in greater detail later.

The third category of donors were the Chinese overseas already holding foreign passports. With the rise of China and interactions with the *xin yimin*, these foreign Chinese began to have new expectations of China. They were drawn emotionally closer to China. In the wake of the earthquake, the appeals of Hong Kong artists, the campaign staged by Taiwan's professionals, and the reports and pictures published in the Chinese mass media and overseas Chinese media had major impact on the Chinese overseas.

Yang Bao'an (Yong Pow Ang), a senior editor of *Lianhe Zaobao*, wrote:

> For many individual donors, he/she might have made donations owing to his/her natural sympathy with the victims and given donations as fellow human beings. It might have been more likely that they did that because they were touched after seeing the pictures of the tragedy and influenced by the atmosphere created by the campaign.

> Objectively, the source of private donations was largely the Chinese overseas, which reflects transnationalism as well as the sentiment of 'blood is thicker than water'. The Prime Minister of China, Wen Jiabao, in his speech thanking the international community for helping the victims of the earthquake, also stated the donations made by 'the compatriots from Hong Kong, Macao and Taiwan and the Chinese overseas in the world.'[5]

Yang also noted that during the drives to assist the earthquake victims, "Beijing has regarded *huaqiao* and *huaren* as one entity; it has also transformed cultural identity into China's economic and political resource."[6]

THE BEIJING OLYMPICS

In July 2001, Beijing won the right to host the prestigious Olympic Games in 2008, beating four other competitors. China was the third Asian country to host the main games after Japan (1964) and South Korea (1988). It was reported that the Beijing Olympic Games were the most watched Olympics in history, drawing 4.7 million viewers worldwide. Some 43 world records and 132 Olympic records were set at the Beijing Olympics. China won the most gold medals (51) and 100 medals altogether, while the US won the most medals (110), with 36 gold medals. Japan was placed in 8th position, with 9 gold medals and 25 medals in all.[7] China emerged as some sort of sports giant in the world, crushing the image of a backward and sick Asian country portrayed by its defeat during the Sino–Japanese war of 1894–95.

It can be argued that the Olympics was important for Beijing's international image and was a matter of national pride; hence, it sought to make the games a success. However, China encountered some difficulties in the preparation for the games and during the ritualistic torch relay from Greece to the host country. It was unfortunate for China that the timing of the games was close to the commemoration date of an uprising in Tibet, which Beijing considers to be Chinese territory.[8]

Trouble erupted in Tibet in March 2008. On 10 March, following a demonstration by monks from various monasteries in Lhasa in commemoration of the 49th anniversary of the failed Tibetan uprising of 1959, wide-scale riots broke out. The riots spread from Lhasa to parts of western China, where there were considerable numbers of Tibetans. The riots culminated on 14 March in open attacks on non-ethnic Tibetans and the looting of Han Chinese-owned shops in Lhasa. The "Tibetan problem" regained international attention. This served as a challenge to the Beijing authorities.

In Beijing's view, Tibet is part of China, and any attempt to challenge its territorial integrity would not be tolerated. However, Tibetans exiles used the Olympic opportunity to force Beijing to give in to their demands. They staged anti-Beijing demonstrations in several countries, especially in the West. The exiles and sympathizers of the Tibetan cause were particularly active during the Olympic torch relay from Greece to China that traversed several major cities. They successfully disrupted the torch relay in several cities, especially London and Paris.

In London, on 7 April, the torch relay was disrupted several times by pro-Tibetan demonstrators before it arrived in Paris the following day. In Paris the number of demonstrators sympathetic to the Tibetan exiles was larger. The torch was extinguished four times, and the "journey of harmony" was cut short. China was embarrassed by these accidents. Its embassies in several other cities then decided to mobilize "overseas Chinese and Chinese compatriots" to guard the torch during the relay. "Donned in red shirts, the Chinese students overseas, together with the Chinese new migrants and overseas Chinese waved the five-star red flag and turned the relay route into a sea of red to drown out the protest groups."[9]

As a result of this new strategy, the subsequent torch relay in Thailand, Malaysia, Australia, Japan, and Korea went relatively smoothly. Still, the sea of red formed by the "overseas Chinese and Chinese compatriots" left a deep, if not menacing, impression among the Japanese and the Koreans as the torch passed through their countries.

The scenes of pro-PRC demonstrators also left negative impressions on Western observers. *The Economist* commented in an editorial, "The recent glimpses of a snarling China should scare the country's government as much as the world".[10] The American China watcher David Shambaugh, writing in the *International Herald Tribune,* commented that "the world should brace itself for more such xenophobic outbursts in the run-up to —and possibly during — the Olympics."[11] But to the Chinese leaders, this outburst was the natural response of a victim. When asked about the mobilization of the Chinese overseas, Jiang Yu, a Foreign Ministry spokeswoman, said: "Why is that only the saboteur has the right to disrupt the relay while the ardent Olympic supporter is denied the right to welcome the Olympic flame?"[12]

For Beijing, the success of the Olympics was thus not just about the reputation of the PRC but also about its "territorial integrity" as the obstruction came from what it sees as "splitist pro-Tibetan groups" and its supporters. The PRC has projected the Beijing Olympics as a symbol of the success of the Chinese people in general, regardless of their citizenship. Indeed, many *huaren* were enthusiastic to assist Beijing and some even served as volunteers to help Beijing during the Olympics.

RESPONSES OF THE CHINESE OVERSEAS

Southeast Asian Chinese responses to the Sichuan earthquake and Beijing Olympics can be divided into two categories. First, the earthquake. As this was a natural disaster and well publicized, it appealed to many ethnic Chinese, especially those who still understand the Chinese language. In Singapore, for instance, the Chinese TV channel held special programmes, expressed condolences to the victims and their families, and also urged the audience to donate to the earthquake victims. Many Chinese Singaporeans made generous donations. Their donations in general were based both on universal humanitarian grounds and on Chinese ethnicity. Nevertheless, in Singapore there are also many *huaqiao* and new migrants, who responded more as Chinese compatriots rather than on humanitarian grounds.

The Malaysian Chinese were also responsive to the earthquake. Special evening gatherings were held to raise funds for the earthquake victims. One of the gatherings was called "Earthquake is cruel, Malaysia has love". It was reported that many ethnic Chinese organizations were quite enthusiastic to donate money. In Thailand and the Philippines, local Chinese organizations, especially Chinese chambers of commerce, came together to make contributions. In Indonesia, too, many Chinese made generous contributions. A Chinese language newspaper in Surabaya, *Qiaodao Ribao,* appealed to the ten million (sic) Indonesian Chinese to help the victims of their *Zhuji Guo* (Ancestral Land or Country of Forefathers) in this most difficult moment.[13] However, there were reports suggesting that while many Chinese in Indonesia had made generous donations, others among them did not display such generosity.

Perhaps more indicative of the expression of ethnicity was the Southeast Asian Chinese response to the Beijing Olympics.

The countries chosen for the torch relay were Indonesia, Malaysia, Thailand, and Vietnam. The Philippines was not selected. In each country, Chinese embassies played an important role in ensuring that the torch relay was successful. It was said that the embassies mobilized both local Chinese and overseas Chinese to "guard" the torch relay.

In Indonesia, for instance, prior to the arrival of the torch, Chen Dajiang (alias Sukanta Tanudjaja), a Chinese Indonesian tycoon, was reported to have led members of the Chinese Chamber of Commerce to liaise with the locals, who, together with the Chinese embassy in Jakarta, succeeded in delivering an uninterrupted torch relay.[14] The relay was done at the Senayan Stadium and many Chinese Indonesians participated. Some were old businessmen who felt proud to be selected by the embassy. It was said that each carried the torch for only 100–200 metres.[15]

While the torch relay was held at a stadium rather than on the streets of Indonesia for fear of disruption, in the other three countries, the torch relay was held on the street under tight security. It was only in Thailand that some Tibetan supporters managed to hold protests but the relay was nevertheless successfully completed without any major incident.[16]

CONCLUSION

If we view the Beijing Olympics in the context of the Tibetan challenge, we can undertand why Beijing mobilized *huaqiao* and *huaren* to safeguard the Olympic torch relay. Nevertheless, the overzealousness of Chinese embassy staff in some countries in organizing the Chinese overseas regardless of citizenship raised some concerns. Some observers began to ask whether China had returned to its old policy of supporting dual nationality for the Chinese overseas. And, indeed, there have been indications that top Chinese leaders in recent years have begun to embrace Chinese overseas regardless of their nationality. However, PRC officials denied that there was any change in Beijing's policy towards the "Chinese overseas".

Both the Sichuan earthquake and the Beijing Olympics can be seen as examples where China utilized the Chinese overseas regardless of their nationality. Beijing used the "national (ethnic?) and cultural belonging" of the Chinese overseas to serve the interests of China. If the earthquake touched on the universal value of sympathy towards human suffering, in the Beijing Olympics, ethnicity was used to achieve China's objective of being recognized as a modern country and a heavyweight in sports. Nevertheless, the case of the Beijing Olympics was more complex as it involved the territorial integrity of the PRC. Therefore China was determined to ensure the safe and smooth conduct of the torch relay. But the involvement of foreign nationals of Chinese descent in guarding the torch relay and waving PRC flags was controversial for they came across as if they were still nationals of China.

It is also important to note that the responses of the Chinese overseas to the two events were not entirely unanimous. Those who still have close business links with China appeared to be more enthusiastic than those who do not. With regard to the Beijing Olympics, many Southeast Asians of Chinese descent were proud that China had succeeded in organizing a major world event, but they were not as enthusiastic as those who have business or direct cultural links with Beijing.

Notes

1. David Barboza, "China Struggles to Shelter Millions of Quake's Homeless", *New York Times*, 26 May 2008, <www.nytimes.com/2008/05/26/world/asia/26china.html> (accessed 11 December 2015).
2. Ibid., also Jake Hooker, "Toll Rises in China Quake", *New York Times*, 26 May 2008, <www.nytimes.com/2008/05/26/world/asia/26quake.html> (accessed 11 December 2015).
3. Yang Bao'an 杨保安, "Zhongguo younan, huaren zhiyuan" 中国有难, 华人支援, *Zaobao Xingqitian*《早报星期天》, 8 June 2008.
4. Ibid.
5. Ibid.
6. Ibid.
7. BBC Sport Olympics, "Beijing 2008 Medal Table", 13 August 2012, <http://www.bbc.co.uk/sport/olympics/2012/medals/historical-medals-beijing-2008/countries> (accessed 10 April 2016).
8. For a brief discussion of the Olympics and China, see Leo Suryadinata, "A New Orientation in China's Policy towards Chinese Overseas? Beijing Olympic Games Fervour as a Case Study", *CHC Bulletin*, no. 12 (November 2008): 1–4.
9. Yong Pao Ang, "Angry China Fuels Fear", *CHC Bulletin*, no. 12 (November 2008): 5–6.
10. *The Economist*, 3 May 2008, cited in ibid.
11. Ibid.
12. Ibid.
13. Xinhua Wang 新华网, "Yinni huaren huaqiao xiang Zhongguo da dizhen zaimin shenchu yuanshou" 印尼华人华侨向中国大地震灾民伸出援手, 16 May 2008, <http://news.xinhuanet.com/overseas/2008-05/16/content_8184254.htm> (accessed 19 April 2016).
14. Chuansong men 传送门, "Quanqiu huashang mingren tang — Yinniyouguang jituan mingyu dongshi zhang Chen dajiang" 全球华商名人堂 — 印尼友光集团名誉董事长陈大江, 28 May 2014, <chuansong.me/n/2750948> (accessed 10 April 2016).

15. Xinhua Wang 新华网, "Fang Yinni huaren huoju shou: wei dangxuan aoyun huojushou er yisheng rongguang" 访印尼华人火炬手: 为当选奥运火炬手而一生荣光, 21 April 2008.
16. Thai Military Information Blog, "Thailand to give High-Caliber Welcome to Olympic Flame", 25 March 2008, <https://thaimilitary.wordpress.com/2008/04/16/security-tighten-asolympic-torch-will-arrives-thailand-tomorrow> (accessed 19 April 2016).

Chapter 10

DIRECT CONTROL? BEIJING AND THE WORLD CHINESE ENTREPRENEURS CONFERENCE

As China develops economically, it needs to have a larger overseas market as well as overseas projects in which to invest its surplus capital. This chapter deals with China's efforts to utilize the Chinese overseas, especially Chinese capitalists, in its economic growth and development, and the establishment of its own world Chinese entrepreneurs conference in 2015, rivalling a similar conference established some years earlier by other parties.

INTRODUCTION

China held its first "World Overseas Chinese [*huaqiao huaren*] Entreprenuers Conference" (世界华侨华人工商大会) in Beijing on 6–7 July 2015. As noted in Chapter 1, in mainland China, the term *huaqiao* is used to refer to Chinese nationals overseas while *huaren* refers to foreign nationals of Chinese descent. According to China press reports, over 300 overseas guests from 79 countries and areas participated in the conference, and Prime Minister Li Keqiang met them at the People's Great Hall and delivered a speech.[1] The China Central TV (CCTV) report mentioned only the presence of a Thai "overseas Chinese businessman",[2] Xie Guoming (谢国民, Thai name: Dhanin Chearavanont) of the Charoen Pokphand Group (better known as the CP Group), who also made a speech at the conference. No other Chinese entrepreneurs were mentioned. However, from CCTV video clips of Li Keqiang's speech,[3] it would seem that many ethnic Chinese tycoons from Southeast Asia were also present at the conference.

BEIJING'S *HUASHANG* CONFERENCE

The Beijing world overseas Chinese entrepreneurs conference was jointly organized by the Overseas Chinese Affairs Office (侨务办公室 OCAO, also known in Chinese as Qiaoban 侨办) under the State Council and China's Overseas Exchange Association. It was held after China had proposed its "One Belt One Road" Strategy. Wang Xiaotao, the vice-chairman of the State Development and Reform Committee, gave a speech entitled "To exhibit the function of *huaqiao huaren*, to assist 'One Belt One Road' development". The chairperson of OCAO, Qiu Yuanping, also made a speech, noting that "Overseas Chinese made major contributions to the countries where they reside and to China's development. According to incomplete statistics, overseas Chinese businessmen (*qiaoshang*)[4] had a net capital worth of more than US$5,000 billion."[5] She went on to say that "China for *huaqiao huaren* is the root of the nation, the soul of culture, and also...the big stage for them to realize their dreams".

The statements of the two top Chinese leaders clearly show that they considered Chinese overseas as "Chinese nationals" who, therefore, had the obligation to help China's "One Belt One Road" Strategy. They also show that the overseas Chinese businessmen (including those who are foreign citizens) are rich and command US$5,000 billion. It is not clear how Qiu Yuanping got the figure for the net capital worth of these businessmen and who these businessmen are, but the fact is that she mentioned it in the context of supporting China's economic development not only within China but also overseas. It implies that their wealth is also part of China's assets that may be used for promoting Beijing's interests.

This line of argument, i.e., all Chinese overseas are part of the Chinese nation, is further elaborated by Premier Li Keqiang, who told the conference participants:

> Six million overseas compatriots (*haiwai qiaobao*) are important members of the large Chinese nation (*zhonghua minzu*). Generation after generation of *huaqiao* and *huaren*, their feelings are still linked to the homeland, their hearts are tied to Zhonghua, ... they have made special and important contributions to the independence and liberation of the Chinese nation, the reform, the opening and the modernization of China.[6]

Li Keqiang went on to express three expectations from *huaqiao huaren*:

> Firstly, to be the 'New Effective Forces' in fostering the economic transformation and development of China, and to widely and deeply participate in the economic construction of China. ... Secondly, to build a 'Rainbow Bridge' for the economic cooperation between China and foreign countries, so that the 'One Belt One Road' constructions can be pushed ahead. ... Thirdly, to establish a 'New Image' of Chinese entrepreneurs to reflect the traditional good virtue of the

> Chinese nation, i.e., to live in harmony with the local population where they live, to be sincere, honest and law-abiding when doing business, and to take social responsibility...[7]

Earlier, however, in 1991, several *huashang* from across the world established a "World Chinese Entrepreneurs Convention" (WCEC) or *Shijie Huashang Dahui* (世界华商大会), under the leadership of the Chinese Chambers of Commerce and Industry of Singapore, Bangkok, and Hong Kong.[8] Its objective was to foster mutual understanding between Chinese entrepreneurs across the world, to build Chinese entrepreneurial networks, to foster ethnic Chinese integration into the local society (*luodi shenggen*), and to make contributions to the economy and development of the countries where they reside.[9] This conference, which is held every two years, was first held in Singapore in August 1991. About 800 representatives from 30 countries and areas and 75 cities participated. The conference proceedings were held in both Chinese and English.

The WCEC has provided Chinese entrepreneurs with forums and networks to facilitate their contributions to the countries where they reside. Twelve meetings of the WCEC had been organized prior to Beijing's *huashang* conference and the thirteenth was held between 25 and 27 September 2015 in Bali, Indonesia, about two and a half months after Beijing's conference. About 2,700 Chinese entrepreneurs from 23 countries attended the Bali meeting. The theme of the convention was "Gather Chinese Entrepreneurs, Win-Win in Indonesia" (融聚华商, 共赢在印尼). Many top officials from Beijing, such as the chairperson of both OCAO and the Federation of Returned Overseas Chinese Associations (FROCA, also known as Qiaolian), the deputy chairman of China's

Overseas Exchange Association, and China's ambassador to Indonesia, were present and gave speeches. The guest of honour was former Indonesian President Megawati Sukarnoputri. Other Indonesian officials present were then Coordinating Minister for Political, Security, and Legal Affairs Luhut Panjaitan and Chairman of the Indonesian People's Consultative Assembly Zulkifli Hasan. These indigenous Indonesian leaders, together with the Chinese Indonesian entrepreneurs at the conference, were unanimous in welcoming China to invest in Indonesia.[10]

The WCEC should have been beneficial for both China and the organizing country, and Beijing's presence at its regular conferences was also felt. In fact, in the short twenty-five years of the WCEC's existence, two of its conferences were held in China, namely, 2001 in Nanking (Nanjing) and 2013 in Chengdu. However, the WCEC apparently did not satisfy a rising China's interests, hence, Beijing felt it necessary to establish its own conference. The Thai Chinese tycoon Xie Guomin noted that Beijing's *huashang* conference constitutes the "Diplomacy of a Big Country" (*daguo waijiao*).

Indeed, it was the "Diplomacy of a Big Country", whose purpose was to serve the interests of China. Even prior to the establishment of Beijing's *huashang* conference, Zhuang Rongwen, the deputy chairman of OCAO, stated that Beijing's aim was to establish an organization of world Chinese entrepreneurs to lead Chinese businessmen overseas to participate in China's development, especially the "One Belt One Road" Strategy.[11] Li Keqiang openly admitted in his speech at the conference that he would like Chinese entrepreneurs to be the "New Effective Forces" (*shengli jun*) of China's economic transformation and development. In other words, Chinese entrepreneurs should serve the interests of China first, with mutual gains for China and the country of origin of these businessmen taking second place, and establishing the new image of Chinese entrepreneurs coming third in China's hierarchy of aims.

Li Keqiang came across as addressing himself to Chinese nationals, but the majority of the Chinese entrepreneurs who participated at the conference were *huaren* rather than *huaqiao*. To ask foreign nationals to serve the interests of China first appears to be unreasonable; this would also put the participants in an awkward position.

As stated in previous chapters, during the Deng Xiaoping period, the distinction between *huaqiao* and *huaren* was quite clear. Deng's China promulgated the first PRC Nationality Law in 1980, which stipulated that China recognizes only single citizenship; once a Chinese person living overseas became a citizen of another country voluntarily, he or she would cease to possess PRC citizenship. The clear distinction that the law made between Chinese nationals and foreigners appeared to have resolved the historical problem of dual nationality for the Chinese overseas.

As China modernized and began to be plugged into the global economy, new waves of Chinese migration to the West and Southeast Asia have occurred. The new Chinese migrants in the West proposed that China revive the dual nationality policy for ethnic Chinese, which is a policy practised in several countries in the West. The proposal was debated in the Chinese People's Consultative Body, but the 1980 Chinese Nationality Law remained unamended.

As noted in Chapter 4, the most striking example of the distinction between Chinese nationals and foreigners could be seen in Beijing's attitude towards the anti-ethnic Chinese violence in Indonesia in May 1998. Many Chinese Indonesians were affected by the violence but Beijing did not want to get involved as they were Indonesian nationals.

BEIJING'S CHANGING POLICY TOWARDS CHINESE OVERSEAS

It appears that Beijing's policy towards the Chinese overseas started to change after the 1998 anti-ethnic Chinese riots in Indonesia. This was reflected in 2001 after Beijing revitalized OCAO and the aforementioned ACFROCA. ACFROCA established the honorary positions of "Overseas Advisors" (*Haiwai Guwen*) and "Overseas Committee Members" (*Haiwai Weiyuan*) for Chinese overseas. Initially, there were only 31 overseas advisors and overseas committee members.[12] But, by December 2013, ACFROCA had appointed 581 such members representing 94 countries. The majority of the advisors and committee members are *huaren*, not *huaqiao*. Legally speaking, the semi-official ACFROCA is for the *huaqiao* in the mainland, but *huaren* have been included in the group, resulting in some criticism among *huaren* in Southeast Asia and scholars in China.[13]

More significant is the establishment of the Conference of World Federation of *Huaqiao Huaren* Associations (CWFHHA)[14] by OCAO in the same year (2001). Soon after its establishment, the first conference was held in 2001. By 2014, there had been seven such conferences. The 6th conference, in 2012, was attended by 570 participants from 110 countries and areas; by 2014, when the 7th conference was held, there were over 500 participants from 119 countries and areas.[15] President Xi Jinping, made a speech at the 7th conference, referring to the Chinese overseas as members of "*Zhonghua* big family". When he addressed the meeting, he used the term "*haiwai qiaobao*" (海外侨胞 overseas compatriots) rather than "*haiwai huaren*" (海外华人 Chinese overseas),[16] but the fact is that the occasion was a world *huaqiao* and *huaren* conference, not a *huaqiao* gathering.

As shown in the preceding chapters, China's merging of *huaqiao* and *huaren* became clearer during the anti-Chinese violence in the Solomon Islands in 2006, the Sichuan earthquake of 2008, and the Beijing Olympic Games, also in 2008.

It should be noted that OCAO has been involved in the reformulation of Beijing's policy towards the Chinese overseas. Nevertheless, the systematic formulation of the policy was believed to have begun in 2011, when an OCAO committee member, Dai Bingguo, coined the term "*Qiaowu gonggong waijiao*" (侨务公共外交, Diaspora Affairs Public Diplomacy).[17] In the same year, Li Haifeng, then the director of OCAO, talked about the use of the "overseas Chinese" as a bridge to link China and the world and to strengthen "public diplomacy". In subsequent policy papers, it becomes clear that OCAO considered the "overseas Chinese" as a great asset and that Beijing would like to use them to promote the interests of China. This is sometime also called *Da Qiaowu Zhengce* (大侨务政策) or the Great Overseas Chinese Affairs Policy. Some mainland Chinese scholars have noted that to use ethnic kinship in diplomacy is not new, and that the Israelis have been using it quite extensively. Yet, the same scholars claimed that the *Qiaowu gonggong waijiao* is unique and an "invention" of China.[18]

However, in this "Great Overseas Chinese Affairs Policy", China uses *huaqiao* (overseas Chinese) to refer to both *huaqiao* and *huaren*, erasing the citizenship boundary. One of the pro-PRC networks in Hong Kong commented that such usage was incorrect and improper.[19] Nevertheless, the comment was ignored.

After 2011, the lumping together of *huaqiao* and *huaren* became more obvious. The Director of the Beijing branch of OCAO Li Yinze gave a speech at the Chinese Chamber of Commerce in Jakarta in April 2012, urging young Chinese Indonesians to learn *hanyu* (the Han Language) "in order to strengthen their identification with the Chinese nation."[20] The chairperson of OCAO, Qiu Yuanping, made a speech at the Perhimpunan INTI (Indonesians of Chinese Descent Association) in September 2014 in which she noted that "The ancestral land [of the Chinese] will never forget the major contributions of the *huaqiao huaren* overseas; China will always be the strong backer of the people of Chinese descent overseas."[21]

This habit of not differentiating between *huaqiao* and *huaren* is worrying. At the 2015 "World Overseas Chinese Entreprenuers Conference", China's top leaders referred in their speeches to *huashang* (foreign businessmen of Chinese descent) as *qiaoshang* (China's businessmen overseas), ignoring their citizenship. They also referred to *haiwai huaren* (Chinese overseas) as *haiwai qiaobao* (overseas compatriots), attempting to return to their past practice.

CONCLUSION

The holding of Beijing's "World Overseas Chinese Entreprenuers Conference" in 2015 cannot be separated from the rise of China. Beijing believes that the realization of its "One Belt One Road" Strategy requires the assistance and support of Chinese entrepreneurs worldwide. Perhaps Beijing felt that because the existing "World Chinese Entrepreneurs Convention" (WCEC) was not initiated and controlled by China, it was unable to fulfill China's requirements; hence, Beijing had to quickly establish another world overseas Chinese entrepreneurs conference. The establishment of China's own conference creates the impression that Beijing cannot accept the "World Chinese Entrepreneurs Convention" initiated by the Chinese overseas.

More significant than this is Beijing's changing policy towards the Chinese overseas, as reflected in its approach and the terms used to refer to ethnic Chinese outside China. In the recent past *huaqiao* and *huaren* have been widely used to distinguish between China's citizens overseas and foreign citizens of Chinese descent. The 1980 Nationality Law, in fact, stresses this distinction, and the law remains in place. However, in recent practice, the terms have been used together and *haiwai huaren* is often replaced by *haiwai qiaobao* in the speeches made by China's top leaders. This practice may have more significant implications in international politics and diplomacy.

Notes

1. Guancha Zhe 观察者, "Shoujie shijie huaqiao huaren gongshang dahuikaimu, haiwai qiaoshang ziben chao 5 wan yi meiyuan" 首届世界华侨华人工商大会开幕海外侨商资本超5万亿美元, 7 July 2015, <http://www.guancha.cn/Industry/2015_07_07_325893.shtml> (accessed 10 July 2015); Xinhua Wang 新华网, "Li Keqiang huijian shoujie huaqiaohuaren gongshang dahui quanti daibiao" 李克强会见首届华侨华人工商大会全体代表, 6 July 2015, <http://news.xinhuanet.com/politics/2015-07/06/c_1115833826.htm> (accessed 10 July 2015).
2. The term used is *qiaoshang* (侨商) not *huashang* (华商), indicating that he is a *huaqiao* (Chinese national residing overseas). In fact, he is a *huaren* (foreign citizen of Chinese descent).
3. Xinhua Wang 新华网, "Li Keqiang huijian shoujie huaqiaohuaren gongshang dahui quanti daibiao", op. cit.

4. The original meaning of *qiaoshang* is compatriot businessmen.
5. Guancha Zhe 观察者, "Shoujie shijie huaqiao huaren gongshang dahui kaimu, haiwai qiaoshang ziben chao 5 wan yi meiyuan", op. cit.
6. Ibid.
7. Ibid. It is worth noting that Li Keqiang's speech was criticized by both Singaporean and Indonesian presses. Li started to adjust his view when he received the 8th World Federation of *Huaqiao Huaren* Associations Conference on 2 June 2016. This time he still expressed his three expectations to the delegates, but changed their order. The first expectation was to be "the golden ribbon (金丝带) of China-Foreign countries friendly cooperation", the second was to be the "participants" (参与者) in transforming China's economy and the third was to be the "heart connecting bridge" (连心桥) for the peaceful unification of the fatherland. Nevertheless, the overall tune of the entire speech remains unchanged. He continued to use *haiwai qiaobao* (Chinese compatriots overseas) to refer to *huaqiao* and *huaren* in his speech, blurring the distinction between China's nationals and foreign nationals of Chinese descent. See Xinhua Wang 新华网, "Li Keqiang huijian dibajie shijie huaqiao huaren shetuan lianyi dahui daibiao" 李克强会见第八届世界华侨华人社团联谊大会代表, 2 June 2016, <http://news.xinhuanet.com/politics/2016-06/02/c_1118980966.htm> (accessed 4 June 2016).
8. A secretariat was established for the WCEC, with each of the three Chinese chambers of commerce serving as secretariat in rotation for a term of six years.
9. Tan Eng Joo, "Speech", in *1st World Chinese Entrepreneurs Convention: A Global Network: 10–12 August, 1991*《首届世界华商大会专辑: 环球网 络: 一九九一年 八月十日至二十日, 新加坡》(Singapore: Singapore Chinese Chamber of Commerce and Industry, 1992), pp. 18–19.
10. *Yinhua Ribao* (Inhua Daily《印华日报》), 26 and 28 September 2015.

11. Guancha Zhe 观察者, "Shoujie shijie huaqiao huaren gongshang dahui kaimu, haiwai qiaoshang ziben chao 5 wan yi meiyuan", op. cit.
12. *Guoji Ribao*《国际日报》, "Ershi wei yinhua jingying shoupin danren zhongguo qiaolian haiwai guwen he weiyuan" 二十位印华精英受聘担任中国侨联海外顾问和委员, 9 December 2013, <http://www.guojiribao.com/shtml/gjrb/20131209/134060.shtml> (accessed 2 April 2015).
13. The most outspoken critics are scholars from Peking University, namely Professors Zhou Nanjing 周南京 and Liang Yingming 梁英明. Both are also returned overseas Chinese from Indonesia.
14. The Chinese name is 世界华侨华人社团联谊会, but the mainland Chinese translation is the Conference for Friendship of Overseas Chinese Associations, which does not reflect its original meaning.
15. Zhongguo Xinwen Wang 中国新闻网, "Diliujie shijie huaqiao huaren shetuan lianyi dahui zai Beijing kaimu" 第六届世界华侨华人社团联谊大会在北京开幕, 9 April 2012, <http://www.chinanews.com/zgqj/2012/04-09/3804392.shtml> (accessed 22 July 2015); Zhongguo Qiao Wang 中国桥网, "Diqijie shijie huaqiao huaren shetuan lianyi dahui" 第七届世界华侨华人社团联谊大会 [The 7th Conference for Friendship of *Huaqiao Huaren* Associations], 5–8 June 2014 <www.chinaqw.com/z/2014/sjhqhrstlydh/index.html> (accessed 22 July 2015).
16. *Renmin Wang-Renmin Ribao*《人民网-人民日报》, "Xi Jinping huijian diqijie shijie huaqiao huaren shetuan lianyi dahui daibiao" 习近平会见第七届世界华侨华人社团联谊大会代表, 7 June 2014, <http://pic.people.com.cn/n/2014/0607/c1016-25116878.html> (accessed 18 March 2016).
17. Xianggang Huasheng Wang 香港华声网, "Qiaowu gonggong waijiao" 侨务公共外交, in "2015 Guancha yu guanzhu" 2015 观察与关注, 3 March 2015, <https://groups.google.com/forum/#!topic/gelora45/VBDSgzZPFMo> (accessed 4 December 2015).
18. Zhao Kejin 赵可金 and Liu Siru 刘思如, "Zhongguo qiaowu gonggong waijiao de xingqi" 中国侨务公共外交的兴起, *Dongbeiya*

Luntan《东北亚 论坛》, no. 5 (2013), <http://www.imir.tsinghua.edu.cn/publish/iis/7236/20120308004952896512257/2013-8-16.pdf> (accessed 8 January 2016).

19. Xianggang Huasheng Wang 香港华声网, "2015 Guancha yu guanzhu" 2015 观察与关注, 3 March 2015, <https://groups.google.com/forum/#!topic/gelora45/VBDSgzZPFMo> (accessed 4 December 2015). See also footnote 11 of this chapter.
20. *Guoji Ribao*《国际日报》. "Beijing shi qiaoban zhuren Li Yinze fang Yinni jianghua yingqi qiaojie buman" 北京市侨办主任李印泽访印尼讲话引起侨界不满 [The speech of Beijing's Qiaoban director Li Yinze caused worries among the Chinese community], 21 April 2012.
21. See *Guoji Ribao*, 19 September 2014.

Chapter 11

"ONE BELT ONE ROAD" STRATEGY AND THE CHINESE OVERSEAS

The usefulness of the Chinese overseas to the PRC became apparent when Beijing's top leadership began mentioning in their speeches that the Chinese overseas were crucial for their "One Belt One Road" Strategy. This belief in the usefulness of the Chinese overseas, which was also shared by many Chinese scholars in China, resulted in the further blurring of the distinction between Chinese citizens and foreign citizens of Chinese descent. This chapter addresses briefly the concept of "One Belt One Road", its ambiguity, and the misperceived role of the Chinese overseas in this strategy. It also discusses its possible impact on China's relations with Southeast Asia.

THE ORIGINS

The "One Belt One Road" Strategy was first proposed by President Xi Jinping in his speech in Kazakhstan in September 2013 and in another speech a month later in Indonesia. In his Kazakhstan speech, Xi mentioned the economic belt of the overland Silk Road, which linked China with Central Asia and Europe, while in the Indonesian speech he proposed a 21st Century Maritime Silk Road, which would link China to Southeast Asia and beyond.

Soon after the two speeches, Xi's proposal became known as the "One Belt One Road" (OBOR) Strategy or *Yidai Yilu Zhanlue* (一带一路战略) in Mandarin. There are many explanations for why the OBOR Strategy was proposed. Some believe that the existing global economic institutional framework limits the economic and political role of China. As China becomes developed and stronger, it wants to play a major role in the world arena, freeing itself from the domination of the United States, Europe, and Japan. OBOR and the Asian Infrastructure Investment Bank (AIIB) are being used to achieve this objective.

President Xi himself links the OBOR Strategy to his "China Dream". He would like to lead the rejuvenation of the Chinese nation in order to make China strong again, as in ancient times. In fact, the rapid economic development of China has resulted in three requirements — the need for raw materials, the need to export surplus products, and the need to channel surplus capital — that pit China against Western capitalist countries, which are in a scramble to fulfill similar needs. The proposed OBOR Strategy would be able to meet these requirements.

Nevertheless, reviving the historical concept of the silk road is not without problems. When the term was first revived, it is possible that the Chinese leader, or at least his advisors, had the historical trade route in mind.[1] In the past, especially during the Ming Dynasty of the fifteenth century, China had indeed built a maritime silk road. However, the concept is also often linked to the tributary system, where China, considering itself the "Middle Kingdom" and overlord of the region required the surrounding smaller countries to pay tributes.[2] In reality, the returns that the tributary states received from China's emperor were always greater than the tributes they paid him.

However, in the twenty-first century, this kind of tributary relationship is not only anachronistic, but also inimical to China's international relations. Perhaps to avoid embarrassment, China's leaders seem to have avoided talk about the historical tributary system, referring instead only to the routes that the historical silk road had passed through. It is said that the cities and countries through which the silk road passed had been prosperous. However, the OBOR Strategy is still China-centred in the sense that China is still the hub of both the "belt" and "road".

The actual contents of the OBOR Strategy as reflected in President Xi's two speeches are not very concrete. At Kazakhstan's Nazarbayev University, Xi stated on 7 September 2013 that:

> In order to foster closer and deeper economic cooperation among many countries, and enlarge the space for development, we can use a new cooperation model — jointly build the "Silk Road economic belt", starting from one point, making it to a line, and from a line to a space, and gradually we would have a large area of cooperation.[3]

This was the origin of the "One Belt" concept. In his speech before the Indonesian Parliament on 3 October 2013, about a month after his speech in Kazakhstan, Xi said:

> China is willing to strengthen maritime cooperation with the ASEAN countries, make a good use of the China–ASEAN Cooperation Fund, which has already been established, develop partnership in maritime cooperation, and jointly build a 21st Century "Maritime Silk Road".[4]

This was the origin of the "One Road" concept.

THE CONTENTS

The OBOR Strategy is considered to be an outline, whose details are left to observers to fill. There is no clear official blueprint on the OBOR Strategy, but there are many interpretations of its outline by both Chinese scholars and officials, who have tried to flesh out its contents.[5] Also, soon after the launch of OBOR, the AIIB was established by Beijing in July 2014. The AIIB is perceived as part of the OBOR Strategy. China believed that with the establishment of the bank, the OBOR proposal became more concrete.

OBOR is the strategy through which China has sought to link itself with the world, mainly Southeast Asia, Central Asia, Europe, and Africa. The construction of railways and harbours has become important for this linkage. Hence, once the OBOR Strategy was proposed, China began to build railways extending beyond China. It has started building a railway linking Central Asia to Xinjiang (China). Railways linking China to other regions, however, are still being planned; there is no schedule for their completion.

On 1 February 2015, an OBOR Leadership Working Committee was established. It is headed by Deputy Prime Minister Zhang Gaoli, but its office is located in the State Development and Reform Committee Office, which is also the committee that oversees the implementation and day-to-day work of the OBOR Strategy.

On 28 March 2015, Xi Jinping made a keynote speech at the annual conference of the Bo'ao Forum for Asia, reiterating the OBOR Strategy. He explained the origin and the broad objective of the strategy. He stated that the OBOR cooperation proposal met "the development needs of China, countries along the routes and the region at large." It would "serve the call of our time for regional and global cooperation. They will be a real chorus comprising all countries along the routes, not a solo for China itself....Currently, more than 60 countries along the routes and international organizations have shown interest in taking part in the development of the Belt and the Road".[6] Soon after the speech, the "official map of the One Belt One Road", showing the regions and countries along the belt and road, was produced (see Figure 11.1).

In January 2016, the State Development and Reform Committee Office published a five-volume set of books entitled "One Belt One Road and Two-Directional Investment".[7] The

FIGURE 11.1
One Belt One Road Map

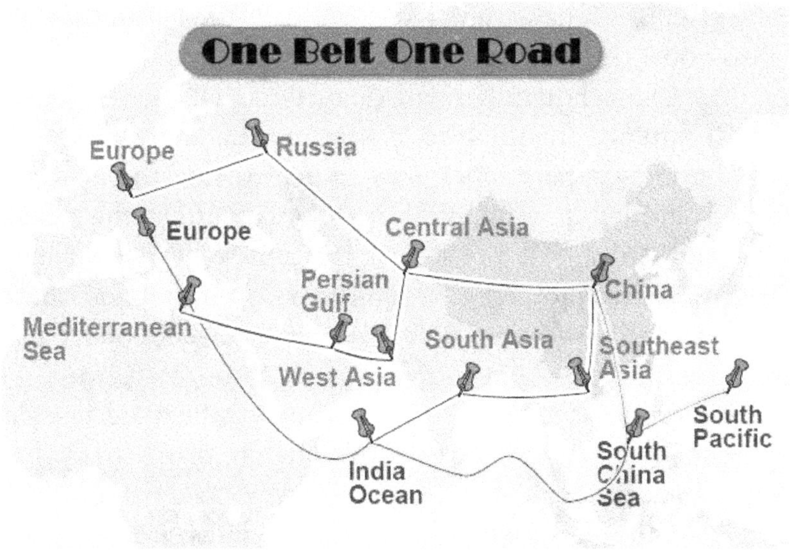

Source: Redrawn from the map published in Guancha Zhe 观察者, "Yangshi fabu quanwei 'Yidai Yilu' bantu" 央视发布权威"一带一路"版图, 13 April 2015, <http://www.guancha.cn/Neighbors/2015_04_13_315767.shtml> (accessed 2 January 2016).

books, which attempt to describe what the OBOR Strategy is, are mainly compilations of speeches and case studies on some Chinese joint projects overseas, data on twenty-four countries, and 2014 statistics showing two-way investments between China and the OBOR countries. Notwithstanding claims that the strategy was not just intended for China's benefit, Xu Shaoshi, the chief editor of the series, who is also the director of the State Development and Reform Committee, noted that the objective of the OBOR Strategy was to help China in two-way investments, i.e., "to get investments into China and to get China's capital out" (*Yin jinlai, zou chuqu* 引进来, 走出去).[8]

OBOR remains a grand design for China to connect with the world with a view to becoming a stronger power, but the initial focus is still on countries and areas along the historical Silk Road, both land and maritime. Therefore, Beijing has placed all of China's economic activities in these countries and areas under the OBOR umbrella.

The China–Britain Business Council sees OBOR as a vehicle for Xi Jinping's intention to "create new trading routes, links and business opportunities with China, passing through over sixty countries along the way, across Asia, Europe, the Middle East and Africa."[9] It noted that the aims of OBOR include: (1) developing prosperity for underdeveloped parts of China, particularly in the west of the country; (2) developing new opportunities for China to partner and cooperate with the various countries along the routes, many of which are developing countries; and (3) increased integration, connectivity, and economic development along both routes.[10]

From the perspective of overseas business groups, OBOR provides various opportunities for them in the following sectors: infrastructure, financial and professional services, advanced manufacturing, transport, and logistics. Nevertheless, infrastructure projects will play an important role in connecting China, and hence are likely to be the focus of the OBOR initiative.

The China–Britain Business Council admitted that investments may be affected by the fact that China and some Southeast Asian countries still have conflicting claims to parts of the South China Sea. Therefore, the council noted that business groups should be careful when selecting projects to avoid areas where issues had not yet been resolved and conflict was likely to occur.

OBOR AND THE CHINESE OVERSEAS

China welcomes countries in the OBOR area to participate in the OBOR project, but in 2014 it unexpectedly began linking the project to the Chinese overseas. Chinese leaders, especially Chinese scholars, consider that OBOR could only succeed with the full participation of the "Chinese Overseas". Thus, China has appealed to Chinese transnationalism to promote the OBOR project as it is assumed that the Chinese overseas reside not only in countries within the "One Road" maritime zone but also in countries along the "One Belt" overland zone.

But, in fact, the presence of the Chinese overseas is uneven in the countries and areas mentioned in the OBOR Strategy. The "One Belt" zone includes Central Asia (e.g., Kazakhstan, Kyrgyzstan, Tajikistan, Turkmenistan, and Uzbekistan), West Asia (Iran and many Arab countries), and some European countries (including Italy and the countries of Eastern Europe). The Chinese population in these areas is small and they are hardly rich and powerful. Even in the "One Road" zone, the spread of the Chinese population is uneven: the zone not only includes many Southeast Asian countries, which have large numbers of ethnic Chinese, but also India, Sri Lanka, and Africa, where the number of Chinese is small and they are economically weak. However, mainland Chinese leaders and scholars ignore this fact and lump "One Belt" and "One Road" together and treat the two regions as one homogeneous group.

The linkage between OBOR and the Chinese overseas was proposed during the World Conference of the Federation of Chinese Clan Associations in 2014 by OCAO leaders as well as President Xi Jinping. Discussions, seminars, and conferences on "OBOR and the Chinese overseas" took place in 2015, echoing the views of the top leader of China. These meetings culminated in July 2015 in the holding of the "World *Huaqiao Huaren* Businessmen and Industrialists Conference" by OCAO, mentioned in Chapter 10.

Why is the full participation of the Chinese overseas so important for China? And what is the actual role of the Chinese overseas in the OBOR Strategy? In seminars and interviews, Chinese leaders and scholars[11] talked only about the large number of Chinese overseas who are patriotic and would help China in realizing the "China Dream". These Chinese who live in the OBOR countries and areas are, in their view, economically strong and rich. In addition there are a large number of ethnic Chinese professionals who could assist China in realizing the objectives of the OBOR. From Beijing's perspective, regardless of their citizenship, wealthy Chinese should be mobilized to invest in China, the professionals should be encouraged to work in China, and those who remain overseas should serve as a bridge between China and the governments and people of their respective countries with a view to promoting the interests of China. In short, Chinese leaders and scholars have spoken only in general terms, with no specifics.

It seems that there was no detailed discussion of concrete projects that the Chinese overseas could undertake in the OBOR Strategy. Who are these Chinese overseas and what are they able to do in China or in their countries of residence? Would there be any conflict of interest between the interests of China and those of the countries along the OBOR route? Are the Chinese overseas expected to pressurize their respective governments to choose the PRC's state-owned enterprises (SOEs) for domestic mega projects? Are they expected to pay for the OBOR projects in their respective countries of residence? Are there rich and influential Chinese residing in the "One Belt" countries/areas? Are all Chinese overseas oriented towards mainland China?

It is difficult to answer all of the above questions. It is also not easy to talk about the role of the Chinese overseas in the OBOR Strategy as the terms have not been properly defined by the Beijing authorities. If we use the vague definition provided above, i.e., socio-economic activities, especially economic activities in any country in the historical OBOR countries/areas, including mainland China, we may find some small and medium joint-venture projects undertaken by Chinese businessmen overseas. However, when we look at mega projects where large capital investments and a lot of expertise are required, it appears that only the state would be able to do it. If there are to be state projects, the most important precondition is still friendly relations between China and the states concerned.

Joint projects between China and Singapore can be cited as one example. The Suzhou Industrial Park project, which was undertaken in 1994, prior to the surfacing of the OBOR Strategy, was not a project undertaken by the Chinese overseas. Instead, it was a joint project between the governments of China and Singapore. Likewise, the more recent projects such as the Sino–Singapore Tianjin Eco City project, the Singapore–Sichuan Hi-Tech Innovation Park project, and the Nanjing Eco High-Tech

Island project are all joint projects between the governments of China and Singapore, or between government-linked companies of the two countries.[12] In short, they are state projects rather than "Chinese overseas" projects from Singapore.

In fact, the Singapore Business Federation and Singapore Press Holdings saw OBOR as an opportunity to promote Singapore's economic development. In February 2016 they formed a "One Belt One Road" Internet portal based on the website of *Lianhe Zaobao,* Singapore's largest circulation Chinese language newspaper. Chan Chun Sing, a minister in the Singapore Prime Minister's Office and chief of the labour union movement, who attended the event, told the press that the Chongqing Connectivity Initiative (CCI), a new Singapore–China government-led project in the western Chinese city, would launch its master plan in March 2016. "This will be a blueprint to guide the development of the project for the next two to three years .... The plan aims to integrate the air, land and sea dimensions of connectivity, which will allow Chongqing to become the node of western China in terms of transport and logistics."[13]

Another recent example is in Indonesia, i.e., the Jakarta–Bandung high speed train project, which was approved by both Beijing and Jakarta in 2015. This mega project is being undertaken by the China Development Bank and the China State Railway Company, on the one hand, and four Indonesian state-owned enterprises, on the other hand. The capital required is US$5.5 billion and it would take at least two and half years to complete.[14] This will be the first overseas bullet train project undertaken by China and is seen by President Xi Jinping as representing "early strategic connection between China and Indonesia". Here again, no Chinese overseas company is involved.

In addition, there is no evidence that China won the Indonesian high speed train project over Japan because of an Indonesian Chinese business connection. The available evidence at the moment is that China was able to offer Indonesia a better deal than Japan. Both of the prime movers of the project on the Indonesian side — Indonesian President, Joko Widodo, who would like to stimulate the sluggish Indonesian economy, and Rini Sumarno, the state owned enterprises minister who was eager to showcase her abilities to her colleagues — are Javanese, not ethnic Chinese. Ironically, the Indonesian minister who had the strong reservations about the project was the transportation minister, Ignatius Jonan, who is said to be of Chinese descent.

For many informed observers, to use ethnicity and race as the foundation of international relations or international projects is dangerous as it tends to promote ethno-nationalism, which could lead to ethnic conflict in multi-ethnic countries. The promotion of Chinese transnationalism may backfire and hurt the interests of the Chinese overseas as well as the interests of China. This is especially the case in the plural societies of Southeast Asia, where Chinese transnationalism would only increase ethnic tension. In fact, China's good relations with states along the "One Belt One Road" zones would be the key to the success of the OBOR Strategy.

INVESTMENTS IN CHINA BY OVERSEAS CHINESE CAPITALISTS

From my earlier study[15] of big Chinese businesses in Southeast Asia, it appears that the absolute majority, with the exception of those in Thailand, are led by first generation Chinese who have adopted local citizenship. They are still able to speak

Chinese or Chinese dialects, and hence had been able to extend their business beyond borders.

When China began to open its doors to foreign investment, many of these ethnic Chinese started investing in China. Of these business tycoons, the most notable are those from Thailand, Malaysia, and Indonesia. Xie Guomin (谢国民 alias Dhanin Cheavanont) of Thailand, Robert Kuok (郭鹤年) of Malaysia/Singapore, and Liem Sioe Liong (林绍良 alias Sudono Salim), Oei Ek Tjhong (黄亦聪 Eka Cipta), and Li Wenzheng (李文正 alias Mochtar Riady) of Indonesia.[16] Their investments in China were made prior to the OBOR Strategy. After the announcement of the strategy, it is not known whether their investments in China, or those made by their descendants, are directly linked to the OBOR Strategy.

It should be noted that many of the ethnic Chinese capitalists in Southeast Asia invested in China more for economic rather than ethnic or patriotic reasons. Younger generation Southeast Asian capitalists of Chinese descent, for their part, may find it more difficult to invest in China as they are not familiar with the business and political environment in China. However, it may be different for Chinese new migrants who were born and brought up/educated in China. They still have close emotional links to China and are familiar with the situation in China. The four examples cited in Chapter 1 may substantiate this point. However, at the moment, it seems that there are not many such big Chinese capitalists in Southeast Asia.

CONCLUSION

Maintaining cordial relations with the states along the OBOR zones is crucial for the success of China's OBOR initiative. The role of the "Chinese overseas" in the OBOR Strategy appears to be quite limited, especially in the areas along the "One Belt" zone, where the number of Chinese overseas is small. Ethnic Chinese capitalists in Southeast Asia who are Chinese-speaking, particularly the older generation, may be able to help China, in order to help themselves, but they may not have the wherewithal to participate in mega projects, which tend to involve states-owned entities rather than private Chinese capital.

It should also be noted that ethnic Chinese capitalists in some Southeast Asian countries, being part of a minority, have often found it prudent to undertake projects jointly with their non-Chinese counterparts so that the latter could be able to share the benefits and in turn guarantee the security of their investments against possible anti-Chinese backlashes in the country. If China insists on using Chinese ethnicity as the basis for establishing relations with Southeast Asian countries and beyond, it would only deepen the suspicion of the Southeast Asian governments towards their ethnic Chinese communities. It would also hinder cooperation between the ethnic Chinese and non-Chinese communities, create tension in local societies, and in turn jeopardize China's state-to-state relations with the countries in question.

Notes

1. See Zheng Yongnian 郑永年, "'Sichou zhi lu' yu zhongguo de 'shidai jingshen'" "丝绸之路" 与中国的 "时代精神", *Lianhe Zaobao* 《联合早报》, 10 June 2014; Zheng Yongnian 郑永年, "Zhongguo chongfan sichou zhi lu de jige zhongyao wenti" 中国重返丝绸之路的几个重要问题, *Lianhe Zaobao* 《联合早报》, 17 June 2014.
2. Ibid.
3. Wang Jingwen 王敬文, "Xi Jinping ti zhanlue gouxiang: 'yidai yilu' dakai 'zhumeng kongjian'" 习近平提战略构想: "一带一路" 打开

"筑梦空间", Zhongguo Jingji Wang 中国经济网, 11 August 2014, <http://www.ce.cn/xwzx/gnsz/szyw/201408/11/t20140811_3324310.shtml> (accessed 18 March 2016).

4. Ibid.
5. For various interpretations by China's scholars, see Zhao Hong, "China's One Belt One Road: An Overview of the Debate", *Trends in Southeast Asia*, no. 6 (Singapore: ISEAS – Yusof Ishak Institute, 2016). Note, however, that Zhao failed to mention the role of the Chinese overseas in OBOR.
6. See "Towards a Community of Common Destiny and a New Future for Asia", Keynote Speech by Xi Jinping at the Boao Forum for Asia Annual Conference 2015, 28 March 2015, <http://english.boaoforum.org/hynew/19353.jhtml> (accessed 1 June 2016). Note that Xi Jinping used *hezuo changyi* (合作倡议 cooperation proposal), not strategy, to refer to OBOR, indicating the inappropriateness of the term "strategy". Nevertheless, in Chinese documents, for instance, the preface of the books by Xu Shaoshi, the term *zhanlue* (strategy) is still used, showing that OBOR is, in fact, a strategy used by China to achieve certain objectives.
7. The book series is entitled *Yidai yilu shuangxiang touzi congshu* (一带一路双向投资丛书) published by Jixie Gongye Publishing in Beijing (北京: 机械工业出版社, 2016).
8. Xu Shaoshi 徐绍史, chief editor 主编, *Zhongguo shuangxiang touzi: zhengce zhinan* 《中国双向投资: 政策指南》 (Beijing 北京: Jixie gongye chubanshe 机械工业出版社, 2016), p. vii.
9. China–Britain Business Council, "One Belt One Road" 一带一路, <www.cbbc.org/sectors/one-belt,-one-road> (accessed 18 March 2016).
10. Ibid.
11. See, for instance, the special report of *China Social Science Journal* (March 2015) which published interviews of a few Chinese professors on "One Belt One Road" and the Chinese overseas.
12. Narendra Aggarwal, "Singapore-China Ties Reach New Heights", *Business Times*, 6 November 2015; Chong Koh Ping, "Bilateral Trade and Investment Going Strong", *Straits Times*, 6 November 2015.

13. Chong Koh Ping, "Lianhe Zaobao and Singapore Business Federation Launch 'One Belt, One Road' Portal", *Straits Times*, 8 March 2016, <http://www.straitstimes.com/business/economy/lianhe-zaobao-and-singapore-business-federation-launches-one-belt-one-road-portal> (accessed 12 May 2016).
14. For a detailed report on this project, see "Sayonara Shinkansen", *Tempo*, 12–18 October 2015, pp. 86–95.
15. Leo Suryadinata, "Ethnic Chinese in Southeast Asia and their Economic Role", in *Chinese Populations in Contemporary Southeast Asian Societies: Identities, Interdependence and International Influence*, edited by M. Jocelyn Armstrong, R. Warwick Armstrong and Kent Mulliner (Richmond, Surrey: Curzon, 2001).
16. Ibid., pp. 55–73.

Chapter 12

BEIJING'S SOFT POWER BID: PROMOTION OF THE CHINESE LANGUAGE AND CONFUCIUS INSTITUTES

Since China's arrival as an economic and political power, Beijing has started efforts to project soft power.[1] Its main mode of developing soft power is the setting up of schools known as "Confucius Institutes" to spread knowledge of the Chinese language and culture across the world, including Southeast Asia. The idea is that grassroots appreciation of the Chinese language and culture would advance China's traditional diplomacy and foreign policy interests.

China's soft power projection, in fact, is not targeted at the Chinese overseas but at the non-Chinese. However, in the process, China has realized that it can also make use of the Chinese overseas to spread the Chinese language and culture. Moreover, it can "re-sinicize" the Chinese overseas and strengthen their cultural ties with China in the hope that they would serve China's national interests.

China's promotion of the Chinese language and the establishment of Confucius Institutes/Confucius Classrooms are done through Hanban (汉办), or the executive body of the Chinese Language Council International (国家汉语国际推广领导小组办公室), which is under China's Ministry of Education.

This chapter[2] attempts to briefly examine the revival of the Chinese language (known in China as the Han Language or *Hanyu* 汉语) and Chinese education in Southeast Asia. The questions it will examine are: What is the current state of Chinese language learning in Southeast Asia? Is there a revival of Chinese-medium schools in these states? How have local Chinese communities and governments reacted to the teaching of the Chinese language, especially the establishment of Confucius Institutes/Confucius Classrooms? Have the local Chinese been re-sinicized, thus hindering or slowing down the "nation-building" process in these young nations?

REGIONAL OVERVIEW

During the Cold War, while communism as well as Chinese influence was perceived to be a threat, many Southeast Asian countries implemented assimilationist policies. They restricted or even prohibited Chinese schools and the use of the Chinese language. The most extreme cases could be found in Vietnam, Indonesia, Laos, and Cambodia, where the three pillars of Chinese culture (Chinese organizations, Chinese newspapers, and Chinese schools) were eliminated. These restrictions contributed to the further indigenization of the ethnic Chinese in the region.

However, the end of the Cold War in 1990 and the rise of the PRC have changed the regional political landscape. Communist ideology is no longer perceived as a problem by Southeast Asia because the PRC has moved to a capitalist system dubbed "Socialist economy with Chinese characteristics". China's relations with the Southeast Asian states have thus improved, and economic and cultural exchanges have intensified. In addition, both the developed and developing countries witnessed a new wave of Chinese migration from the 1980s.

Having attained the hard power attributes of big powers, namely, military and economic power, the PRC is now intent on also projecting soft power. Not surprisingly, Hanban, which was first established in 2004, has been active in Southeast Asia and beyond to promote the Chinese language and culture. One of its instruments is the Confucius Institute (CI) or Kongzi Xueyuan (孔子学院).[3] Confucius institutes are usually established in partnership with selected universities in target countries. The first CI was established in South Korea in 2004. By 2007, it was reported that there were about 120 CIs in 24 countries;[4] by 2015, the number had increased to about 500 CIs in 125 countries.[5]

The number of CI and Confucius Classrooms (孔子课堂, CC) in Southeast Asia is fairly large, and some countries have more than one CI or CC (see Table 12.1). According to the Confucius Institute Online (网络孔子学院), there were 41 CIs and CCs in eight Southeast Asian countries. The earliest CIs were established in Singapore and Thailand in 2005. The establishment of CIs and CCs is linked to the state of the respective countries' relations with China as well as local conditions. Among the Southeast Asian countries that have CIs and CCs, the largest number is in Thailand (23), followed by Indonesia (7), the Philippines (3), Malaysia (2), Singapore (2), and Cambodia and Laos (1 each). Although there is no CI in Myanmar, there are two CCs within local computer institutes (电脑学苑). Brunei and Vietnam are the two Southeast Asian states that have neither CIs nor CCs. According to a report, a Chinese commercial delegation had visited Brunei in 2008, hoping to set up a CI, but nothing has happened since then.[6] Another report stated that in 2009 Vietnamese scholars appealed to their government to set up a CI but without success.[7]

TABLE 12.1
Confucius Institutes/Confucius Classrooms in Southeast Asia

Country	CI First Established	Number	CI/CC
Thailand	2005	23	Chiang Mai University (July 2005) Chulalongkorn University, Bangkok (December 2006) Burapha University, Chonburi (November 2006) Suan Dusit Rajabhat University, Bangkok (June 2006) Prince of Songkla University, Songkhla (December 2006) Khon Kaen University (May 2006)
Indonesia	2010	7	Surabaya University (June 2010) Hasanuddin University, Makassar (June 2010) Malang University (June 2010) Tanjung Pura University, Pontianak (June 2010) Maranatha Christian University, Bandung (June 2010) Al-Azhar University, Jakarta (June 2010) Kursus Mandarin July 2007.
Philippines	2006	3	Angeles University, Angeles City (October 2009) Bulacan University, Malolos (November 2007) Ateneo de Manila University, Quezon City (October 2006)

TABLE 12.1 *(continued)*

Singapore	2005	2	Nanyang Technological University (June 2005) Singapore Kong Zi School (July 2007)
Malaysia	2010	2	University of Malaya, Kuala Lumpur (July 2009) Global Hanyu Malaysia (2005/September 2006)
Cambodia	2009	1	Royal Academy of Cambodia, Phnom Penh (August 2009)
Laos	2009	1	National University of Laos, Vientiane (September 2009)
Myanmar	2008	2	Fuxing Language & Computer School, Yangon (February 2008) Fuqing Language & Computer School, Mandalay (February 2008)
Vietnam	–	0	–
Brunei	–	0	–

Source: Compiled from Confucius Institute Online 网络孔子学院, <http://www.chinesecio.com/> (accessed 20 September 2012). Translation to English is by the author.

Although not all countries are enthusiastic about the establishment of CIs, many welcome Beijing to send Chinese teachers to the region to conduct free Chinese classes. Many Southeast Asian states have also been happy to have their language teachers trained in Chinese universities.

China's initiatives aside, the Chinese language has also organically spread in several Southeast Asian countries as there are now fewer reservations about the language and culture of a country that today is plugged into the global economy. In the Indochinese states and Myanmar, the three cultural pillars of Chinese have been allowed to re-emerge. Chinese schools in a different format have begun to appear. In Laos and Cambodia, for instance, enrolments at local Chinese schools have increased, with many of the students being ethnic Chinese and some non-Chinese. Nevertheless, as the Chinese language and culture had been suppressed for several decades, these Chinese children have low Chinese language standards. Many have been learning Chinese using local languages as a learning medium. However, the children of new Chinese migrants are better equipped to study the language.

CAMBODIA

During the reign of Prince Norodom Sihanouk, Cambodia had Chinese medium schools. One of the most famous ones in Phnom Penh was named Duanhua (端华). In 1970, General Lon Nol staged a coup, which brought into power a right-wing military group. Almost all Chinese schools in Cambodia, totalling more than 200, were closed down. Nevertheless, in Kratie, a border province between Cambodia and Vietnam that was under the control of the Khmer Rouge communist rebel forces, Chinese schools were still allowed to operate. However, this tolerance was short-lived: in March 1974, the Khmer Rouge changed its policy and closed down all Chinese schools in Kratie. In 1975, the Khmer Rouge "liberated" Cambodia and began to establish a "socialist state". It decided to eradicate those who were considered "enemies of socialism", including the ethnic Chinese who were urban dwellers. In theory, the policy was without ethnic overtones but it was soon revealed that the Khmer Rouge not only prohibited the ethnic Chinese from using their language but also induced them to abandon their traditions. Later, the use of the Chinese language and practice of Chinese culture were prohibited. Whoever spoke the Chinese language or dialects was considered to have committed a crime. Therefore, many Cambodian Chinese hid their ethnic identity, fearing punishment.

Thus, the Chinese language and culture had not only been suppressed by the pro-American Lon Nol government but also by the communist regime led by Pol Pot. Pol Pot's policy was more extreme as it was aimed at eradicating both the Chinese language and culture. In December 1978 Vietnamese troops invaded Cambodia and installed a pro-Hanoi regime. But the position of Chinese language and culture did not improve much. As there had been no Chinese schools in Cambodia for more than twenty years, the ethnic Chinese community in Cambodia gradually lost their "mother tongue". The younger generation could only communicate in Khmer.

It was only after the end of the Cold War and the withdrawal of Vietnamese troops from Cambodia in 1989 that Chinese schools were re-established. In September 1992, the Duanhua School was officially re-opened. Many former Chinese school teachers returned to their teaching positions. According to one source, the local Chinese community sponsored the Chinese schools, as in the past, because ethnic Chinese leaders were eager to revive the Chinese language and culture in Cambodia.[8] By 2006, there were about seventy Chinese schools in Cambodia, of which eleven were located in Phnom Penh. Many of the promoters of Chinese education in Cambodia are former local Chinese school teachers and students.

Duanhua School has about 11,000 students on the main and branch campuses. Apart from day-time students, it has 2,000 students who attend evening school. The teaching and administrative staff number approximately 300. Most subjects, such as General Knowledge, Mathematics, Geography and History, are taught in Mandarin, while the Cambodian language is taught four or five periods a week. The school uses primary school textbooks jointly prepared by the Cambodian General Chinese Association and Jinan University (Guangdong). However, its high school textbooks are prepared by Dong Jiao Zong (董教总), the Malaysian United Chinese Schools Teachers' Association and United Chinese School Committees' Association. Since there are not enough Chinese school teachers to teach in Cambodia, the Cambodian Chinese community has asked for assistance from the PRC government to send Chinese language teachers, especially to teach the more advanced courses.

Nevertheless, the Chinese standards of Chinese Cambodian students are low as they generally speak Khmer rather than Chinese at home. And, in view of their low standards, the Khmer language is increasingly used in schools to help students understand Mandarin. Recent changes in the Cambodian school system have also affected the Chinese schools. Previously, Cambodia had a half-day school system, with many Chinese students attending two schools: a Cambodian school and a Chinese school. However, in 2006 the Cambodia government changed the school system to a whole-day system. This affected the ability of the Chinese schools to attract enough students. As a result, the Chinese community in Cambodia began to transform Chinese schools into bilingual or even trilingual schools in order to keep their students. They strengthened their courses in Khmer and English in order to survive. The transformation apparently was quite successful as Duanhua School has managed to maintain its high student enrolments.

In recent years, as Sino–Cambodian relations improved significantly, a Confucius Institute was set up within the Royal Academy of Cambodia in Phnom Penh in 2009.

LAOS

The situation in Laos is quite similar to that of Cambodia as it was heavily influenced by Vietnam. Between 1975 and 1990, the Chinese community in Laos encountered suppression. Only after the end of the Vietnamese occupation of Cambodia did the Laotian government revise its policy. Chinese schools started to re-emerge. There are now five "Chinese medium schools" in Laos. One of the largest Chinese schools is Liaodu Gongxue (寮都公学). All the Chinese schools are under the management of the Zhonghua Lishihui (Chinese Council). The schools use some teaching materials from mainland China while others are produced locally. However, as most of the Chinese Laotian children have low commands of the Chinese language, these schools in reality are bilingual schools.[9] Owing to its better quality compared to state schools, many Laotians (including non-Chinese) sent their children to Liaodu Gongxue. Those who can afford it, send their children overseas for further studies, either to the West or to China (Beijing and Guangzhou are their favorite destinations). Similar to Cambodia, Laos has allowed the establishment of a Confucius Institute. This is within the National University of Laos in Vientiane.

VIETNAM

Following the unification of South and North Vietnam in 1975, about 300 Chinese medium schools were closed down. Chinese Vietnamese were unable to study Chinese for a long time. The Sino–Vietnamese war of 1979 made the study of the Chinese language even more difficult. Only in the 1980s, when Sino–Vietnamese relations improved, were the restrictions on the study of Chinese relaxed. The restrictions were further relaxed in the

1990s. Nevertheless, there is no full-fledged Chinese medium school, as there had been in the pre-1975 period.

However, there are Chinese language institutes or learning centres. Most of the Chinese Vietnamese have been attending Vietnamese schools and have lost their command of the Chinese language. However, some keen Chinese parents send their children to these Chinese language centres. In Ho Chi Minh City there are around twenty such Chinese language centres. But, according to one publication, the number of Chinese children studying at these centres has declined.

As in the two other Indochinese states, the standard of Chinese language in Vietnam has declined. But, unlike in Cambodia and Laos, there is no Confucius Institute in Vietnam.

THAILAND

Thailand is well known for its assimilationist policy towards the ethnic Chinese, which has been successful. Nevertheless, it allows the existence of ethnic Chinese organizations and Chinese language newspapers. But Chinese medium schools were transformed into Thai medium schools, with allowance for the teaching of Chinese up to Primary Four level.

Since 1992, with better relations between China and Thailand, the facilities for Chinese language learning in Thailand have also improved. The teaching of the Chinese language in Chinese medium schools that were transformed to Thai medium schools has been extended from Primary Four to up to Primary Six level. Although no Chinese medium schools have been established, Chinese language institutes, language centres, and evening schools (yexue 夜学) have emerged. Currently, there are seventy-six such Chinese language learning facilities throughout Thailand, of which the largest and most famous is Dongfang Wenhua Xueyuan (Academy of Eastern Culture).

There is a serious shortage of Chinese language teachers in Thailand. Therefore, Mae Fah Leung University in Thailand's Chiang Rai province established the Association of Fostering Chinese Language Teaching (泰国华教促进会) to train Chinese language teachers. It also plans to set up a teachers' training centre in Bangkok to train Chinese language teachers. Some Sino–Thai organizations send their teachers to China to upgrade their Mandarin standards.

In addition, "Chinese studies" programmes have been established in a number of Thai universities, including Chulalongkorn University. However, the standards of Chinese among the Chinese Thai students are low as they prefer to speak Thai. In fact, Thai has become the language of the Chinese Thai. It seems that the Chinese language can flourish in Thailand only with a large number of Chinese new migrants.

THE PHILIPPINES

Prior to 1975, Chinese schools in the Philippines used Taiwanese textbooks and were controlled by Taiwan groups, if not by the Taiwanese government. However, in 1975 the Philippine government started a Filipinization process, which gradually indigenized the Chinese schools. These new schools have been mistakenly called Filipinized "Chinese" schools as they are run by the Chinese community and the students are mainly Chinese. The schools had a restriction on the teaching of the Chinese language. According to one source, Chinese could not be taught for more than 100 minutes a day.[10] Besides, the curricula had to be changed and the use of Taiwan textbooks was no longer permitted.

After the Philippines established diplomatic ties with the PRC in 1975, PRC influence began to penetrate into Chinese language education in the Philippines. Chinese *Pinyin* and *Jiantizi* began to be introduced but many pro-Taiwan Chinese schools refused to accept the reform. Therefore, there was a kind of dualism in Chinese language learning in the Philippines.

As in many Southeast Asian countries, the ethnic Chinese in the Philippines experienced a nation-building process. Many study English and Tagalog in school and there has been a decline in the enrollment of students in the so-called Chinese schools. Currently, there are still around 160 "Chinese schools" in the Philippines[11] but, according to one publication, the standard of the Chinese language among Chinese students is not high.[12] Some observers have noted that the rise of China is likely to boost the learning of the Chinese language and culture in the Philippines.

INDONESIA

It is common knowledge that the thirty-two years of President Suharto's "New Order" rule (1966–98) witnessed the introduction of total assimilation for the Chinese community in Indonesia. The three Chinese cultural pillars, i.e., Chinese socio-political organizations, Chinese schools, and Chinese newspapers (mass media), were eradicated. But the fall of Suharto in May 1998 and the democratization process that followed led to the end of the suppression of the Chinese language and culture. Chinese organizations and Chinese mass media re-emerged. However, the full-fledged Chinese medium schools that had existed in the pre-Suharto era did not reappear. Instead, so-called trilingual schools (三语学校) were established. The reasons for not re-establishing full-fledged Chinese schools are complex: the thirty-two years of the "New Order" had indigenized Chinese Indonesians, not only in terms of citizenship but also language and culture.

The new Chinese schools in theory follow the curriculum of Indonesia's national schools, except that the Chinese language and English are also taught in addition to Bahasa Indonesia. Some trilingual schools have tended to spend more time teaching Chinese in order to attract those parents who are eager to have their children learn their "mother tongue". In the past decade, quite a few of the old Chinese schools in major cities such as Jakarta and Surabaya have been "revived". For instance, Pah Hwa (八华) School and Pah Chung (巴中) School have been revived in Jakarta. But these schools, in fact, are different from the original schools as they are trilingual schools rather than Chinese medium schools.

It is worth noting that the activists behind the promotion of the Chinese language and Chinese schools are former Chinese school teachers or students. Many of them had obtained degrees or certificates from Chinese universities (e.g., Xiamen University) through correspondence courses. However, most of the trilingual schools charge higher than average school fees and the number of these schools is relatively small. Therefore, their impact has not been significant. The majority of Chinese Indonesian students attend regular Indonesian national schools; many parents even send their children to school in Singapore and the West. Those who go to China to study are still rather small in number.

Hanban has been active in Indonesia. Initially, the Indonesian government was not keen on establishing Confucian Institutes. However, in the past few years, a few have been established.

The most recent Confucius Institute in Indonesia was set up at an Islamic university in Jakarta, Al Azhar University. A local Chinese businessman, Burhan Uray (Bong Swan An 黄双安), donated a building to be used for the Confucius Institute via the good offices of a foundation known as Yayasan Nabil, set up by Eddie Lembong (汪友山). The institute has facilities for students of Al-Azhar to learn Mandarin. In addition, it provides for Al-Azhar students to go to Fujian Teachers Training University in China to take a Mandarin course.

The setting up of the Confucius Institute at the Islamic university seems to have been a fairly sensitive issue. It is interesting to note that while the Confucius Institute is still known by its usual name in Chinese characters, i.e., Kongzi Xueyuan, its Indonesian equivalent, Pusat Bahasa Tionghoa (Chinese Language Centre), has no mention of the word "Confucius". This omission could be because Confucianism, known as Agama Khonghucu (Confucian Religion), is recognized as an organized religion in Indonesia. The dropping of the word "Confucius" may be due to concerns that some Indonesians may mistake the language institute for a religious one.

It should be noted that Hanban's activities in Indonesia are not without problems. On 20 April 2012, for instance, Li Yinze (李印泽), the chief of Hanban in Beijing, who was visiting Indonesia and was invited to give a talk by the Indonesian Chinese Chamber of Commerce (印尼中华总商会), made a speech that ruffled both Chinese Indonesians and the indigenous population. Li was reported to have stated:

> The purpose of my visit this time is to help the younger generation Chinese overcome the problem of learning the Han language. To study the Han language and understand Chinese

> culture is significant for enhancing the cohesiveness of the Chinese nation (中华民族). Therefore, I hope overseas young Chinese will be willing to study the Han language, in order to strengthen communication and interaction between them and young people in China, to strengthen their national identity (民族认同感).[13]

The speech, which was reported in the *Guoji Ribao*, a Chinese language newspaper in Jakarta, triggered negative reactions. The Chinese daily criticized Li Yinze for not understanding the overseas situation, while an Indonesian newspaper published a letter from a reader urging the Indonesian government to dissolve Chinese organizations and associations in Indonesia as they were a potential "fifth column" for the PRC. A professor from Peking University, Liang Yingming (梁英明), wrote an article criticizing Li Yinze's speech for being confusing and contrary to historical developments.

However, the above incident did not spiral out of control. In fact, many Indonesian newspapers were not aware of it, and, unlike in the past, the Indonesian government did not launch any official protest, indicating that Sino–Indonesian relations are cordial and Indonesian politicians have been preoccupied with other issues.

MALAYSIA

Malaysia is the only country in Southeast Asia where a complete Chinese education system has been in existence since even before independence. Not only does it have Chinese primary schools but also Chinese secondary schools as well as colleges. More recently, in 2012, a Chinese college in Johor was permitted to upgrade to a university, Southern University College (Nanfang Daxue Xueyuan 南方大学学院). But the existence of Chinese schools has not been uncontentious.

It should be noted that while the state tolerated Chinese primary schools, in the post-independence years, Chinese secondary schools were forced to convert to national-type schools in exchange for state funding. Those schools that refused to convert and have remained essentially Chinese medium schools are known as Chinese independent schools (or Duli Zhongxue 独立中学). They are financially independent. In 1955 there were only twenty such independent schools but by the 1980s the number had increased to sixty. Subsequently, the government refused to let the Chinese community establish more independent schools.

However, the socio-political landscape in Malaysia has changed in recent years. The political system has been gradually democratized and a stronger political opposition and civil society forces have emerged, forcing the UMNO-dominated Barisan Nasional government to adopt a more relaxed policy towards Chinese education. Responding to Chinese pressure, the government eventually allowed the Chinese to set up a new independent school — Chong Hwa High School — in Kuantan, Pahang, in 2012.[14] In fact, "Chinese colleges" such as New Era (新纪元) in Kuala Lumpur and Han Chiang (韩江) in Penang had already been established in the late 1990s. This relaxed approach to Chinese education has taken place against the backdrop of the globalization of education, which has led to a mushrooming of private international educational institutes.

In 2009, a Confucius Institute (Kongzi Xueyuan) was established at the University of Malaysia. The Chinese name for it is Malaixiya kongzi hanyu xueyuan (马来西亚孔子汉语学院). The insertion of the term *hanyu kongzi* and *xueyuan* is understandable because, as in Indonesia, Kongzi (Confucius) is often associated with Kongjiao (Religion of Kongzi). Earlier, another language centre had been established, also by Hanban, but outside a local university. That centre, too, does not carry the Kongzi Xueyuan name.

The recognition of Chinese university degrees will have a positive impact on the Chinese language and Chinese education in Malaysia. However, the Malay community is not united on the issue of Chinese education and independent Chinese schools; the issue could become problematic again if inter-ethnic politics intensifies.

SINGAPORE

In the early post-independence years, Singapore had a sizeable number of Chinese schools. Upon independence, as part of its nation-building efforts, the Singapore government introduced a bilingual education policy. This policy required all students attending English medium schools to learn their respective "mother tongues" as a second language (in the case of the ethnic Chinese, the mother tongue is Mandarin or *Putonghua*), while students at the vernacular schools, including Chinese schools, had to learn English as well. With the rising importance of English as a global language of commerce, science, and technology, enrolment at the vernacular schools gradually declined, and many of these schools closed down as parents saw the utility of sending their children to English schools.

By the late 1970s, the government began to realize that the standard of Chinese had declined seriously, threatening the survival of Chinese culture and Chinese heritage. The government then introduced a "Speak Mandarin" campaign that sought to discourage the use of Chinese dialects, whose use was perceived to be eroding the standards of Chinese literacy among Chinese Singaporeans and also dividing the Chinese community. Nevertheless, since most Chinese Singaporeans were learning Mandarin as a second language, their Mandarin standards remained lower than that of their first language. Then, in 1979, the government introduced a limited number of what are known as "Special Assistance Plan" (SAP) schools. These are Chinese schools where students learn both Chinese and English at first language level.

Nevertheless, as Chinese Singaporeans are not a homogeneous group, many children with non-Chinese education backgrounds have not been able to perform well in their mother tongue subject. The government again reviewed its policy in recent years to allow students who were struggling with the mother tongue to take modules that gave greater weightage to their oral, rather than written, skills. This policy is not without its critics.

Singapore, in short, does not have pure Chinese medium schools. Nevertheless, Chinese education has not disappeared. Through bilingual education the Chinese language has been retained. However, in general, the standards of the Chinese language among average young Chinese Singaporeans are not high. This has raised the concern of many Chinese parents and Chinese educators. Although efforts have been made to try to improve the standards of the Chinese language among Chinese Singaporeans, English remains the first language for many of them.

Singapore was one of the first countries in Southeast Asia to establish a Confucius Institute, which is located at the Nanyang Technological University. Although the institute offers Chinese language courses, most of its courses are advanced ones on Chinese culture (including Confucianism) to cater to the needs of Singaporeans who already have a fairly good foundation in the Chinese language.

CONCLUSION

Chinese language learning and Chinese education in Southeast Asia regained popularity after the 1990s, when the threat of communism receded and China plugged into the global economic system became an economic heavyweight. However, the popularity of the Chinese language and education differs from country to country. It is linked to the state of China's relations with each country in the region, as well as the size of the ethnic Chinese population in each country. Using the learning of the Chinese language and the establishment of Confucius Institutes as indicators of China's soft power, we may be able to judge how successful China has been in Southeast Asia.

In Singapore and Malaysia, where there are sizeable numbers of ethnic Chinese, Chinese language learning has continued. Nevertheless, while Chinese medium schools have survived in Malaysia, in Singapore they have died out. Instead, all ethnic Chinese children in Singapore are required to study their "mother tongue", i.e., Mandarin or *Huayu*, as defined by the Singapore state. With the rise of China and improvement of Sino–Malaysian and Sino–Singapore relations, the demand for the learning of the Chinese language and culture has also increased. Nevertheless, one needs to note that the contents of the Chinese publications and media in these countries are different from those of mainland China; they do not reflect the national contents of China but their own national contents. In other words, the establishment of CIs has managed to increase the influence of China in these countries but has not enhanced China's soft power as yet.

If the Chinese language learning has been popular in both Malaysia and Singapore, this is not the case with many other Southeast Asian countries. Some countries at one time discouraged and restricted the study of the Chinese language and even banned Chinese schools. They were suspicious of Beijing's intentions and were not enthusiastic about Chinese language learning and Chinese education. Nevertheless, the collapse of communism and the rise of China as a major economic and political power have forced many countries to re-examine their policy towards the Chinese community and Chinese language. These countries have relaxed the regulations on their Chinese communities and on the use of the Chinese language. Many (e.g., Indonesia, the Philippines, Thailand, Cambodia, and Laos) have allowed the establishment of CIs but others (e.g., Myanmar, Brunei, and Vietnam) have only allowed the establishment of Chinese language centres. These differences show the limited and uneven success of Beijing in spreading its soft power in the Southeast Asian region.

Concerned about nation-building, the Southeast Asian countries fear that the revival of the Chinese language and culture may hinder the cohesiveness of their young nations. On the other hand, they cannot ignore the rapid rise of China. They recognize that knowledge of the Chinese language is necessary for dealing with the economic heavyweight that China has become. Faced with this dilemma, the Southeast Asian countries have often given in to economic reality, provided that the price they pay is not too high.

Owing to the past policy of hostility or neglect towards the Chinese language, the Southeast Asian countries (with the exception of Malaysia and possibly Singapore) face a shortage of Chinese language teachers. Also, the standards of the Chinese language among their ethnic Chinese populations are low. Therefore, in the past few years, if not the past decade, many of these countries began taking steps to catch up. The road ahead is still long and bumpy.

Southeast Asian Chinese students have to learn their respective local languages and English, often at the expense of the Chinese language. Politically, this may be the way to resolve the problem of national identity. Interestingly non-Chinese Southeast Asians have also been learning the Chinese language, which helps to deflect concerns that only the ethnic Chinese learn the language. Nevertheless, anti-Chinese and anti-Chinese-language forces have not gone away. At the same time, China's policy towards the ethnic Chinese and the Southeast Asian states will continue to affect the Chinese community and Chinese language. Comments such as those by Hanban's director on the relationship between learning Chinese and Chinese nationalist identity, together with China's blurring the distinction between *huaqiao* and *huaren*, may generate ethnic divisions within Southeast Asia and also impede the development of the Chinese language.

Notes

1. "Soft power", as coined and defined by Joseph Nye, i.e., "the ability to co-opt others through the attractiveness of one's institutions, ideas, values, culture, and the perceived legitimacy of policies". See Joseph S. Nye Jr., *The Future of Power* (New York: Public Affairs, Perseus Books Group, 2011), p. 20. However, the PRC has different interpretation of the term, which refers to Chinese business and other non-military elements. For a discussion on China's soft power from the Chinese perspective, see Ooi Kee Beng, ed., *The Eurasian Core and its Edges: Dialogues with Wang Gungwu on the History of the World* (Singapore: Institute of Southeast Asian Studies, 2015), pp. 173–77.

2. This chapter is mainly based on the author's keynote speech at the regional conference on "Chinese Language Teaching and Education in a Globalizing Southeast Asia", organized jointly by the Confucius Institute of the Ateneo de Manila University and International Society for the Study of Chinese Overseas (ISSCO), held in Manila on 17–18 August 2012.
3. For a brief introduction on the Confucius Institute in the world, see Grace Chew Chye Lay, "The Confucius Institute in the World: An Overview", *CHC Bulletin*, no. 9 (May 2007): 13–19.
4. Ibid., p. 15.
5. The official Hanban website mentioned that by 2015 there were about 500 CIs in 125 countries: Asia (32 countries/areas) 110 CIs; Africa (32 countries/areas): 46 CIs; Europe (40 countries/areas): 169 CIs; the Americas (18 countries/areas): 157 CIs; Oceania (3 countries): 18 CIs. See 汉办官网-孔子学院-国家汉办 <www.hanban.edu.cn/confuciousinstitutes> (accessed 12 May 2016).
6. Guangxi zhongxiao qiye wang 广西中小企业网, "Zhongguo jihua zai Wenlai sheli Longzi Xueyuan" 中国计划在文莱设立孔子学院, 19 September 2008, <http://smegx.gov.cn/gxsme/xwpt/article.jsp?id=7110> (accessed 20 September 2012).
7. Kongmeng zhi xiang wang 孔孟之乡网, "Yuenan xuezhe huyu jinkuai chengli Kongzi Xueyuan" 越南学者呼吁尽快成立孔子学院, 31 October 2009, <http://www.kmzx.org/Article/ShowArticle.asp?ArticleID=4284> (accessed 20 September 2012).
8. Huang Zhaoxian 郑昭贤, "Lijing cangsang de lao xiaozhang" 历经沧桑的老校长, in *Dongnanya huaren de jingshen: jianren buba*《东南亚华人的精神: 坚韧不拔》(Selangor: Celue Zixun yanjiu zhongxin 策略资讯研究中心, 2009), pp. 161–64.
9. Cui Guiqiang 崔贵强, ed. 主编, *You yangguang de difang jiuyou huaren*《有阳光的地方就有华人》[Where the Sun Shines, There Are Chinese], (Singapore, 2009), p. 165.
10. Ibid., p. 135.

11. See the short write up "Chinese Language Education in the Philippines: From Taiwan to China", by Clark Alejandrino and Ellen Palanca, *CHC Bulletin*, no. 18 (October 2012): 12–13.
12. Cui Guiqiang, ed. *You yangguang de difang jiuyou huaren*, op. cit., p. 135.
13. *Guoji Ribao*《国际日报》, "Beijing shi qiaoban zhuren Li Yinze fang Yinni jianghua yingqi qiaojie buman" 北京市侨办主任李印泽访印尼讲话引起侨界不满 [The Speech of Beijing's Qiaoban Director Li Yinze Caused Worries Among the Chinese Community], 21 April 2012.
14. *Lianhe Zaobao*《联合早报》, "Guandan duzhong zhengshi huozhun chengli" 关丹独中正式获准成立, 28 July 2012; Moe Clarifies Decision on Chong Hwa High School Kuantan, <http://schooladvisor.my/news/moe-clarifies-decision-on-chong-hwa-high-school-kuantan> (accessed 2 March 2016).

PART IV

New Policy and Its Impact

Chapter 13

BEIJING'S NEW POLICY: A RETURN TO CHINESE TRANSNATIONALISM?

The previous chapters dealt with Beijing's responses to both external events involving the Chinese overseas and domestic events or domestic needs in which the Chinese overseas were involved. These events occurred around the turn of the century, coinciding with the rise of China. This chapter summarizes various case studies showcasing China's new policy towards the Chinese overseas and their relationship with China's national interests. It becomes clear that, increasingly, Beijing has perceived the Chinese overseas as a form of social and economic capital for the development of China and hence fine-tuned its policy towards them. It would appear that Beijing is adopting Chinese transnationalism once again. It even had plans to introduce a *Huayi* Card that would allow persons of Chinese origin residency, but not voting, rights in China but the project was shelved owing to unfavourable responses from some Chinese overseas and non-Chinese.

BEIJING'S RESPONSES TO EXTERNAL EVENTS FROM NON-INTERVENTION TO DIRECT INTERVENTION

As noted in Chapter 4, in 1998, Beijing adopted a "hands-off policy" towards the Chinese overseas during the anti-Chinese violence in Indonesia. However, Beijing's responses to external events differ from country to country as the objective conditions in each have not been the same. As noted earlier in this study, there are various types of responses, which produce different models.

The so-called Indonesian model, the non-intervention (non-protection) model, was unique and is unlikely to be repeated. At that time, China was diplomatically isolated and required the support of a major country in Southeast Asia. As Indonesians of Chinese descent were being beaten up and raped and their homes looted, China watched helplessly as these people were no longer Chinese citizens. Many Chinese Indonesians fled to safer places and China did not stage any protest. It was only a few months later that Beijing appealed to the newly-installed Indonesian government to protect its own citizens, including those of Chinese descent.

However, it seems that there was some debate in China's foreign policy circles as to whether non-intervention was the right decision, but the policy prevailed as it served the national interests of the PRC. However, if large-scale anti-Chinese riots were to occur in Indonesia today, it is likely that Beijing would intervene.

The other five cases that took place since the turn of the century show different degrees of interference in anti-Chinese violence or ethnic tension and of protection of ethnic Chinese.

The so-called Solomon model and the Tonga saga were examples of direct intervention/protection. In April 2006, when anti-Chinese violence occurred in the Solomon Islands, Beijing repatriated those Chinese who were affected by the riots regardless of their citizenship. A few hundred Chinese were taken to Hong Kong and Guangdong to be resettled. The Solomon Islands had diplomatic ties with Taipei, not Beijing, and China's actions were intended to show that the PRC was the protector of the Chinese overseas, and, equally important, well placed to replace Taipei. Nonetheless, Beijing still failed to persuade the Solomon Islands to switch recognition.

Beijing also evacuated the Chinese in Tonga during anti-Chinese riots there several months later. It should be noted that most of the Chinese in these two South Pacific island-states were new migrants and their numbers were extremely small. Nevertheless, these two instances were the beginning of Beijing's policy of evacuating Chinese from distant lands.

In fact, the largest evacuation took place in 2011, when there was a political upheaval in Libya. About 35,000 Chinese, mainly Chinese workers employed in China's state-owned enterprises (SOEs), were affected and Beijing sent naval vessels and military aircraft to evacuate them. The protection of the "overseas Chinese" coincided with China's interest in protecting its SOEs, which represent a vital national interest.

The fourth example involved the evacuation of the Chinese during the anti-China/Chinese riots in Vietnam in May 2014. Beijing immediately sent ships and airplanes to repatriate the Chinese victims, mainly labourers or other employees of China's SOEs. This incident showed that Beijing was able and willing to protect its citizens overseas, and, again, there was no conflict between the interests of these "overseas Chinese" and China's higher order national interests. Unlike in the case of the Solomon Islands, the repatriation from Vietnam did not include Chinese overseas of other nationalities. Taiwanese and Hong Kong residents were not included either.

The fifth example was China's response to the "Nude Squat" incident in Malaysia in 2005 and the saga of the Chinese ambassador to Malaysia in 2015. The former was a case of mistaken identity that was quietly resolved, while the latter was seen as an intervention by the Malay elite and was more significant than the former case. While some Malaysian Chinese were happy with the ambassador's visit and speech, others, however, were apprehensive and concerned.

The last example discussed was China's response to the conflict between the Kokang regional army and Myanmar government forces, which took place in February 2015. The Kokang affair has a Chinese element as the Kokang are ethnically Chinese, with many of them originally from Yunnan. Therefore, the rebels were believed to have been supported by the Yunnanese and local authorities. The attitude of Beijing's government towards the Kokang rebels was ambiguous, and many rebels took refuge in Yunnan province. The festering problem can only be resolved if the Myanmar government offers the Kokang minority autonomous status and the Beijing government ceases its support for the rebels.

The examples highlighted above are varied in nature, but they also have many things in common. All of them involved the "Chinese overseas" and all took place after the rise of China and the new waves of Chinese migration. Most of the Chinese that Beijing evacuated were "new migrants". Nevertheless, the principles of China's foreign policy continue to be applicable: the Chinese overseas are protected if doing so does not come into conflict with the higher priorities in China's national interests (such as in the Solomon Islands and Tonga cases), or if their interests coincide with the higher priorities in China's national interests (such as in the case of Libya and Vietnam).

The number of overseas Chinese involved is also relevant. The repatriation of the overseas Chinese can only be done if they are in the hundreds rather than in the hundreds of thousands (e.g., the Solomon Islands and Tonga). Libya was, of course, an exception, as the Chinese involved were not just ordinary overseas Chinese but Chinese nationals working for China's SOEs. It is also important to note that the majority of the Chinese overseas repatriated were Chinese nationals or recent migrants, although in some cases (e.g., the Solomon Islands) some foreign nationals were also included. However, it would be more difficult for China to repatriate a large number of Chinese who are neither Chinese citizens nor new migrants, as in the case of Indonesia. Nevertheless, the more critical factors determining China's policy towards the Chinese overseas are China's security, economic and political interests.

In the case of Vietnam, Beijing was able to protect the overseas Chinese there because of proximity and because the majority of the Chinese there were PRC citizens. Also, they were working for Chinese companies (or at least joint venture companies between China and Vietnam). Moreover, the number involved was relatively small and more manageable. Equally important, because China has an ongoing territorial dispute with Vietnam, it needed to show its strength to the Vietnamese.

The Malaysian cases are interesting. The first case, the "Lock-up Girl" incident, involved Chinese nationals being abused by the Malaysian police and a videotape of the abuse of one of the victims allegedly being circulated. It turned out later that the woman featured in the videotape was a non-Chinese. The second case involved the Chinese ambassador visiting

Chinatown and delivering a prepared speech on extremism and racism in the wake of a racial riot following an attack on a Chinese shopkeeper by a Malay man and his friends. The Chinese involved in this case were Malaysian, not PRC, citizens. Both these incidents took place amidst Beijing's growing interest in "protecting" the Chinese overseas. Again, Beijing's behaviour in these two cases did not deviate much from the foreign policy principles discussed earlier: China's highest order national interests prevailed.

The case of Myanmar is unique as the Kokang Chinese are a "homeland minority". In other words, unlike other Chinese overseas, their traditional homeland is within Myanmar itself although they are a minority in the country. Not surprisingly, the Kokang rebels want a separate nation within Myanmar but their struggle is not fully supported by China as mainland China has its own minority separatist problem. Beijing felt that it was not in its national interest to support the Kokang rebels.

Apart from the above examples, there have been other minor conflicts since the turn of the century between the Chinese overseas and Western authorities, in which the Chinese foreign ministry later became involved. For instance, a curious incident occurred in April 2007 when the Chinese foreign ministry issued a strongly-worded statement following clashes between Chinese immigrants and Italian police in Milan. A ministry spokesperson, Qin Gang, made a statement noting, "We hope the Italian side will resolve the situation in a spirit of fairness and equity, give serious considerations to the reasonable demands of the overseas Chinese and protect their legitimate rights."[1] The Chinese government's response, however, seems disproportionate, considering that the clashes were sparked off by an ethnic Chinese woman's minor traffic offence.[2]

Anti-Chinese violence in developing countries is a complex phenomenon. The stronger economic position of the ethnic Chinese relative to that of indigenous populations has always been a factor behind anti-Chinese sentiments. Anti-Chinese violence amid these circumstances is usually triggered by some political event in which the Chinese overseas are involved or are perceived to have been involved. Occasionally, the invisible hands of Beijing or Taipei can also be identified as an important factor. Therefore, it is difficult to avoid anti-China/Chinese violence from breaking out in the future.

Nevertheless, ethnic conflicts in the West between Chinese migrants and the locals are rare. But in the future, such conflicts may flare up in countries where there are sizeable numbers of new Chinese migrants. If so, it is yet unclear where China's foreign ministry will get involved. If it does, Beijing's policy towards the Chinese overseas can be considered to have indeed changed, and the likely impact on the world needs to be carefully re-examined.

BEIJING'S RESPONSES TO INTERNAL NEEDS: FROM DUAL NATIONALITY TO SINGLE NATIONALITY TO THE *HUAYI* CARD

Beijing had long realized that the Southeast Asian states were suspicious of China and distrusted the Chinese overseas in general and the overseas Chinese in particular, fearing that they could be used by the PRC to promote its political and economic interests. To establish good relations with the Southeast Asian states, which was crucial for the security and prosperity of China, Beijing was prepared to offer a practical solution to this historical legacy, one that would be acceptable to the host countries: resolving the dual nationality (dual citizenship) problem. In 1955, during the Afro-Asian conference, Prime Minister Zhou Enlai proposed a solution to the dual nationality status of the overseas Chinese: Beijing was ready to abandon its jurisdiction over the "Chinese overseas" in countries that adopted a One-China policy and signed a dual nationality treaty with China. However, only Indonesia responded positively to the proposal at that time.

It was only after 1974, as several of the Southeast Asian countries established diplomatic relations with the PRC that Beijing declared that it no longer considered those Chinese who adopted local citizenship willingly citizens. Nevertheless, the nationality status of the Chinese was still a problem in those countries that did not have diplomatic relations with the PRC. In 1980, Beijing under Deng Xiaoping promulgated the first PRC Nationality Law, introducing single nationality status. In other words, an ethnic Chinese ceases to be a PRC national once he/she acquires foreign citizenship voluntarily. This was tantamount to declaring that China would no longer intervene in affairs of non-PRC citizens.

Following the promulgation of the Chinese Nationality Law, Beijing appeared to have ceased to "intervene" in the ethnic Chinese affairs of other countries. In April 1994, when an anti-Chinese riot took place in Medan, Indonesia, resulting in the destruction of ethnic Chinese property, Beijing's foreign ministry spokesman issued a statement to show China's concern. The Indonesian foreign ministry took exception to this statement and accused China of intervention in its domestic affairs. However the two sides decided not to pursue the matter and there was no diplomatic uproar.[3]

More significant was the May 1998 anti-Chinese riot in Indonesia. Unlike previous anti-Chinese riots, which were mainly anti-Beijing, this riot was focused on the ethnic Chinese in Indonesia. Also, unlike previous riots, this riot involved not only arson, looting, and killing but also the systematic raping of Chinese women. The barbaric event stunned the world and Chinese communities across the world condemned the violence. Yet, the PRC did not respond until two months later. Even then, the statement it issued was weak — it said China was concerned (*guanzhu* 关注) over the fate of Indonesians of Chinese descent and urged the new Habibie government to protect its citizens.

Beijing did not launch a strong protest, probably because the riots were not directed at China. Moreover, Beijing considered Jakarta an important strategic partner with which it wanted to maintain friendly relations. One could argue that the 1998 anti-Chinese riot showed that Beijing kept its promise not to intervene in the affairs of non-Chinese citizens owing to a conflict with its core national interests.

However, China's growing economic muscle by the turn of the century caused the Beijing leadership to change its attitude towards the Chinese overseas. It is essential to note that by this time, China had also begun to experience a new exodus of Chinese citizens (*xin yimin* or new migrants) to various destinations. The number of new migrants is large and many of them have skills and capital. This new wave of migrants will be fairly important for Beijing's future development. Around the same time, China began to revitalize the Overseas Chinese Affairs Office (OCAO; also known as Qiaoban), which is under the Chinese State Council.

Beijing's leaders began to rethink the importance of the Chinese overseas for China's economic development, for its economic expansion overseas, and for enlarging its political space abroad. Beijing began to blur the distinction between *huaqiao* and *huaren* and began to consider both categories of

Chinese overseas as members of one Chinese nation (*Zhonghua Minzu*) regardless of their citizenship. The purpose, it seems, was to invoke Chinese transnationalism. Beijing appealed to *huaqiao* and *huaren* to get involved in aid efforts after the Sichuan earthquake of 2008 and the torch relay and celebrations of the Beijing Olympics.

When President Xi Jinping proposed the "One Belt One Road" Strategy, the role of the Chinese overseas, especially in Southeast Asia, was considered to be important, if not crucial, for its success. Beijing thus expected the Chinese overseas, many of them in big business and or the professions, to help China's economic expansion overseas. In 2015, Beijing even initiated its own "World Overseas Chinese Entrepreneurs Conference" to appeal to the Chinese overseas to help China realize its "One Belt One Road" Strategy. This was despite the existence of the "World Chinese Entrepreneurs Convention" organized by ethnic Chinese in Southeast Asia.

To promote the spread of the Chinese language and culture, since 2004, Beijing began to establish Confucius Institutes, first in South Korea, and in the following year in Southeast Asia and beyond. The targets are not solely ethnic Chinese though in many countries they have become the prime targets. Beijing's intention was to teach those ethnic Chinese children who had lost their language skills and culture so that future generations of Chinese overseas would again identify themselves with the Chinese nation.

As stated earlier, of the new waves of Chinese migrants in recent years many went to the Western countries. Some of the migrants who had obtained citizenship in these countries began to urge Beijing in the 1990s to re-introduce dual nationality for the Chinese overseas, emulating a practice prevalent in many Western countries.[4] The issue was discussed in the China's

People's Political Assembly but the proposal was rejected.[5] Apparently, Beijing realized that it would not be in the national interest of the PRC to return to the practice of dual nationality as this would only enhance the suspicions that many countries harboured of China, especially the countries of Southeast Asia. To resolve the problem, Beijing in 2004, introduced a "Green Card" (Permanent Residency) policy, but the requirements for this card have been too rigid and not many people have been able to obtain it. It should also be noted that the Green Card system is not for the ethnic Chinese overseas only; but for all foreigners who qualify. However, at the end of 2015 Beijing announced that it would introduce a new Green Card system which is specially designed for *huaren*, i.e. Chinese with foreign citizenship.

HUAYI CARD

On 5 December 2015, *Ming Bao*, a major Chinese language daily in Hong Kong, reported that on 27 November 2015 Guo Hong 郭洪, the director of the management committee of the Zhong Guan Cun 中关村 (known as the "Silicon Valley of China", located in Beijing), had made an unexpected announcement of a pilot project known as the *Huayi* Card (*Huayi Ka* 华裔卡) system.[6] According to the announcement, the card would be issued to any qualified person of Chinese origin so that he/she could stay in China as a permanent resident and enjoy almost all the privileges of a Chinese citizen. This card is different from dual nationality status as the card holder does not have the right to vote and to be voted.

According to the report, the project was being introduced because of the need for China to recruit more professionals for high technology and economic development. The idea came from the Indian practice of issuing two types of identity cards for Indians overseas known as Persons of Indian Origin (PIOs) cards and Overseas Citizens of India (OCI) cards.[7] According to the report, after the introduction of these two card systems, some 4 million OCIs and 7 million POIs had returned to India to work, as of 2010.[8]

The report also said that between 1978 and 2005, US$622.4 billion worth of investments were injected into the Chinese economy, of which 67 per cent came from the Chinese overseas. Some 550,000 companies with foreign capital had been registered during the same period, of which 70 per cent were owned by ethnic Chinese. In Zhong Guan Cun, there were 2 million entrepreneurs (*chuangye renshi* 创业人士), both foreign nationals and "returned overseas Chinese", constituting only 1.5 per cent, while in California's Silicon Valley some 36 per cent of the entreprenuers were from overseas.

It was reported that after the reform era in China, about 7 million Chinese had migrated, and there were also more than one million Chinese students overseas. The report noted that as of 2015 there were about "60 million overseas Chinese all over the world", of which about 4 million were entrepreneurs. These are the targets of the *Huayi* Card policy.

About ten years since China introduced the Green Card permanent residency system, it has issued fewer than 10,000 Green Cards to foreigners, including people of Chinese origin. China's appears to be the hardest Green Card to obtain in the world. The *Huayi* Card system is meant to help ease the problem of obtaining some sort of status in China for the Chinese overseas. Many Chinese new migrants in the West would like to have dual nationality status and the *Huayi* Card is a form of compromise. Some have even argued that the *Huayi* Card would be a prelude to the introduction of a dual nationality law in China. The difference between the Green Card and *Huayi Ka* is that the former is ethnicity-blind, while the latter is based on ethnicity.

The announcement has caused a lot of confusion. Some thought the *Huayi* Card had already been introduced but the authorities said that this was not the case. It would only be a pilot and would be tried out in 2016. Presumably, the system would be tested on a small group of foreign Chinese first and if the result was promising, it would then be implemented on a larger scale.

It seems that Beijing has now started thinking along the lines of ethnicity. Observers may hastily conclude that China is advocating Chinese transnationalism. But the term *huayi* has not been clearly defined. Is the term used to refer to Han Chinese only or to both Han and non-Han Chinese overseas? In any case, the *Huayi* Card system will have a tremendous impact on the Chinese overseas as their loyalties to their host countries may come under suspicion. Owing to its sensitivity, there were suggestions that the card be tried out in Canada first, where dual nationality is allowed and the ethnic Chinese issue is not sensitive.

As stated earlier, the *Huayi* Card system was criticized by many observers who understand the Chinese overseas situation, especially in Southeast Asia. In China, Professor Liang Yingming of Peking University commented on its shortcomings and the risks associated with adopting the ethnic principle in issuing permanent residency rights.[9] The Chinese press in Singapore also published reports that were unflattering of the *Huayi* Card.[10] Probably because of such criticisms, OCAO had second thoughts on introducing the system at the moment. The director of OCAO, Qiu Yuanping, announced on 8 March 2016 that the report concerning the *Huayi* Card was untrue.[11] Later, there was a similar report which quoted her as saying that OCAO did not have any plans to issue *Huayi* Cards. However, OCAO would amend the existing regulations to make it easier for foreigners of Chinese descent (*waiji huaren*) to get permanent resident status and enjoy other facilities in China.[12] In other words, the scheme has been shelved for the time being.

Notes

1. People's Daily Online 人民网, "China Hopes Italy to Resolve Police-Chinese Clash Fairly", 13 April 2007, <http://en.people.cn/200704/13/eng20070413_366343.html> (accessed 12 December 2015).
2. Ibid.
3. For a discussion of this event, see *Tempo*, "Mencari Kerok dan Intimidasi", 30 April 1994, pp. 21–32.
4. Zhou Nanjing 周南京, ed., *Jingwai huaren guoji wenti taolun ji*《境外华人国籍问题讨论辑》(Hong Kong 香港: Hong Kong Press for Social Science Ltd. 香港社会科学出版社, 2005), pp. 175–76.
5. Ibid., pp. 177–78.
6. See *Ming Bao*《明报》, "Zhongguo shixing 'huayi ka', zhenshi chengren shuangchong guoji" 中国试行"华裔卡"真实承认双重国籍, 6 December 2015, <www.mingpaocanada.com/tor/htm/News/20151205/taa1_r.htm> (accessed 10 December 2015). The discussion in this section is mainly based on this report.
7. For Chinese studies on PIO and OCI, see Zhang Yinglong 张应龙 and Huang Chaohui 黄朝辉, "Yindu qiaomin zhengce yanjiu" 印度侨民政策研究, in *Jingwai huaren guoji wenti taolunji*《境外华人国际问题讨论辑》, edited by Zhou Nanjing 周南京 (Hong Kong 香港: Hong Kong Press for Social Science Ltd. 香港社会科学出版社, 2005), pp. 290–311; Qiu Li Ben 丘立本, "Yindu Guoji yimin yu qiaowu gongzuo de lishi yu xianzhuang" 印度国际移民与侨务工作的历史与现状, *Huaqiao huaren lishi yanjiu*《华侨华人历史研究》, no. 1 (March 2012): 24–35. According to these studies, the Indian government introduced the PIO card in March 1999 and the OCI card in

January 2003. Both cards have a common feature, i.e., the card holders do not have political rights in India. The PIO card was merged into the OCI card on 9 January 2015. See Indian Ministry of Home announcement at <http://mha1.nic.in/pdfs/Merge_PIO_OCI.pdf> (accessed 5 February 2016).

8. The *Ming Bao* report, op. cit., cited figures of 40 million OCI and 70 million POI, which seem to be unrealistically excessive and erroneous.
9. *Lianhe Zaobao*《联合早报》, "Beida jiaoshou liang yingming: zhongguo yao lizhi kandai haiwai huaren lichang" 北大教授梁英明: 中国要理智看待海外华人立场, 22 February 2016.
10. For instance, *Lianhe Zaobao*《联合早报》, "Bendi xuezhe: mohu huaqiao huaren jiexian" 本地学者: 模糊华侨华人界限, 19 February 2016.
11. Zhongguo Xinwen Wang 中国新闻网, "Qiu Yuanping huiying qiaojie guanzhu redian: 'Huayi Ka' baodao bushushi" 裘援平回应侨界关注热点: "华裔卡" 报道不属实, 10 March 2016, <http://www.chinanews.com/gn/2016/03-10/7792404.shtml> (accessed 20 April 2016).
12. China Daily 中国日报中文网, "Guowuyuan qiaoban zhuren Qiu Yuanping: muqian hai wei kaolü chutai Huayi Ka" 国务院侨办主任裘援平:目前还未考虑出台华裔卡, 13 March 2016, <http://cn.chinadaily.com.cn/2016lianghui/2016-03/13/content_23844522.htm> (accessed 20 April 2016).

Chapter 14

THE IMPACT OF BEIJING'S CHANGING POLICY

As the Chinese overseas are not a homogeneous group, and their situation differs from country to country, it is difficult to make generalizations regarding the impact of Beijing's changing policies on them. Nevertheless, this chapter discusses some broad and general impacts of China's changing policies on the Chinese overseas in Southeast Asia, with special reference to three countries: Singapore, Malaysia, and Indonesia. It concludes with a brief comment on the responses of some governments in the region.

GENERAL IMPACT ON THE CHINESE OVERSEAS

For ethnic Chinese businessmen who have business links with mainland China, the rise of China and the opportunities it allows them are a welcome development. Some are proud that China considers them a part of the great Chinese nation, probably unaware of the political implications of being grouped as such.

However, many are uncomfortable to be called *huaqiao* again as they are no longer citizens of the PRC. They are aware that they live in Southeast Asia, where local nationalism is at its height. They know that their political loyalties might be questioned by the indigenous people and governments of their adopted countries. This is particularly the case as China becomes more assertive in the South China Sea, which may affect ethnic relations in the Southeast Asian states that have territorial dispute with Beijing.

Most of the Chinese who moved to Southeast Asia before the new waves of Chinese migration have become local citizens,[1] but many new migrants may not have qualified for citizenship or become citizens yet. New migrants who have been naturalized may still have strong links with China and may welcome having dual nationality status, but the majority of local-born Chinese and earlier migrants do not want dual nationality, fearing that their loyalties would be questioned by the governments and peoples of their adopted lands. This is the case not only in Southeast Asia, but also in many other countries.[2]

Moreover, China's recent tendency to blur the distinction between *huaqiao* and *huaren* and its appeals to Chinse transnationalism are likely to have a negative impact on nation-building, especially in Southeast Asia, where the process is relatively new. The impact would be more serious for those new Chinese migrants who have been naturalized and expect to be accepted as loyal citizens of their adopted countries.

Apart from the difference between new and old migrants (and their descendants), it seems that the responses of the Chinese overseas to Beijing's new policy depends on the degree of their integration into local society, their economic background, and self-interest.

MALAYSIA, SINGAPORE, AND INDONESIA

As stated at the beginning, the Chinese in Southeast Asia are heterogeneous. Even within any one country, the Chinese are far from homogeneous. Understandably, their responses to Beijing's policies differ from group to group. While the region's small number of *Peranakan* Chinese[3] would be uneasy with China's policy to embrace them as part of the Chinese nation, they might also feel uneasy about China's assertiveness in the region, especially China's claims in the South China Sea.

Some Chinese Malaysians might have felt relieved that Beijing's ambassador's intervened on their behalf in 2015 to deal with Malay extremists. But in the long run they will be aware that, as citizens of another country, they will have to fend for themselves when there are ethnic conflicts. They need to live in peace with the other ethnic groups who share the same citizenship. They do not want to be called *huaqiao* or citizens of China living overseas as Malaysia is their homeland.

In Singapore, the national education policy has been quite successful. The state has introduced a bilingual policy, where students are expected to learn both English and their respective "mother tongues". For Chinese Singaporeans, the Chinese mother tongue is known as *Huayu* (华语, the language of the Hua people), to distinguish it from the mainland Chinese language, which is known as *Hanyu* (汉语, the language of the Han people). They call themselves *Huazu* (华族, Hua people), not *Hanzu* (汉族, Han people). Many have adopted English as their first language or working language. Chinese Singaporeans are proud of being citizens of the island-state and of their country's achievements.

On 7 April 2016, Josephine Teo (also known as Yang Liming), senior minister of state for foreign affairs, speaking at the Singapore Parliament in Mandarin, stated clearly that "China actively pushes its overseas Chinese affairs policy, its target perhaps extends to include the local Chinese communities who are Chinese descendants overseas."[4] She also said that in terms of culture and customs, Chinese Singaporeans have some similarities with those in mainland China, so they are sometimes mistaken for Chinese citizens living overseas. "But in reality, Chinese Singaporeans (*Huazu Xinjiapo ren* 华族新加坡人) are *Huayi* (华裔, of Chinese descent), not *Huaqiao* (华侨). [We] are *Huazu* who are citizens of an independent state, with [our own] loyalty and identity."[5] Teo went on to say that Singapore,

> is a multi-cultural society, Chinese Singaporeans have been living with other races in peace and maintain friendly relationship with them, and this cultural structure of multiculturalism and tolerance, has created the unique identity of Singaporeans, this is also the pride of being a Singaporean.[6]

Likewise, Professor Wang Gungwu observes that "The Chinese in Singapore will not blindly follow China. Each generation sees more Singaporeans embracing a Singapore identity that binds more of the local-born together. The Singapore identity is avowedly multi-cultural." However, he notes that there is a group of Chinese Singaporeans who are sympathetic to China. In his view, when an ASEAN country comes into conflict with China, the Singapore government may have to spend more efforts to convince this group to stand with that ASEAN country or remain neutral.[7] However, there has also been tension between new Chinese migrants and Chinese Singaporeans owing to economic competition and cultural prejudices.

It is worth noting that in Singapore, there are many *Peranakan* Chinese who have lost active command of the Chinese language. This group of Chinese still maintain that they are of Chinese descent but culturally are Westernized and localized.

In Indonesia, too, the responses of Chinese Indonesians to China's policy are varied. The so-called *totok* or the Mandarin-speaking Chinese were quite excited about the rise of China. This was especially the case with the older generation *totok* who received Chinese education before Chinese medium schools were banned in Indonesia. As many of them became Indonesian citizens only during the Suharto era, they still have lingering sentiments towards China. Some of them are not aware of the distinction between *huaqiao* and *huaren*, but others who are aware are happy to be considered both. However, this group consists of older Chinese and they constitute a minority among the Chinese Indonesians.[8]

The *Peranakan* Chinese, who form the majority of the Chinese population in Indonesia, have been localized, and most have lost command of the Chinese language. They have stronger Indonesian national and provincial identities and disapprove of China's blurring of their nationality status.

Benny Setiono, a *Peranakan* who is the president of the Indonesian Chinese Association (Perhimpunan INTI), Jakarta branch, criticized some of the *totok* community leaders who have become Indonesian citizens but continue to be close to Beijing's embassy in Jakarta. Setiono accused these Chinese leaders of maintaining such ties for personal benefit.[9]

Setiono also criticized the Chinese embassy for being too close to Chinese Indonesians and not respecting their Indonesian nationality. He complained that the embassy no longer follows Prime Minister Zhou Enlai's policy of encouraging the

Chinese in Indonesia to integrate into local society. He said he expected the Chinese embassy staff to behave like Zhou Enlai, guiding the Chinese to be integrated into Indonesian society.[10]

IMPACT ON ETHNIC TENSION BETWEEN THE CHINESE AND NON-CHINESE

China and the Causes of Anti-Chinese Violence

There are at least two sources of anti-Chinese sentiments in Southeast Asia: domestic and external (China). With regard to domestic factors, owing to ethnic politics and the superior economic status of the Chinese *vis-a-vis* the non-Chinese (indigenous) populations, anti-Chinese tensions and anti-Chinese violence cannot be entirely avoided in these countries. The Chinese overseas are divided in their views on protection from China when they are targets of violence. Many local Chinese do not want China's involvement as external intervention might make the situation worse, and the results may not be beneficial for them.

Gradually, the external factor may become important as the cause of anti-Chinese violence. As China becomes more assertive on the South China Sea islands disputes and the conflict between China and the Southeast Asian claimants to the islands intensifies, anti-China/Chinese riots are likely to recur. The Chinese overseas would be caught in between in such circumstances. Beijing's policy of blurring the distinction between *huaqiao* and *huaren*, together with its advocacy of Chinese transnationalism, would only give ammunition to local politicians and indigenous populations in Southeast Asia to stage anti-Chinese campaign/riots. And, these are beyond the control of the Chinese overseas. If Beijing continues its recent policies, they would result in further ethnic tensions and even anti-Chinese violence in some Southeast Asian countries. Let us look at some countries briefly.

Ethnic Tension in Malaysia

As Malaysia's political structure and government policies are based on race, the divisions between the Chinese and Malays are obvious and difficult to bridge. A major racial riot occurred in 1969. In subsequent years, there have been instances of heightened ethnic tension, though not as serious as in 1969. The Malaysian government seems to have been able to control the situation thus far.

While growing civil society movements in Malaysia have cut across ethnic lines, the mainstream political parties continue to be ethnic-based, or seen as ethnic-based parties. In recent years, as UMNO, the backbone of the ruling National Front multi-ethnic coalition government, is perceived to be losing power, party leaders have focused on ethnic issues, directed especially at the Chinese, to reverse their political fortunes, resulting in heightened ethnic tensions. Chapter 7 discussed the July 2015 incident at Low Yat Plaza in Kuala Lumpur, which caused a small riot involving the Chinese and Malays. The Chinese ambassador's speech two months later against what he called terrorism, racism and extremism was seen by UMNO as "intervention in Malaysian domestic affairs". Tensions might have escalated into ethnic conflict had it not been controlled by both the Malaysian and Chinese governments. As the South China Sea dispute with Malaysia has not been settled and Beijing has intensified its outreach towards the Chinese overseas, there is no guarantee that anti-

China, if not anti-Chinese, demonstrations and violence will not recur.

Ethnic Tension in Myanmar

Multi-ethnic Myanmar had major anti-Chinese violence in 1967 during the Cultural Revolution in China. Prior to this ethnic violence in the country was more directed against the Indian minority rather than the ethnic Chinese. Elements of the Myanmar Chinese economic elite have been quite well integrated into the society and they tend to have good relations with the army and the ruling elite. Thus, anti-Chinese riots in Myanmar were few and far between during the era of military rule. However, with the ascension to power of the National League for Democracy (NLD) led by Aung San Suu Kyi, Myanmar economic nationalism may rise, which could lead to ethnic conflict in Myanmar. This may be the case if China selects only Myanmar Chinese, especially the less well-integrated tycoons, to participate in economic projects in Myanmar. At the moment though, the main problem is still that of the Kokang Chinese minority group in the north, who are defiant towards the Myanmar authorities. If Myanmar's new authorities are not friendly with Beijing, China could conceivably use the Kokang Chinese to advance its interests.

Ethnic Tension in Cambodia

During the time of Sihanouk, the ethnic Chinese in Cambodia were well treated, and the relationship between the Chinese and Khmer people was cordial. But discrimination against the Chinese rose after the coup by General Lon Nol in 1970. The Chinese suffered greatly after 1975, when the country fell to the Khmer Rouge regime. Under its despotic rule, ethnic

Chinese were either put in concentration camps or killed. The Vietnamese occupation of Cambodia (1979–90) did not improve the plight of the Chinese, who continued to be discriminated against.

But under the current Hun Sen regime dating from 1985, relations between Phnom Penh and Beijing have improved, and the ethnic Chinese appear to be welcome. Because many Chinese were either killed or left Cambodia during the Pol Pot time, there are now many new Chinese migrants in the country. Nevertheless, at the moment, there is not much ethnic tension between the Chinese and the Khmers. Perhaps this is due to the fact that Cambodia is poor and needs to rely heavily on China and the Chinese for its economic development.

Ethnic Tension in the Philippines

The Chinese in the Philippines have been quite well integrated, if not assimilated, into the larger Philippine society. Nevertheless, the Philippine Chinese are not homogeneous. There is still a division between Chinese *mestizos*[11] and Chinese migrants. And, among the Chinese migrants, one can also note differences between new and old migrants and there has been tension between them. Major conflict between Chinese Filipinos (or *Tsinoys*)[12] and ethnic Filipinos appears to be rare. The Philippine government had issued anti-Chinese regulations in the early 1950s but these are a thing of the past. Nevertheless, kidnappings of Chinese Filipino tycoons by indigenous Filipinos have taken place quite frequently. The Chinese Filipinos' superior economic position *vis-à-vis* indigenous Filipinos is a source of some low-level tension in the country.

However, China's display of military muscle in the South China Sea and the dispute over the Spratly islands between

Beijing and Manila have caused concern among the Chinese in the Philippines. If the conflict escalates, the Chinese in the Philippines would be forced to choose sides, and many of them, especially the new migrants, would become the targets of Filipino nationalism.

Ethnic Tension in Vietnam

The conflict between Chinese and Vietnamese nationalisms has a long history, but it intensified after the unification of North and South Vietnam in 1975. The unified Vietnam introduced a socialist transformation programme, and the ethnic Chinese, many of whom belonged to the trading class, became the targets, which caused an exodus of the Chinese from Vietnam. This exodus reached its peak during the Sino–Vietnamese war (1979) and after. The war seems to have had a long-term impact on ethnic relations in Vietnam, especially in the north.

The dispute over the South China Sea between Beijing and Hanoi has intensified the ethnic animosity. Nevertheless, each of these two governments knows it needs to accommodate the other in order to maintain stability on its borders, which is a necessary condition for delivering the economic development that will continue to legitimate its authoritarian rule. Yet, Beijing appears to be firm on the South China Sea issue. Anti-China and anti-Chinese violence may recur if Hanoi feels that its core national interests have been violated.

Ethnic Tension in Indonesia

Anti-Chinese violence in Indonesia has been a frequent occurrence since the country's independence. The five major instances of anti-Chinese violence took place during the revolutionary period in 1945–46; in 1960 after the promulgation of the 1959 regulation banning the Chinese from the retail trade sector; the 13 May 1963 racial riots in West Java; the 1965 anti-Communist and anti-China riots, which affected the Chinese who were suspected to be leftists/communists' and the 1998 anti-Chinese violence before the fall of Suharto.

The causes of anti-Chinese violence are complex, ranging from politics, the superior economic position of the ethnic Chinese relative to that of indigenous Indonesians, negative perceptions of the ethnic Chinese, and the *pribumi*-based concept of the Indonesian nation. In addition, suspicion of the links that the ethnic Chinese had with China and of their loyalties have never disappeared from the minds of many Indonesian nationalists. The ethnic Chinese factor has been periodically used by politicians in Indonesia to discredit their rivals in the political struggle.

The 2014 presidential election is a good example. Joko Widodo (Jokowi) almost lost his chance to become president owing to the smear campaign by his opponents accusing him of being a Chinese and a Christian. Jokowi managed to fight back and won the presidential election. However, his opponents branded him as a president who was pro-Chinese and pro-China. In another example, an anti-Chinese party, Partai Priboemi was established in August 2015, demanding that the Indonesian Parliament restrict the rights of non-indigenous Indonesians (i.e., Chinese Indonesians). The ones behind the party are henchmen of then General Prabowo Subianto, suspected to be one of the masterminds behind the anti-Chinese riots of 1998.

Recently, the employment of Chinese labour from mainland China in China–Indonesia joint-venture companies was highlighted in the Indonesian press and was made an issue.

Many Indonesians demanded that Indonesians should be hired in place of labourers from China. Chinese Vice President Liu Yandong's speech at the University of Indonesia in 2015 also became an issue.[13] She was misquoted as saying that Jokowi had agreed to allow 10 million mainland Chinese migrants into Indonesia over an unspecified period of time. In fact, Liu only mentioned that China and Indonesia had a special relationship and that their combined population would be 1.6 billion, which would be significant in the region.[14]

However, Chinese officials visiting Indonesia did stress the ethnic links between mainland Chinese and Chinese Indonesians, stating that they are part of the Chinese nation. Even Ambassador Liu Jianchao declared in 2012 that Chinese Indonesians had blood ties and hence special feelings towards China and its people. He was speaking during a ceremony of the Confucius Institute at the Al-Azhar University in Jakarta.[15] Such comments have been used by those who are anti-Chinese as "evidence" that the Chinese Indonesians continue to be loyal to China.

The award in 2015 of the Jakarta–Bandung high-speed train project to the China State Railway Company was criticized by the anti-Chinese group. They saw it as Chinese domination "through the establishment of a political and economic alliance between ethnic Chinese in Indonesia, Indonesian bureaucrats and China."[16]

THE IMPACTS ON, AND RESPONSES OF, FOREIGN GOVERNMENTS

As of the time of writing, only Singapore minister Josephine Teo has responded to Beijing's policy of blurring the distinction between *huaqiao* and *huaren*. She noted in the Singapore Parliament that Chinese Singaporeans have a separate identity from that of Chinese nationals and that they are loyal to Singapore. Nevertheless, she did not launch any protest against Beijing's policy (see above). Apart from Singapore, it seems that none of the Southeast Asian governments have openly commented on or criticized Beijing's changing policy towards the Chinese overseas or made it a major diplomatic issue. There are many possible explanations for this reticence: the Cold War has ended, China has moved away from its communist foundations and no longer exports communism, and this is the era of globalization, where countries need trade and investment with China. Besides, many Southeast Asian countries do not feel the impact of China's changing policy yet as China continues to uphold the 1980 Nationality Law, which allows for the recognition of only one nationality.

China's changing policy towards the Chinese overseas so far has been implemented more dramatically outside the Southeast Asian region rather than in the region, and its impact on Southeast Asia has not been serious. Those aspects of the policy that are being applied to Southeast Asia have not alarmed the Southeast Asian states. For their part, the Southeast Asian governments generally are weak. In addition, all Southeast Asia countries are concerned with improving their economic situation, and, China as an economic power is a major trading partner for them and a source as well as destination for investments.

The Southeast Asian countries also need their ethnic Chinese to help improve their economies. Moreover, many of the Southeast Asian countries are too preoccupied with domestic issues to pay attention to the nuances in Beijing's policy towards the Chinese overseas. However, if these countries experience severe economic downturns, the ethnic Chinese may again be held as scapegoats and become targets of anti-Chinese violence. In such circumstances, the governments of these countries could begin to focus on China and the Chinese overseas issue again.

CONCLUSION

This study examined Beijing's changing policy towards the Chinese overseas since the rise of China, highlighting the internal and external drivers behind the change. Beijing's actions appear to have emulated the foreign policies of the great powers, for whom pursuing the national interest is paramount. Despite the increasing importance of the Chinese overseas in Beijing's national interest calculations over the past sixteen years or so, the reality is that the Chinese overseas still rank rather low in its national interests, compared to other, higher order interests, such as national security and territorial integrity, economic performance, and the survival of the CPC. Nevertheless, owing to a rising China's need for resources overseas, external markets, and external expertise, which many new and old Chinese migrants are able to help fulfil, China's interest in the Chinese overseas often coincides with the higher order priorities in China's national interest. Some observers have misinterpreted this coincidence of interests as a sign that China's interest in the Chinese overseas is now the highest order priority in China's national interest.

As the Chinese overseas are now seen by the twenty-first-century leadership of China as essential social and economic capital for a rising China, they are expected to make major contributions to the economic transformation of China and for its "One Belt One Road" Strategy. Not surprisingly, Beijing has introduced a series of new measures that appear to be aimed at mobilizing the Chinese overseas regardless of their citizenship. Beijing also seeks to develop soft power by spreading the Chinese language and culture through the establishment of Confucius Institutes and Confucius Classrooms. One of the objectives of this initiative has been to re-sinicize foreign citizens of Chinese descent.

This policy resembles that of the Kuomintang's policy of promoting Chinese transnationalism in the part of the twentieth century. Beijing has attempted to blur the distinction between Chinese citizens and foreign citizens of Chinese descent, as reflected in various recent external and internal events involving the Chinese overseas. China also began to show its intention to protect not only Chinese nationals overseas but also those Chinese overseas who have become foreign nationals. It seems that Beijing has forgotten its earlier policy of encouraging the Chinese overseas to integrate into local society and respect the rules and regulations of their adopted countries.

In fact, not all Chinese are citizens of China, and China promulgated the Nationality Law in 1980, which recognizes single citizenship. The blurring of the distinction between *huaqiao* and *huaren,* in fact, goes against China's own Nationality Law; it infringes upon the rights of other citizens and could also spark off ethnic tensions in plural societies. This may harm the interests of the Chinese overseas as they would be distrusted by their adopted lands. It would also harm China's friendly relations with the governments of the countries concerned.

Notes

1. The possible exceptions are perhaps the Chinese in Brunei, many of whom are still permanent residents rather than citizens as the requirements for Brunei citizenship are more rigorous than that of other Southeast Asian states.
2. Even in the United States, a scholar cum social activist, Professor Wang Ling-chi, disagreed with the idea of a dual nationality law for the Chinese overseas.
3. Peranakan refers to the offspring of intermarriage between a native (Malay/Indonesian) female and a foreign male. But increasingly Peranakan Chinese is used to refer to locally-born Chinese who speaks Malay/Indonesian as their first language. For a discussion of the term, see Leo Suryadinata, ed., *Peranakan Chinese in a Globalizing Southeast Asia* (Singapore: Chinese Heritage Centre and Baba House, 2010), pp. 2–3.
4. Yang Liming 杨莉明, "Juyou dute shenfen rentong he xiaozhong" 具有独特身份认同和效忠, *Lianhe Zaobao*《联合早报》, 8 April 2016, p. 10; also Charissa Yang, "Singapore's Value Lies in its 'Unique Culture'", *Straits Times*, 8 April 2016.
5. Yang Liming, "Juyou dute shenfen rentong he xiaozhong", op. cit., p. 10.
6. Ibid.
7. Wang Gungwu, "Singapore's 'Chinese Dilemma' as China Rises", *Straits Times*, 1 June 2015.
8. To be fair, there are also quite a few Chinese-speaking writers who are Indonesia-oriented and want to have a clear distinction between *huaqiao* and *huaren*. See for example the Chinese magazines published in Jakarta such as *Bazhong huixun* 巴中会讯 and *Hu Sheng* 呼声 for articles urging the Chinese-speaking Chinese to be proud of their Indonesian citizenship.
9. Benny G. Setiono, "Beberapa catatan mengenai perkembangan organisasi-organisasi Tionghoa di Indonesia", *Yinni Jiaodian*《印尼焦点》[Indonesia Focus], HKSIS, July 2008, pp. 74–77.
10. Ibid.

11. Chinese of mixed Filipino and Chinese ancestry.
12. *Tsinoy*, which refers to Chinese Filipinos in the Philippine language, is a term coined by Kaisa Para Kaunlaran Inc., known in Chinese as 菲律宾华裔青年联合会 [Association of Young Filipinos of Chinese descent]. The association which was established in 1987 is made up of younger *Tsinoys* who actively promote the integration of ethnic Chinese into mainstream Philippine society.
13. Liao Jianyu 廖建裕, "Yinni fanhua shili zaiqi" 印尼反华势力再起, *Lianhe Zaobao*《联合早报》, 29 September 2015.
14. Ibid.
15. Embassy of the People's Republic of China in the Republic of Indonesia, "Liu Jianchao dashi chuxi Alazhadaxue kongzi xueyuan xinzhi jiebei yishi" 刘建超大使出席阿拉扎大学孔子学院新址揭牌仪式, 9 November 2012, <http://id.china-embassy.org/chn/sgsd/t987391.htm> (accessed 16 February 2016).
16. See Johanes Herlijanto, "What Does Indonesia's Pribumi Elite think of Ethnic Chinese Today?", *ISEAS Perspective*, no. 32 (14 June 2016): 1 and 6.

Appendix

THE NATIONALITY LAW OF THE PEOPLE'S REPUBLIC OF CHINA

(Adopted at the Third Session of the Fifth National People's Congress on September 10, 1980)

Article 1: The law is applicable to the acquisition, renunciation, and restoration of the nationality of the People's Republic of China.

Article 2: The People's Republic of China in a unified, multi-national country; Persons belonging to any nationalities of China have Chinese nationality.

Article 3: The People's Republic of China does not recognize dual nationality for any Chinese national.

Article 4: Any person born in China whose parents are Chinese nationals or one of whose parents is a Chinese national has Chinese nationality.

Article 5: Any person born abroad whose parents are Chinese nationals, or one of whose parents is a Chinese national has Chinese nationality. But a person whose parents are Chinese nationals and have settled abroad or one of the parents who is a Chinese national has settled abroad and who has acquired foreign nationality on birth does not have Chinese nationality.

Article 6: Any person born in China whose parents are stateless or of uncertain nationality and have settled in China has Chinese nationality.

Article 7: Aliens or stateless persons who are willing to abide by China's Constitution and laws may acquire Chinese nationality upon the approval of their application provided that:

(1) they are close relatives of Chinese nationals; or

(2) they have settled in China; or

(3) they have other legitimate reasons.

Article 8: Any person who applies for naturalization in China acquires Chinese nationality upon approval of his or her application; no person whose application for naturalization in China has been approved is permitted to retain foreign nationality.

Article 9: Any Chinese national who has settled abroad and who has been naturalized there or has acquired foreign nationality of his own free will automatically loses Chinese nationality.

Article 10: Chinese nationals may renounce Chinese nationality upon approval of their applications provided that:

(1) they are close relatives of aliens; or

(2) they have settled abroad; or

(3) they have other legitimate reasons.

Article 11: Any person whose application for renunciation of Chinese nationality has been approved loses Chinese nationality.

Article 12: State functionaries and army men on active service should not renounce Chinese nationality.

Article 13: Aliens who were once of Chinese nationality may apply for restoration of Chinese nationality provided that they have legitimate reasons; those whose applications for restoration of Chinese nationality are approved shall not retain foreign nationality.

Article 14: The acquisition, renunciation and restoration of Chinese nationality, with the exception of the cases provided in Article 9, shall go through the formalities of the application. Applications under the age of 18 may be filed by the minors' parents or other legal representatives.

Article 15: The organs handling nationality applications are local, municipal and country public security bureau at home and China's diplomatic representations and consular offices abroad.

Article 16: Applications for naturalization and for renunciation or restoration of Chinese nationality are subject to examination and approval by the Ministry of Public Security of the People's Republic of China. The Ministry of Public Security issues a certificate to any person whose application is approved.

Article 17: The nationality status of persons who have acquired or lost Chinese nationality before the promulgation of this law remains valid.

Article 18: The law comes into force from the day of promulgation.

(Taken from *Selected Articles from Chinese Yearbook of International Law*, edited by Chinese Society of International Law, Beijing: China Translation and Publishing Corporation, 1983).

BIBLIOGRAPHY

"2014 nian 5 yue yuenan paihua zhenxiang, luji ganbu: yuenan baomin jiushi yao baofu taishang xuehan gongchang" 2014 年5月 越南排华真相,陆籍干部: 越南暴民就是要报复台商血汗工, 19 May 2014. <http://blog.udn.com/t612/13456054> (accessed 16 December 2015).

Achariam, Timothy. "Rais Slams Ambassador Over Petaling Street Visit", 27 September 2015. <www.thesundaily.my/news1564767> (accessed 5 October 2015).

Aggarwal, Narendra. "Singapore-China Ties Reach New Heights". *Business Times*, 6 November 2015.

Alejandrino, Clark and Ellen Palanca. "Chinese Language Education in the Philippines: From Taiwan to China". *CHC Bulletin*, no. 18 (October 2012).

Apple Daily. "Paihua baodong waijiaobu yintiezhi gongtaishang quge/jishixinwen" 排华暴动外交部印贴纸供台商区隔/即时新闻, 15 May 2014. <http://www.appledaily.com.tw/realtimenews/article/new/20140515/398104> (accessed 16 December 2015).

Arase, David. "Strategic Rivalry in the South China Sea: How can Southeast Asian Claimant States Shape a Beneficial Outcome?" *ISEAS Perspective*, no. 57 (13 October 2015).

Atkinson, Joel. "Big Trouble in Little Chinatown: Australia, Taiwan and the April 2006 Post-Election Riot in Solomon Islands". *Pacific Affairs* 82, no. 1 (Spring 2009): 47–65.

Baidu Baike 百度百科. “Bai Soucheng” 白所成. <http://baike.baidu.com/view/2764210.htm> (accessed 20 May 2015).

———. “Peng Jiasheng” 彭家声. <http://baike.baidu.com/view/932349.htm> (accessed 20 May 2015).

Barboza, David. “China Struggles to Shelter Millions of Quake’s Homeless”. *New York Times*, 26 May 2008. <www.nytimes.com/2008/05/26/world/asia/26china.html> (accessed 11 December 2015).

BBC News. “Yemen’s Crisis: China Evacuates Citizens and Foreigners from Aden”, 3 April 2015. <www.bbc.com/news/world-middle-east-32173811> (accessed 1 June 2016).

BBC Sport Olympics. “Beijing 2008 Medal Table”, 13 August 2012. <http://www.bbc.co.uk/sport/olympics/2012/medals/historical-medals-beijing-2008/countries> (accessed 10 April 2016).

BBC Zhongwen Wang, BBC 中文网. “Miandian fandui pai lingxiu ang shan su ji jieshu lishixing fang hua” 缅甸反对派领袖昂山素季结束历史性访华, 14 June 2015. <http://www.bbc.com/zhongwen/simp/world/2015/06/150614_burma_aungsansuukyi> (accessed 17 June 2015).

———. “Zhongguo dashi yanlun ganshe neizheng, damajiang chuanzhao” 中国大使言论干涉内政，大马将传召, 27 September 2015. <http://www.bbc.com/zhongwen/trad/world/2015/09/150927_malaysia_china_diplomacy> (accessed 5 June 2016).

CCTV新闻. “李克强会见首届华侨华人工商大会全体代表”, 6 July 2015. <http://www.yangshi13.com/cctv/xinwenlianbo/2015/0706/28389.html> (accessed 10 July 2015).

Chew Chye Lay, Grace. “The April 2006 Riots in the Solomon Islands”. *CHC Bulletin*, nos. 7 and 8 (May and November 2006): 11–21.

———. “The Confucius Institute in the World: An Overview”. *CHC Bulletin*, no. 9 (May 2007): 13–19.

China-Britain Business Council. “One Belt One Road” 一带一路. <www.cbbc.org/sectors/one-belt,-one-road> (accessed 18 March 2016).

China Daily 中国日报中文网. “Guowuyuan qiaoban zhuren Qiu Yuanping: muqian hai wei kaolü chutai Huayi Ka” 国务院侨办主任裘援平:

目前还未考虑出台华裔卡, 13 March 2016. <http://cn.chinadaily.com.cn/2016lianghui/2016-03/13/content_23844522.htm> (accessed 20 April 2016).

China.org.cn. "Large-scale Evacuation of Chinese from Solomon Islands", 25 April 2006. <www.china.org.cn/english/2006/Apr/166694.htm> (accessed 23 October 2015).

———. "Taiyang: yuenan paihua yuanqi nanhai, gen zai guonei" 太阳: 越南 "排华" 缘起南海, 根在国内, 24 May 2014. <http://www.china.org.cn/chinese/2014-05/24/content_32472465.htm> (accessed 16 December 2015).

China View. "China asks Malaysia to probe Assault Cases", 29 November 2005. <http://news.xinhuanet.com/english/2005-11/29/content_3853442.htm> (accessed 16 April 2016).

The Chinese American Professors and Professionals Network 美国华裔教授专家网. "Guowuyuan qiaoban: haiwai huaqiao huaren da 6000 wan Zhongguo jiang zhubu jiangdi 'luka' menkan-qianzheng" 国务院侨办: 海外华侨华人达 6000 万中国将逐步降低"绿卡"门槛-签证, 3 May 2014. <scholarsupdate.hi2net.com/news.asp?NewsID=14335> (accessed 4 January 2016).

Ching, Frank. "Beijing Seeks Loyalty from Ethnic Chinese Settle Abroad". *Business Times*, 4 May 2016.

Chong Koh Ping. "Bilateral Trade and Investment Going Strong". *Straits Times*, 6 November 2015.

———. "Lianhe Zaobao and Singapore Business Federation Launch 'One Belt, One Road' Portal". *Straits Times*, 8 March 2016. <http://www.straitstimes.com/business/economy/lianhe-zaobao-and-singapore-business-federation-launches-one-belt-one-road-portal> (accessed 12 May 2016).

Chuansong men 传送门. "Quanqiu huashang mingren tang — Yinni youguang jituan mingyu dongshi zhang Chen dajiang" 全球华商名人堂 — 印尼友光集团名誉董事长陈大江, 28 May 2014. <chuansong.me/n/2750948> (accessed 10 April 2016).

Coppel, Charles. *Indonesian Chinese in Crisis*. Kuala Lumpur: Oxford University Press, 1983.

Cribb, Robert. "The 1965 Killings Constituted Genocide". In *Indonesia, Genocide and Persecution Series*, edited by Noah Berlatsky (Farmington Hills, MI: Greenhaven Press, 2014), pp. 91–102.

Cribb, Robert and Charles Coppel. "A Genocide that Never Was: Explaining the Myth of Anti-Chinese Massacre in Indonesia 1965–1966". *Journal of Genocide Research* 11, no. 4 (2009): 447–65.

Cui Guiqiang 崔贵强, ed. 主编. *You yangguang de difang jiuyou huaren* 《有阳光的地方就有华人》 [Where the Sun Shines, There Are Chinese]. Singapore, 2009.

Damar Harsanto. "May Riots Still Burned into Victim's Minds". *Jakarta Post*, 14 May 2002.

Daw Win. "Law Sit Han". In *Southeast Asian Personalities of Chinese Descent: A Biographical Dictionary*, edited by Leo Suryadinata. Singapore: Institute of Southeast Asian Studies, 2012.

Deng Yuwen 邓聿文. "Beijing dui miandian de liangshou zhengce" 北京对缅甸的两手政策. *Lianhe Zaobao* 《联合早报》, 10 June 2015.

Dewi Anggraeni. *Tragedi Mei 1998 dan Lahirnya Komnas Perempuan*. Jakarta: Kompas Pustaka Buku, 2014.

Duiker, William J. *The Communist Road to Power in Vietnam*. Boulder: Westview Press, 1982.

Embassy of the People's Republic of China in Malaysia. "Huang Huikang dashi zai haishang sizhou zhilu Zhongguo-Malaixiya luntan ji Zhongguo-Dongmeng shangwu xiehui, Malaixiya chengli yishi shang de zici" 黄惠康大使在海上丝绸之路中国-马来西亚论坛暨中国-东盟商务协会 (马来西亚) 成立仪式上的致辞, 1 October 2015. <http://my.china-embassy.org/chn/sgxw/t1302809.htm> (accessed 5 October 2015).

Embassy of the People's Republic of China in the Republic of Indonesia. "Liu Jianchao dashi chuxi Alazhadaxue kongzi xueyuan xinzhi jiebei yishi" 刘建超大使出席阿拉扎大学孔子学院新址揭牌仪式, 9 November 2012. <http://id.china-embassy.org/chn/sgsd/t987391.htm> (accessed 16 February 2016).

Embassy of the People's Republic of China in the Republic of Singapore. "2014 nian 5 yue 16 ri waijiaobu fayanren Hua Chunying zhichi lixing jizhe zhaodaihui" 2014年5月16日 外交部发言人华春莹主持例行记者招待会, 16 May 2014. <http://www.chinaembassy.org.sg/chn/fyrth/t1156836.htm> (accessed 16 December 2015).

Embassy of the Republic of the Union of Myanmar in Belgium. "Composition of the Different Ethnic Groups under the 8 Major National Ethnic Races in Myanmar". <http://www.embassyofmyanmar.be/ABOUT/ethnicgroups.htm> (accessed 18 June 2015).

ETTV (Eastern Television). "The Battle of the Solomon Islands". EastSouthWestNorth Blog, 20 April 2006. <www.zonaeuropa.com/20060425_1.htm> (accessed 2 August 2015).

Fang Xiongpu 方雄普, Xie Chengjia 谢成佳, eds. 主编. *Huaqiao huaren gaikuang*《华侨华人概况》. Beijing 北京: Zhongguo huaqiao chubanshe 中国华侨出版社, 1993.

Fitzgerald, Stephen. *China and the Overseas Chinese: A Study of Peking's Changing Policy 1949–1970*. Cambridge: Cambridge University Press, 1972.

Forbes. "Singapore's 40 Richest: #7 Zhong Sheng Jian", 28 July 2010. <www.forbes.com/lists/2010/79/singapore-10_Zhong-Sheng-Jian_ZUOE.html> (accessed 12 April 2016).

———. "Singapore's 50th Richest: #20 Zhong Sheng Jian", 27 October 2016. <http://www.forbes.com/profile/zhong-sheng-jian> (accessed 12 April 2016).

Gill, Parveen. "Police Made Me Strip, says Chinese National". *The Star*, 12 November 2005. <http://www.thestar.com.my/news/nation/2005/11/12/police-made-me-strip-says-chinese-national> (accessed 16 April 2016).

Gleeson, Sean. "Chinese, Burmese Officials Meet to Defuse Kokang Tensions". *The Irrawaddy*, 9 March 2015. <http://www.irrawaddy.com/news/burma/chinese-burmese-officials-meet-to-defuse-kokang-tensions.html> (accessed 22 May 2015).

Global Times Editorial. "North Myanmar Peace Imperative for China", 16 February 2015. <www.globaltimes.cn/content/907884.shtml> (accessed 15 April 2015).

GovHK 香港政府一站通. "Explanations of Some Questions by the Standing Committee of the National People's Congress Concerning the Implementation of the Nationality Law of the People's Republic of China in the Hong Kong Special Administrative Region (Adopted at the 19th Session of the Standing Committee of the 8th National People's Congress on 15 May 1996)". <http://www.gov.hk/en/residents/immigration/chinese/law.htm> (accessed 15 May 2016).

Guancha Zhe 观察者. "Shoujie shijie huaqiao huaren gongshang dahui kaimu, haiwai qiaoshang ziben chao 5 wan yi meiyuan" 首届世界华侨华人工商大会开幕 海外侨商资本超5万亿美元, 7 July 2015. <http://www.guancha.cn/Industry/2015_07_07_325893.shtml> (accessed 10 July 2015).

———. "Yangshi fabu quanwei 'Yidai Yilu' bantu" 央视发布权威"一带一路"版图, 13 April 2015. <http://www.guancha.cn/Neighbors/2015_04_13_315767.shtml> (accessed 2 January 2016).

Guangxi zhongxiao qiye wang 广西中小企业网. "Zhongguo jihua zai Wenlai sheli Longzi Xueyuan" 中国计划在文莱设立孔子学院, 19 September 2008. <http://smegx.gov.cn/gxsme/xwpt/article.jsp?id=7110> (accessed 20 September 2012).

Guo Qingjiang 郭清江. "Zongbianji shijian, laolian guabuzhu" 总编辑时间·老脸挂不住". *Sin Chew Jit Poh*《星洲日报》, 29 September 2015. <http://www.sinchew.com.my/node/260087> (accessed 30 September 2015).

Guoji Ribao《国际日报》. "Beijing shi qiaoban zhuren Li Yinze fang Yinni jianghua yingqi qiaojie buman" 北京市侨办主任李印泽访印尼讲话引起侨界不满 [The Speech of Beijing's Qiaoban Director Li Yinze Caused Worries Among the Chinese Community], 21 April 2012.

———. "Ershi wei yinhua jingying shoupin danren zhongguo qiaolian haiwai guwen he weiyuan" 二十位印华精英受聘担任中国侨联海外顾问和委员, 9 December 2013. <http://www.guojiribao.com/shtml/gjrb/20131209/134060.shtml> (accessed 2 April 2015).

Haacke, Jurgen. "Why Did Myanmar's Opposition Leaders Just Visit China?" *The Diplomat*, 15 June 2015. <thediplomat.com/2015/06/why-did-myanmars-opposition-leader-just-visit-china> (accessed 18 June 2015).

Hafiz Yatim. "Ketuk Ketampi bogel 2005: K'jaan bayar pampasan", 27 July 2011. <https://www.malaysiakini.com/news/171157> (accessed 16 April 2016).

Hao Mengfei 郝梦飞. "Qiaomin liyi, lingshi baohu, guojia liyi" 侨民利益, 领事保护, 国家利益. In *Zhongguo guojia liyi yu yingxiang*《中国国家利益与影响》, edited by Xu Jia 许嘉, 主编. Beijing 北京: Shijie zhishi chubanshe 世界知识出版社, December 2006.

Harman, Mike. "Tongan Riots, 2006". Libcom.org, 28 June 2008. <https://libcom.org/history/tongan-riots-2006> (accessed 30 March 2016).

Herlijanto, Johanes. "What Does Indonesia's Pribumi Elite think of Ethnic Chinese Today?". *ISEAS Perspective*, no. 32 (14 June 2016).

Hinton, Harold. *Communist China in World Politics*. Boston: Houghton Mifflin, 1966.

Hong, Carolyn. "Doubts Linger over Nude Video". *Straits Times*, 5 January 2006.

———. "Malaysia: Policewoman in Aabuse Vvideo Iidentified". *Sunday Times*, 27 November 2005.

Hooker, Jake. "Toll Rises in China Quake". *New York Times*, 26 May 2008. <www.nytimes.com/2008/05/26/world/asia/26quake.html> (accessed 11 December 2015).

Huang Jinfa 黄进发. "Haiwai guchu gukushen?" 海外孤雏孤苦甚? Sui Huo Pinglun 燧火评论, 2 October 2015. <http://www.pfirereview.com/20151002> (accessed 10 February 2016).

Huang Zhaoxian 郑昭贤. "Lijing cangsang de lao xiaozhang" 历经沧桑的老校长. In *Dongnanya huaren de jingshen: jianren buba*《东南亚华人的精神: 坚韧不拔》. Selangor: Celue Zixun yanjiu zhongxin 策略资讯研究中心, 2009, pp. 161–64.

Huanqiu Shibao《环球时报》. "Zhefu wunian chongchu jianghu ting 84shui 'guogan wang' jiang mianbei jushi" 蛰伏五年重出江湖听

84岁"果敢王"讲缅北局势, 29 December 2014. <http://world.huanqiu.com/exclusive/2014-12/5307556.html> (accessed 20 May 2015).

Jiefang Ribao 《解放日报》. "Deng Xiaoping ruhe jiejue zhongguo yu zhoubian geguojian de zhengduan?" 邓小平如何解决中国与周边各国间的争端?, 15 September 2010.

Kausikan, Bilahari. "Singapore is Not an Island". *Straits Times*, 6 October 2015.

Keating, Joshua. "Yemen's President Just Stepped Down. Now What?", 22 January 2015. <http://www.slate.com/blogs/the_slatest/2015/01/22/yemen_s_president_just_stepped_down_now_what.html> (accessed 1 June 2016).

Kent, Jonathan. "Video puts Malaysia Police in Dock", 25 November 2005. <http://news.bbc.co.uk/2/hi/asia-pacific/4470422.stm> (accessed 16 April 2016).

Kongmeng zhi xiang wang 孔孟之乡网. "Yuenan xuezhe huyu jinkuai chengli Kongzi Xueyuan" 越南学者呼吁尽快成立孔子学院, 31 October 2009. <http://www.kmzx.org/Article/ShowArticle.asp?ArticleID=4284> (accessed 20 September 2012).

Kurlantzick, Joshua. "Vietnam Protests: More Than Just Anti-China Sentiment". *Council on Foreign Relations*, 15 May 2014. <http://blogs.cfr.org/asia/2014/05/15/vietnam-protests-more-than-just-anti-china-sentiment/> (accessed 16 December 2015).

Kyodo News. "Official Chided for Humiliation of Chinese Women", 2 December 2005. <http://www.chinadaily.com.cn/english/doc/2005-12/02/content_499957.htm> (accessed 12 April 2016).

Larkin, Stuart. "China's 'Great Leap Outward': The AIIB in Context". *ISEAS Persp*ective, no. 27 (9 June 2015).

———. "Multiple Challenges for the AIIB". *ISEAS Perspective*, no. 33 (2 July 2015).

Le Thu, Huong. "The Anti-Chinese Riots in Vietnam: Responses from the Ground". *ISEAS Perspective*, no. 32 (27 May 2014).

Leaf, Paul J. "Learning from China's Oil Rig Standoff with Vietnam". *The Diplomat*, 30 August 2014. <thediplomat.com/2014/08/learning-

from-chinas-oil-rig-standoff-with-vietnam> (accessed 15 December 2015).

Len Xinyu 冷新宇. "Zhongguo guoqi zai libiya shousun 188 yi meiyuan, minqi sunshi weizhi" 中国国企在利比亚受损188亿美元, 民企损失未知. *Zhongguo jingji zhoukan* 《中国经济周刊》, 24 May 2011. <http://news.qq.com/a/20110524/000019.htm> (accessed 5 June 2016).

Li, Peter S. and Eva Xiaoling Li. "The Chinese Overseas Population". In *Routledge Handbook of the Chinese Diaspora*, edited by Tan Chee Beng. London and New York: Routledge, 2013.

Li Yanyun 李艳云. "Malaixiya dai waizhang yuejian dashi yu liangxiaoshi" 马来西亚代外长约见大使逾两小时. BBC, Boxun.com, 28 September 2015. <http://www.bbc.com/zhongwen/simp/world/2015/09/150928_china_malaysia_meeting> (accessed 10 February 2016).

———. "Zhongguo dashi yanlun ganshi neizheng, damajiang chuanzhao" 中国大使言论干涉内政, 大马将传召. BBC, Boxun.com, 27 September 2015. <http://www.bbc.com/zhongwen/simp/world/2015/09/150927_malaysia_china_diplomacy> (accessed 10 February 2016).

Lianhe Ribao 《联合日报》. "Fang Guilun: Dashi wu ganzheng, waijiaobu budong lijie" 方贵伦: 大使无干政, 外交部不懂礼节, 28 September 2015. <www.kwongwah.com.my/?p=21101> (accessed 8 February 2016).

Lianhe Zaobao 《联合早报》. "Beida jiaoshou liang yingming: zhongguo yao lizhi kandai haiwai huaren lichang" 北大教授梁英明: 中国要理智看待海外华人立场, 22 February 2016.

———. "Bendi xuezhe: mohu huaqiao huaren jiexian" 本地学者: 模糊华侨华人界限, 19 February 2016.

———. "Guandan duzhong zhengshi huozhun chengli" 关丹独中正式获准成立, 28 July 2012; Moe Clarifies Decision on Chong Hwa High School Kuantan. <http://schooladvisor.my/news/moe-clarifies-decision-on-chong-hwa-high-school-kuantan/> (accessed 2 March 2016).

———. "Zai Beijing shiyaxia, Mian tongmengjun jieshu yu zhengfu jun jizhan" 在北京施压下, 缅同盟军结束与政府军激战, 12 June 2015.

———. "Zhongguo jinqi zai nan Zhongguo haijunyan, jinzhi chuanzhi feiji shiru" 中国今起在南中国海军演, 禁止船只飞机驶入, 19 July 2016.

Liao Jianyu 廖建裕. "Yinni fanhua shili zaiqi" 印尼反华势力再起. *Lianhe Zaobao*《联合早报》, 29 September 2015.

Lin Xixing 林锡星. "Fansi suoluomen qundao paihua beiju" 反思所罗门群岛排华悲剧. *Yazhou Zhoukan*《亚洲周刊》, 7 May 2008, p. 18.

Lintner, Bertil. "The Sinicizing of the South Pacific". *Asia Times Online*, 18 April 2007.

Lowy Institute for International Policy. "Australian Foreign Aid". <http://www.lowyinstitute.org/issues/australian-foreign-aid> (accessed 23 October 2015).

———. "China and the Pacific Islands". <www.lowyinstitute.org/issues/china-pacific> (accessed 23 November 2015).

Malay Mail Online. "Low Yat was about Racism, deal with it", 14 July 2015. <http://www.themalaymailonline.com/opinion/boo-su-lyn/article/low-yat-was-about-racism-deal-with-it> (accessed 10 February 2016).

Malaysiakini. "Don't Put China's Pride Above Malaysia's, says Khairy", 28 September 2015. <www.malaysiakini.com/news/313794> (accessed 5 October 2015).

———. "Suruhanjaya: Bogel dan ketuk ketampi haram", 23 January 2006. <http://www.malaysiakini.com/news/46110> (accessed 16 April 2016).

———. "Utusan to Chinese Envoy: Deal with Prostitutes, not Petaling Street", 27 September 2015. <http://www.malaysiakini.com/news/313634> (accessed 5 October 2015).

McPhedran, Ian. "Concern Over 'Buying' Islanders". *Adelaide Advertiser*, 26 April 2006.

Ming Bao《明报》. "Zhongguo shixing 'huayi ka', zhenshi chengren shuangchong guoji" 中国试行"华裔卡"真实承认双重国籍, 6 December 2015. <www.mingpaocanada.com/tor/htm/News/20151205/taa1_r.htm> (accessed 10 December 2015).

Morris-Jung, Jason. "Reflections on the Oil Rig Crisis: Vietnamese's Domestic Opposition Grows". *ISEAS Perspective*, no. 43 (30 July 2014).

Mozingo, David. *Chinese Policy toward Indonesia 1949–1967*. Ithaca: Cornell University Press, 1976.

Murty, Michael. "MCA Attacks DAP's 'Calculated Distortion' of China Ambassador's Speech". *The Rakyat Post*, 28 September 2015. <http://www.therakyatpost.com/news/2015/09/28/mca-attacks-daps-calculated-distortion-of-china-ambassadors-speech> (accessed 26 January 2016).

Myin Myint Kyu. "Spaces of Exceptional Shifting Strategies of the Kokang Chinese along the Myanmar/China Border". M.A. thesis, Graduate School of Chiang Mai University, October 2011.

Nanfang Daily (*Nanfang Ribao*, Mainland China), in English translation. "The Battle of the Solomon Islands". EastSouthWestNorth Blog, 24 April 2005. <www.zonaeuropa.com/20060425_1.htm> (accessed 2 August 2015).

Nguyen Manh Hung. "The Politics of the United States–China–Vietnam Triangle in the 21st Century". *Trends in Southeast Asia*, no. 21. Singapore: Institute of Southeast Asian Studies, 2015.

Nurul Nazirin. "Chinese Nationals to Sue for Cruelty, Torture", 14 November 2005. <soc.culture.malaysia.narkive.com/a0sR3EjE/chinese-nationals-to-sue-for-cruelty-torture> (accessed 12 April 2016).

Nye, Joseph S. Jr. *The Future of Power*. New York: Public Affairs, Perseus Books Group, 2011.

Ooi Kee Beng, ed. *The Eurasian Core and its Edges: Dialogues with Wang Gungwu on the History of the World*. Singapore: Institute of Southeast Asian Studies, 2015.

Parello-Plesner, Jonas and Mathieu Duchatel. *China's Strong Arm: Protecting Citizens and Assets Abroad*. London: International Institute for Strategic Studies, May 2015.

Patey, Luke. "China's New Crisis Diplomacy in Africa and the Middle-East". *DIIS Policy Brief*, January 2016.

Peng Nian 彭念. "Wengshan Suzhi fang hua de xuanji" 翁山淑枝访华的玄机. *Lianhe Zaobao*《联合早报》, 11 June 2015.

People's Daily Online 人民网. "China Hopes Italy to Resolve Police-Chinese Clash Fairly", 13 April 2007. <http://en.people.cn/200704/13/eng20070413_366343.html> (accessed 12 December 2015).

"Pola kerusuhan di Jakarta dan sekitarnya" (Dokumentasi Awal no. 1). In *Sujud di Hadapan Korban Tragedi Jakarta Mei 1998* (Laporan Investigasi dan Analisa Data Tim Relawan untuk Kemanusiaan). Jakarta: Divisi Data Tim Relawan, 1998.

Poston, Dudley L. Jr. and Mei-Yu Yu. "The Distribution of the Overseas Chinese in the Contemporary World". *International Migration Review* 24, no. 3 (1990).

Purdey, Jemma. *Anti-Chinese Violence in Indonesia, 1966–1999*. Singapore: NUS Press, 2006.

Qiang wai lou 墙外楼. "Taisu zhaokai xinwen fabuhui: zai yue gangchang 4 ming dalu ji laogong siwang" 台塑召开新闻发布会: 在越钢厂4名大陆籍劳工死亡, 20 May 2014. <https://commondatastorage.googleapis.com/letscorp_archive/archives/71132> (accessed 16 December 2015).

Qiaowu Weiyuanhui (Taiwan) 侨务委员会 (台湾). 2011年侨务统计年报 *2011 Statistical Yearbook of the Overseas Chinese Affairs Council*, p. 11. <www.ocac.gov.tw/OCAC/File/Attach/313/File_2430.pdf> (accessed 4 January 2016).

———. "Haiwai huaren ji Taiqiao renshu" 海外华人及台侨人数, 29 July 2016. <www.ocac.gov.tw/OCAC/Pages/List.aspx?nodeid=33> (accessed 4 January 2016).

Qiu Li Ben 丘立本. "Yindu Guoji yimin yu qiaowu gongzuo de lishi yu xianzhuang" 印度国际移民与侨务工作的历史与现状. *Huaqiao huaren lishi yanjiu*《华侨华人历史研究》, no. 1 (March 2012): 24–35.

Radio Free Asia (RFA). "Kokang Army Recruiting Chinese Nationals as Mercenaries in Yunnan: Sources", 24 March 2015. <http://www.rfa.org/english/news/myanmar/recruit-03242015121255.html> (accessed 22 May 2015).

Rajagopalan, Megha and Ben Blanchard. "China Evacuates Foreign Nationals from Yemen in Unprecedented Move". Reuters Television and Sabine Siebold in Berlin, 3 April 2015.

Renmin Wang-Renmin Ribao 《人民网-人民日报》. "Xi Jinping huijian di qijie shijie huaqiao huaren shetuan lianyi dahui daibiao" 习近平会见第七届世界华侨华人社团联谊大会代表, 7 June 2014. <http://pic.people.com.cn/n/2014/0607/c1016-25116878.html> (accessed 18 March 2016).

Reuters. "Solomons Hell for Chinese". EastSouthWestNorth Blog, 20 April 2006. <http://www.zonaeuropa.com/20060425_1.htm> (accessed 2 August 2015).

———. "Up to 21 Dead, Doctor Says, as Anti-China Riots Spread in Vietnam", 15 May 2014. <http://www.reuters.com/article/us-vietnam-china-riots-casualties-idUSBREA4E03Y20140515> (accessed 16 December 2015).

"Sayonara Shinkansen". *Tempo*, 12–18 October 2015, pp. 86–95.

Setiono, Benny G. "Beberapa catatan mengenai perkembangan organisasi-organisasi Tionghoa di Indonesia". *Yinni Jiaodian* 《印尼焦点》 [Indonesia Focus], HKSIS, July 2008, pp. 74–77.

Shee Poon Kim. "China's Responses to the May 1998 Anti-Chinese Riots in Indonesia". EAI Working Paper No. 37. East Asian Institute, 24 March 2000.

Simpfendorfer, Ben. "The Impact of the Arab Revolutions on China's Foreign Policy". In *The EU-China Relationship: European Perspectives. A Manual for Policy Makers*, edited by Kerry Brown. Singapore: World Scientific, 2015, pp. 201–13.

Sina 新浪网. "CHH: Zhongguo zai feizhou de touzi yuan chao meiguo" CHH: 中国在非洲的投资远超美国. <finance.sina.com.cn/stock/usstock/c/20140806/175719932066.shtml> (accessed 1 June 2016).

Sing Tao (Hong Kong). "The Battle of the Solomon Islands". EastSouthWestNorth Blog, 24 April 2006. <www.zonaeuropa.com/20060425_1.htm> (accessed 2 August 2015).

Slamet Singgih. *Intelijen: Catatan Harian Seorang Serdadu*. Jakarta: Penerbit Kata, 2015.

The Socialist Republic of Vietnam, Online Newspaper of the Government. "PM Orders Urgent Measures to Maintain Security, Order", 15 May 2014. <http://news.chinhphu.vn/Home/PM-orders-urgent-measures-to-maintain-security-order/20145/21039.vgp> (accessed 16 December 2015).

South China Morning Post. "Malaysia: Stripping Scandal Inquiry Widens", 1 December 2005. <web.international.ucla.edu/institute/article/34741> (accessed 16 April 2016).

Spiller, Penny. "Riots Highlight Chinese Tension". BBC News, 21 April 2006. <http://news.bbc.co.uk/2/hi/asia-pacific/4930994.stm> (accessed 2 August 2015).

Squires, Nick. "Beijing Slush Fund to Woo Solomons". *South China Morning Post*, 30 April 2006.

The State Council the People's Republic of China. "Overseas Chinese Affairs Office of the State Council", 12 September 2014. <http://english.gov.cn/state_council/2014/10/01/content_281474991090995.htm> (accessed 19 February 2016).

Straits Times. "Our Future in S-E Asia—Lee", 13 November 1978.

Suara Pembaruan. "Dubes RRC Sesalkan Terjadinya Perkosaan Saat Kerusuhan" [PRC's Ambassador Deplores Raping During Riots], 7 July 1998.

The Sun Daily, quoting the Bernama News. "China Welcomes Vietnam's Compensation on Anti-China Riots", 26 August 2014. <www.thesundaily.my/news/1151177> (accessed 16 December 2015).

Sun, Yun. "The Kokang Conflict: How Will China Respond?" *The Irrawady*, 18 February 2015. <www.irrawaddy.com/contributor/kokang-conflict-will-china-respond.html> (accessed 21 May 2015).

Suryadinata, Leo. "A New Orientation in China's Policy towards Chinese Overseas? Beijing Olympic Games Fervour as a Case Study". *CHC Bulletin*, no. 12 (November 2008): 1–4.

———. "Anti-Chinese Riots in Indonesia: Perennial Problem but Major Disaster Unlikely". *Straits Times*, 25 February 1998.

———. "Book Review: Jingwai huaren guoji wenti taolun ji (The Citizenship Problems of the Chinese Overseas: A Collection of Documents and Articles), edited by Zhou Nanjing". *Journal of Chinese Overseas* 1, no. 2 (November 2005): 286–88.

———. "Can the Kokang Chinese Problem in Myanmar be Resolved?" *ISEAS Perspective*, no. 37 (15 July 2015).

———. *China and the ASEAN States: The Ethnic Chinese Dimension*. Singapore: Singapore University Press, 1985.

———. "China's Hands-off on Indonesia". *Far Eastern Economic Review*, 16 April 1998.

———. "Did the Natuna Incident Shake Indonesia-China Relations?" *ISEAS Perspective*, no. 19 (26 April 2016).

———. *Elections and Politics in Indonesia*. Singapore: Institute of Southeast Asian Studies, 2002.

———, ed. *Ethnic Chinese as Southeast Asians*. Singapore: Institute of Southeast Asian Studies, 1997.

———. "Ethnic Chinese in Southeast Asia and their Economic Role". In *Chinese Populations in Contemporary Southeast Asian Societies: Identities, Interdependence and International Influence*, edited by M. Jocelyn Armstrong, R. Warwick Armstrong and Kent Mulliner. Richmond, Surrey: Curzon, 2001, pp. 55–73.

———, ed. *Migration, Indigenization and Interaction: Chinese Overseas and Globalization*. Singapore: World Scientific, 2011.

———. *"Overseas Chinese" in Southeast Asia and China's Foreign Policy: An Interpretative Essay*. Research Notes and Discussion Paper. Singapore: Institute of Southeast Asian Studies, 1978.

———, ed. *Peranakan Chinese in a Globalizing Southeast Asia*. Singapore: Chinese Heritage Centre and Baba House, 2010.

———. *Pribumi Indonesian the Chinese Minority and China: A Study of Perceptions and Policies*. Kuala Lumpur: Heinamann Asia, 1978.

Sydney Morning Herald. "Mobs Run Riot in Tonga", 16 November 2006.

Taipei Times. "The Battle of the Solomon Islands". EastSouthWestNorth Blog, 21 April 2015. <www.zonaeuropa.com/20060425_1.htm> (accessed 2 August 2015).

Tan Eng Joo. "Speech". In *1st World Chinese Entrepreneurs Convention: A Global Network: 10–12 August, 1991*《首届世界华商大会专辑: 环球网络: 一九九一年八月十日至二十日, 新加坡》. Singapore: Singapore Chinese Chamber of Commerce and Industry, 1992, pp. 18–19.

Tempo. "Mencari Kerok dan Intimidasi", 30 April 1994, pp. 21–32.

Thai Military Information Blog. "Thailand to give High-Caliber Welcome to Olympic Flame", 25 March 2008. <https://thaimilitary.wordpress.com/2008/04/16/security-tighten-as-olympic-torch-will-arrives-thailand-tomorrow> (accessed 19 April 2016).

Tiezzi, Shannon. "Myanmar Apologizes to China for Deadly Strike". *The Diplomat,* 3 April 2015. <http://thediplomat.com/2015/04/myanmar-apologizes-to-china-for-deadly-strike> (accessed 21 May 2015).

To, James Jiann Hua. *Qiaowu: Extra Territorial Policies of the Overseas Chinese*. Leiden: Brill, 2014.

Turley, William S. "Vietnam since Reunification". *Problems of Communism* 26 (March–April 1977): 36–54.

van Genniken, Jaap. *The Third Indochina War: The Conflicts between China, Vietnam and Cambodia*. Amsterdam, n.p., 1983.

VOA (Voice of America). "The Battle of the Solomon Islands". EastSouthWestNorth Blog, 24 April 2006.<www.zonaeuropa.com/20060425_1.htm> (accessed 2 August 2015).

Wang Gungwu. *China and the Chinese Overseas*. Singapore: Times Academic Press, 1991.

———. "Singapore's 'Chinese Dilemma' as China Rises". *Straits Times,* 1 June 2015.

Wang Jingwen 王敬文. "Xi Jinping ti zhanlue gouxiang : 'yidai yilu' dakai 'zhumeng kongjian'" 习近平提战略构想: "一带一路" 打开 "筑梦空间". Zhongguo Jingji Wang 中国经济网, 11 August 2014. <http://www.ce.cn/xwzx/gnsz/szyw/201408/11/t20140811_3324310.shtml> (accessed 18 March 2016).

Wen Wei Po (Wen Hui Bao, Hong Kong). "The Battle of the Solomon Islands". EastSouthWestNorth Blog, 24 April 2006. <www.zonaeuropa.com/20060425_1.htm> (accessed 2 August 2015).

Xi Jinping. "Shixian Zhonghua minzu weida fuxing shi haineiwai Zhonghua ernü de gongtong mengxiang" 实现中华民族伟大复兴是海内外中华儿女的共同的梦. In *Xi jinping tan zhiguo lizheng*《习近平谈治国理政》. Beijing 北京: Foreign Languages Publishing 外文出版社，2014, pp. 63–64.

———. "Shixian Zhonghua minzu weida fuxing shi zhonghua minzu jindai yilai zui weida de mengxiang" 实现中华民族伟大复兴是中华民族近代以来最伟大的梦想. In *Xi Jinping tan zhiguo lizheng*《习近平谈治国理政》. Beijing 北京: Foreign Languages Publishing 外文出版社，2014, pp. 35–36.

———. "Zai di shier jie quan'guo renmin daibiao dahui di yici huiyi shang de tanhua" 在第十二届全国人民代表大会第一次会议上的谈话. In *Xi Jinping tan zhiguo lizheng*《习近平谈治国理政》. Beijing 北京: Foreign Languages Publishing 外文出版社, 2014, pp. 38–43.

Xianggang Huasheng Wang 香港华声网. "2015 Guancha yu guanzhu" 2015观察与关注, 3 March 2015. <https://groups.google.com/forum/#!topic/gelora45/VBDSgzZPFMo> (accessed 4 December 2015).

Xinhua China Daily 中国日报网. "Backgrounder: China's Major Overseas Evacuations in Recent Years". <www.chinadaily.com.cn/china/2015-03/30/content_19954649.htm> (accessed 1 June 2016).

Xinhua Wang 新华网. "China's Libya Evacuation Highlights People-First Nature of Government", 3 March 2011. <http://news.xinhuanet.com/english2010/indepth/2011-03/03/c_13759953.htm> (accessed 6 June 2016).

———. "Fang Yinni huaren huoju shou: wei dangxuan aoyun huojushou er yisheng rongguang" 访印尼华人火炬手：为当选奥运火炬手而一生荣光, 21 April 2008. <http://news.xinhuanet.com/sports/2008-04/21/content_8021910.htm> (accessed 10 April 2016).

———. "Li Keqiang huijian dibajie shijie huaqiao huaren shetuan lianyi dahui daibiao" 李克强会见第八届世界华侨华人社团联谊大会代表, 2 June 2016. <http://news.xinhuanet.com/politics/2016-06/02/c_1118980966.htm> (accessed 4 June 2016).

———. "Li Keqiang huijian shoujie huaqiaohuaren gongshang dahui quanti daibiao" 李克强会见首届华侨华人工商大会全体代表, 6 July 2015. <http://news.xinhuanet.com/politics/2015-07/06/c_1115833826.htm> (accessed 10 July 2015).

———. "Yinni huaren huaqiao xiang Zhongguo da dizhen zaimin shenchu yuanshou" 印尼华人华侨向中国大地震灾民伸出援手, 16 May 2008. <http://news.xinhuanet.com/overseas/2008-05/16/content_8184254.htm> (accessed 19 April 2016).

Xu Shaoshi 徐绍史, chief editor 主编. *Zhongguo shuangxiang touzi: zhengce zhinan*《中国双向投资：政策指南》. Beijing 北京: Jixie gongye chubanshe 机械工业出版社, 2016.

Xue Li. "Can China Untangle the Kokang Knot in Myanmar?" *The Diplomat*, 20 May 2015. <http://thediplomat.com/2015/05/can-china-untangle-the-kokang-knot-in-myanmar> (accessed 22 May 2015).

Yang Bao'an 杨保安. "350 wan pingfang gongli haiyu de geda" 350 万平方公里海域的疙瘩. *Lianhe Zaobao*《联合早报》, 8 December 2011.

———. "Zhongguo younan, huaren zhiyuan" 中国有难，华人支援. *Zaobao Xingqitian*《早报星期天》, 8 June 2008.

Yang, Charissa. "Singapore's Value Lies in its 'Unique Culture'". *Straits Times*, 8 April 2016.

Yang Liming 杨莉明. "Juyou dute shenfen rentong he xiaozhong" 具有独特身份认同和效忠. *Lianhe Zaobao*《联合早报》, 8 April 2016, p. 10.

Yangguang Huaxia 阳光华夏. "Zhongmian bianjing gao junyan, jiefangjun yishi liangniao" 中缅边境搞军演，解放军一石两鸟, 2 June 2015. <http://hk.on.cc/hk/bkn/cnt/commentary/20150602/bkn-20150602012349241-0602_00832_001.html> (accessed 10 June 2015).

Yanlord Land Holdings website. <www.yanlordland.com/en/Corporate_Governance2.asp?> (accessed 12 April 2016).

Yinhua Ribao (Inhua Daily《印华日报》), 26 and 28 September 2015.

Yong Pao Ang. "Angry China Fuels Fear". *CHC Bulletin*, no. 12 (November 2008).

Zhang Xiuming 张秀明. "Guoji yimin tixizhong de zhongguo dalu yimin—Ye tan xin yimin wenti" 国际移民体系中的中国大陆移民 —也谈新移民问题. In *Shijie Shiye: Zouchu guomen de zhongguo xin yimin*《世界视野：走出国门的中国新移民》, edited by Zhao Hongying 赵红英 and Zhang Chunwang 张春旺. Beijing 北京: Zhongguo huaqiao chubanshe 中国华侨出版社, 2013.

Zhang Yinglong 张应龙 and Huang Chaohui 黄朝辉. "Yindu qiaomin zhengce yanjiu" 印度侨民政策研究. In *Jingwai huaren guoji wenti taolunji*《境外华人国际问题讨论辑》, edited by Zhou Nanjing 周南京. Hong Kong 香港: Hong Kong Press for Social Science Ltd. 香港社会科学出版社, 2005, pp. 290–311.

Zhang Zhenguo 张振国. "Waimei: huaren yimin zai Tangjia weihe bushou huanying?" 外媒：华人移民在汤加为何不受欢迎？ Xingdao huanqiu wang 星岛环球网, 31 December 2013. <http://ed-china.stnn.cc/Chinese/2013/1231/4757.shtml> (accessed 30 March 2016).

Zhao Hong. "China's One Belt One Road: An Overview of the Debate". *Trends in Southeast Asia*, no. 6. Singapore: ISEAS – Yusof Ishak Institute, 2016.

Zhao Kejin 赵可金 and Liu Siru 刘思如. "Zhongguo qiaowu gonggong waijiao de xingqi" 中国侨务公共外交的兴起. *Dongbeiya Luntan*《东北亚论坛》, no. 5 (2013). <http://www.imir.tsinghua.edu.cn/publish/iis/7236/20120308004952896512257/2013-8-16.pdf> (accessed 8 January 2016).

Zheng Yongnian 郑永年. "'Sichou zhi lu' yu zhongguo de 'shidai jingshen'" "丝绸之路" 与中国的 "时代精神". *Lianhe Zaobao*《联合早报》, 10 June 2014.

———. "Zhongguo chongfan sichou zhi lu de jige zhongyao wenti" 中国重返丝绸之路的几个重要问题. *Lianhe Zaobao*《联合早报》, 17 June 2014.

Zhong Shengjian 钟声坚. Hudong baike 互动百科 <baike.com>; Shanwei Shimin Wang 汕尾市民网 <http://www.swsm.net/thread-313328-1-1.html> (accessed 12 April 2016).

Zhongguang Xinwen Wang 中广新闻网. "Yuenan fanzhong baodong, lu mei chao ditiao" 越南反中暴动, 陆媒超低调, 17 May 2014. <https://tw.news.yahoo.com/越南反中暴動-陸媒超低調-062949679.html> (accessed 16 December 2015).

"Zhongguo pai zhuanji jie tangjia huaqiao huiguo" 中国派专机接汤加华侨回国. <http://www.tuiwen.org/article/2060404638/> (accessed 30 March 2016).

Zhongguo Pinglun Xinwen Wang 中国评论新闻网. "Tangjia shaoluan 8 ren siwang, huaren shangdian zao xiji" 汤加骚乱 8人死亡, 华人商店遭洗劫, 18 November 2006. <http://hk.crntt.com/crn-webapp/doc/docDetailCreate.jsp?coluid=7&kindid=0&docid=100251880> (accessed 30 March 2016).

Zhongguo qiaoshang touzi qiye xiehui chengli dahui 中国侨商投资企业协会成立大会. <http://www.chinaqw.com/zt/zgqsxh/> (accessed 19 February 2016).

Zhongguo Qiao Wang 中国桥网. "Diqijie shijie huaqiao huaren shetuan lianyi dahui" 第七届世界华侨华人社团联谊大会 [The 7th Conference for Friendship of Overseas Chinese Associations], 5–8 June 2014. <www.chinaqw.com/z/2014/sjhqhrstlydh/index.html> (accessed 22 July 2015).

Zhongguo Ribao Wang 中国日报网. "Meimei: yuenan jiang wei fanhua shaoluan fuchu jingji daijia" 美媒: 越南将为反华骚乱付出经济代价, 19 May 2014. <http://world.chinadaily.com.cn/2014-05/19/content_17517952.htm> (accessed 16 December 2015).

Zhongguo Xinwen Wang 中国新闻网. "Diliujie shijie huaqiao huaren shetuan lianyi dahui zai Beijing kaimu" 第六届世界华侨华人社团联谊大会在北京开幕, 9 April 2012. <http://www.chinanews.com/zgqj/2012/04-09/3804392.shtml> (accessed 22 July 2015).

———. "Jingwai dagong bu qingchu quanli yiwu, haiwai zhongguo laogong jiufen jizeng" 境外打工不清楚权利义务海外中国劳工纠纷骤增, 9 February 2007. <http://www.chinanews.com/hr/news/2007/02-09/871487.shtml> (accessed 1 June 2016).

———. "Qiu Yuanping huiying qiaojie guanzhu redian: 'Huayi Ka' baodao bushushi" 裘援平回应侨界关注热点: "华裔卡" 报道不属实, 10 March 2016. <http://www.chinanews.com/gn/2016/03-10/7792404.shtml> (accessed 20 April 2016).

Zhongguo Zhengxie Wang 中国政协网. "Haiwai liexi zhe: haiwai chuangyezhe de qiusuo zhilu" 海外列席者: 海外创业者的求索之路, 12 March 2014. <http://www.zgzx.com.cn/2014-03/12/content_8619104.htm> (accessed 10 April 2016).

Zhou Nanjing 周南京. "Guanyu Yindunixiya huaren rongru zhuliu shehui de ruogan wenti" 关于印度尼西亚华人融入主流社会的若干问题. First published in *Qiandao Ribao* (Surabaya), 13 November 2007. Republished in *Nushantala huayi zongheng* 《努山塔拉华裔纵横》, by Zhou Nanjing 周南京. Hong Kong 香港: Hong Kong Press for Social Science Ltd. 香港社会科学出版社, January 2011.

———, ed. *Jingwai huaren guoji wenti de taolun ji* 《境外华人国际问题的讨论辑》. Hong Kong 香港: Hong Kong Press for Social Science Ltd. 香港社会科学出版社, 2005.

Zhou Taomo. "30 September 1965 Movement". *Indonesia* (October 2014), pp. 1–34.

Zhu Zhiqun. *China's New Diplomacy: Rationale, Strategies and Significance*. 2nd ed. Surrey, England: Ashgate Publishing, 2013.

Zhuang Guotu 庄国土. "Huaqiao huaren fenbu zhuangkuang he fazhan qushi" 华侨华人分布状况和发展趋势. *Yanjiu yu Tantao* 《研究与探讨》. Zhonghua qiaowu diyi kan 中华侨务第一刊，2010 年 No. 4. <http://qwgzyj.gqb.gov.cn/yjytt/155/1830.shtml> (accessed 4 January 2016).

———. *Huaqiao huaren yu Zhongguo de Guanxi* 《华侨华人与中国的关系》. Guangzhou 广州: Guangdong gaodeng jiaoyu chubanshe 广东高等教育出版社, 2001.

———. "Zhongguo xin yimin yu Dongnanya huaren wenhua" 中国新移民与东南亚华人文化. *CHC Bulletin*, no. 9 (May 2007).

INDEX

Note: Page numbers followed with "n" refer to endnotes.

C

www.ingramcontent.com/pod-product-compliance
Lightning Source LLC
Chambersburg PA
CBHW071844270326
41929CB00013B/2095
* 9 7 8 9 8 1 4 7 6 2 6 4 9 *